"Black Sam" Fraunces

A Revolutionary War Spy

Rosemary J. Palermo

Old Age Press

455 E. Ocean Blvd #303

Long Beach, CA 90802

2nd Edition - Copyright © 2016 by Rosemary J Palermo

3rd edition – 2022

ISBN-13: 978-0-9971618-3-0

For my mother:

You instilled a love of reading and the curiosity to keep learning.

Thank you!

This new 3rd edition includes recently discovered genealogical information that expands upon members of Elizabeth Dally's family as well as genealogical information about the black Fraunces descendants.

It provides supporting information that the Hannah Darrah who married David Kelley and was mother of statesman William Darrah Kelley, was not Hannah Louisa Fraunces, but in fact a different woman whose lineage is noted here. Several additional corrections have been made to prior errors in genealogical records.

Proof has been provided that the "Poison Peas Plot" to assassinate General Washington at the start of the Revolution did happen and is not just a myth although many myths have been spread about the incident. The "lewd woman" mentioned in General Washington's address to the troops at the hanging of Thomas Hickey, the first man hung in America, has now been disclosed as well.

And yes, Samuel Fraunces was a man of mixed race, a successful entrepreneur married to a white woman in the slave state of New York. He risked everything including being sold into slavery to support the American Revolution.

"I am happy to find, by the Concurrent Testimony of many of our suffering Brethren, & others, that you have invariably through the most trying Times, maintained a constant friendship & Attention to the Cause of our Country & its Independence & Freedom. I do therefore hereby recommend you to the several Executives & to all the good People of these States, as a warm Friend—& one who has not only suffered in our Cause, who has deserved well of many Individuals, who have experienced the rigors of Captivity in N. York, and therefore One who is deserving the favor & attention of these U. States."

Letter from George Washington to Samuel Fraunces

"Sir, can you stay a moment?" Sam quietly murmured to General Washington as he and his staff rose to leave their luncheon in the Long Room at Sam's Queen's Head Tavern in New York City that 21st of June 1776. Washington and his military family, key leaders of the Revolution, ate lunch every day at his tavern, just blocks from their headquarters at Kennedy House. Sam knew the General and his men well as he also catered dinners at the Mortier House where they lived.

As Washington stood waiting, Sam removed a bowl of peas from a cupboard. Washington, who loved peas, asked Sam why they had not been served at lunch. He sat suddenly, stunned, as Sam explained that he believed they had been poisoned by one of the General's hand-picked Life Guards. A doctor soon confirmed that the peas contained arsenic.

This was the first time Sam saved Washington's life, but not the last. His actions saved the lives of General Washington and the leading officers of the American Revolution. Had they been assassinated; the war would likely have ended that day because the assassination was part of a larger plot by the British to attack and take over the city.

Sam would go on to save the life of Washington again, spy for the Patriots behind enemy lines and help many prisoners of war with food clothing and money and escapes. He would become the first Steward to the first President of the United States of America.

Why do we not know more about this hero of the Revolution? Sam was a man of mixed race in a time of slavery and prejudice. His story deserves to be told.

Contents

BEFORE THE WAR

THE WAR YEARS

AFTER THE WAR

FRAUNCES GENEALOGY

1700 Ward Map of New York

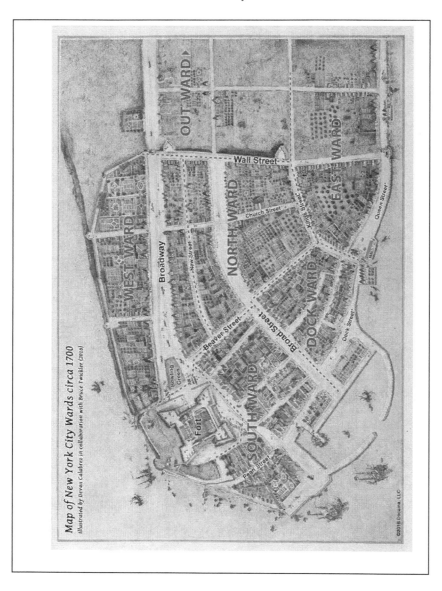

Map of New York City Wards circa 1700
Illustrated by Devan Calabrez in collaboration with Bruce Twickler (2016)

Before the War

1754 – Arrival

On a sunny fall day, a group of bedraggled passengers stumbled down a gangplank to the bustling New York City dock. One gentleman staggered a bit as he regained his land-legs after the difficult 9 week sail from England. Samuel Fraunces had cleaned up before going ashore, putting on his powdered wig and finest clothes. He looked around as the busy harbor clanged, clopped, whinnied, thumped, and shouted in different languages around him. As a brisk cool breeze blew away the stench of horse droppings and sweating, unwashed bodies, Sam inhaled the fresh air and, holding his hat against the breeze, walked up Broad Street towards a new beginning.

Sam was 32 and had planned his arrival well. There was a letter, received on August 20th, waiting when he arrived, probably containing an introduction to someone in NY.[1] He had apparently brought substantial funds as well. Within weeks of his arrival in 1754, he had purchased a partnership with James Taggart selling strong spirits, and 5 months later, in February of 1755, Sam paid his fees and was listed as an English subject, freeholder and innkeeper in New York City.[2]

New York in 1754 was a rapidly growing seaport, 2nd in size only to Philadelphia. Kings College had just been founded and New York welcomed many different churches and a synagogue. The economy was strong as New York merchants provisioned British ships for the

French and Indian War. Merchant privateers brought captured cargo and ships into port every few days. In 1756 there were 28 merchant privateers listed in New York, including the most prominent names in the city. Captured cargos, including the crews, were sold and the ships used for trade. The merchants of New York were used to risk taking, including slavery, piracy, and smuggling.

Freedom of the press had been established in 1733 by a New York jury when they declared John Peter Zenger, printer of the New York Weekly Journal, not guilty of libel for publishing scandalous, but true, articles about the corruption of the Royal Governor. Zenger's attorney defended his printing of the anonymous articles as a cause of liberty, demanding the prosecution prove the accusations false. The jury, against the Judge's instructions, declared Zenger not guilty, establishing forever that you can print anything if it is true.

Eighteen thousand people crowded into Manhattan when Sam arrived in 1754, but only about 6000 were white male residents. The rest were women, children, and slaves - lots of slaves. Over 40% of the households in New York kept slaves, more than 3000 of them, far more than Philadelphia where only 6% held slaves and only 2% in Boston did. This racial imbalance led to constant fears of slave uprisings. These were not completely unfounded.

Manhattan had experienced a series of arson fires. Fire was the city's worst fear as it quickly consumed whole neighborhoods of wooden buildings, killing entire families, and leaving survivors homeless and destitute. A slave was caught fleeing a warehouse fire in 1746 and rumors spread, faster than fire, that slaves were planning a revolt.

Meanwhile, a 16 year old Irish indentured servant named Mary Burton was arrested in an unrelated case. Her master, tavern-keeper John Hughson, was illegally selling liquor to slaves and fencing stolen goods. The authorities, after Hughson for both crimes, arrested Mary for questioning. Mary wouldn't say a word - until she heard that a large reward was offered for information about the fires. Suddenly, Mary Burton began talking about a plot between poor whites and blacks to burn the city, kill all the white men, capture the white women, and elect a king, all planned at Hughson's tavern. News of this plot soon fanned the flames of hysteria. As a result of the panic she created, 13 blacks were burned at the stake, 17 blacks and 4 whites were hung, 70 blacks were transported to slavery in the West Indies and 7 whites were deported. After the first hangings and burnings, arrested slaves panicked and began accusing others, hoping for leniency. At the height of this madness, half the male slaves over the age of 16 were in jail. When the stories became outlandish and began involving prominent citizens, the new Governor realized the trials were out of control and dismissed the remaining cases. Like the Salem witch trials, hysteria had trampled common sense. Mary Burton received a reward of $L100$ from the city. She used it to pay off her indenture and disappeared.

The executed slaves were buried in the Negro Burial Ground, a cemetery just outside the palisade fence, on land inherited by Sara (Jans) Van Borsum. The Van Borsum family enlarged the Negro Burial

3

Ground to about 5 city blocks at the north edge of the city. It remained in use as a Negro Cemetery until its closing in 1795, when land for a new cemetery was donated by Samuel de la Plaine and his wife. Aaron Burr, along with Henry H. Kip, John Kip and Daniel Denniston were owners when the old burying ground was partitioned for development. The Old Negro Burying Ground was rediscovered in 1991 during survey work for a new Federal Courthouse. There were over 20,000 bodies buried in the original cemetery. The remains of 419 people were removed, studied and re-interred in a formal ceremony and the site is now a National Historic Landmark.[3]

So, when Samuel Fraunces arrived in New York in 1754, blacks were viewed with suspicion and fear. New York laws specified that only Blacks could be slaves and Manhattan was the center of the colonial slave trade. Over 70% of the early slaves there had come from the West Indies, but after 1740, most were coming from Africa. Although there had been free blacks under Dutch rule, very few remained after the English took over and passed stringent laws against them. Few blacks were educated, and prejudice was rampant. In 1754, when Sam arrived, the City Council, noted that "*negroes were becoming insolent*", and prohibited "*unlawful meetings of negro slaves*" and strictly enforced laws against "*more than 3 slaves being together under penalty of whipping*".

Sam was a handsome man with a genial personality. He was an excellent cook and baker, knew fine wine and was in every way a gentleman. He arrived with some money and decided the best use of his skills was to open a first class tavern.

Tavern-keepers were at the center of colonial social life. They were well known people in their community. Although usually not of great wealth, they were financially secure. It took a good deal of cash to lease a space, furnish it and supply dishes, silverware and mugs, glasses and cooking and serving utensils for large numbers of people. The costs to purchase local beer, imported wine and stronger spirits were high. Furniture and linens were needed for guest rooms and more staff was needed. Cities closely regulated taverns, charging fees and taxes.

Taverns were originally in the lower floors of a residence. A large taproom with tables and chairs, a fireplace, perhaps a desk for writing and, of course, the bar took up the ground floor along with a kitchen. More elegant establishments had larger private meeting rooms. Upper floors housed the owner and his family, and lodgers if the house was big enough. Governments and courts met in taverns. The Colonial legislature met at Sam's tavern. Attorneys were present, so wills and contracts could be drawn, letters written, documents translated and, of course, politics discussed. Farmers discussed prices and buyers. Ship captains posted word of sailing times and cargo space while merchants bought and sold.

The earliest post offices were also in taverns. For many years Sam's location was specified as a stage depot and post office. Letters were left on a table near the door and stage drivers took them along to their next stop. Eventually, regular mail service and Post Roads were established, but mail was still delivered to taverns. A list of letters was

5

posted in the newspapers and tavern customers let friends and neighbors know they had mail. The addressee went to the tavern and paid the postage to pick up their letter.

Taverns were busy all day. Breakfast was a big meal served primarily for boarders or overnight guests. Lunch or supper at an 'ordinary' was served from 1 to 4 in the afternoon, buffet style. Dinner, when offered, was served about 7 pm. As tavern owners became more prosperous and moved to separate locations, they rented out the family's former rooms. Most taverns served very ordinary food, but Sam built his reputation on his fine food and excellent wine cellar.

Alcohol was believed to cure the sick and strengthen weak constitutions. It was used by men and women to help digestion, lessen pain, and cure colic and laryngitis. A hot toddy was believed to prevent cholera. By 1790 it was estimated that, in the Colonies, everyone over the age of 15 consumed over 34 gallons of beer and cider, 5 gallons of distilled spirits and 1 gallon of wine per year. All good wine was imported, and Madeira fortified with brandy became a favorite libation.

Pictorial signs originated because early customers were illiterate. Some sign painters were apparently illiterate as well, and many curious names evolved based on what they could paint and their misunderstanding of names. The 'Bag o Nails' was originally the 'Bacchanalians', 'Cat and Wheel' was originally 'St. Catherine's Wheel', and the 'Pig and Carrot' was originally 'Pique et Carreau' (spade and diamond suits of playing cards). As literacy grew, many taverns kept the pictorial signs for nostalgic reasons.

We don't know the name of Sam Fraunces and James Taggart's first tavern. Taggart was registered as an innkeeper in 1754 and Sam received one of 218 licenses issued in 1755, the year after he arrived. There were only 2200 homes in Manhattan in 1755 so, at fewer than 10 regulars per tavern, it was a highly competitive business. On March 27th, 1756, they dissolved their partnership as retailers of strong liquors[4]. Taggart kept his business and married. He died 4 years later, in 1760, in debt to Isaac Lattouch and his brother-in-law, Benjamin Stout, proprietor of the Plow and Horse Tavern. Taggart's tavern furnishings were sold to pay his debts.

Most tavern proprietors leased property in expensive cities and moved to different locations when rent got too high or a better location became available, usually taking their signs with them. In 1756 Sam bought his own building uptown, near the new Kings College, on a long term land-lease from Trinity Church. The land lease made it less expensive to buy. Trinity had first leased this lot in 1752 to John Dunscomb and Peter Rushton for 21 years at L4 per year. They built a structure which they sold to James Mills, a peruke (wig) maker, who in turn sold it to Mary Alexander and John Provoost, who then sold to Samuel Fraunces. The building had not been used as a tavern before, so Sam had to completely furnish and stock it. It was located at the SW corner of Broadway, the main thoroughfare in the city, and Warren Street, which was, in 1756, the northernmost street within the palisade wall (later Wall Street). The Negro Burial Ground lay just outside the wall. Across Broadway, on the Commons, was the first city almshouse,

7

city jail and a hospital. British army barracks were situated at the north end of the Commons, but they were not Sam's target clients.

Sam called his first tavern the Free Mason's Arms, appealing to influential Freemasons in the city. This building had 12 fireplaces, 2 dining rooms and 8 other good rooms as well as a large, pleasant garden where patrons of both sexes could sit out on warm afternoons. Sam had clearly arrived with money. He could not have saved enough as Taggart's partner to buy a building and equip it less than 2 years after his arrival, especially uptown, where many of the wealthy were moving to large new homes. Samuel's plan to become the best place in town had just begun.

In 1757, 35 year old Sam asked pretty 19 year old Elizabeth Dally to marry him. It appears from circumstantial evidence that she was a daughter of Hendrick Dally and Sarah Gifford. Their son, Gifford Dally, was godparents to Sam and Elizabeth's daughter Hannah Louisa and to her grandchild, Andrew Gifford Fraunces, son of Andrew and Sarah Pye for whom he was named. Elizabeth's sister Catherine (Dally) Simmons and her husband owned a tavern in NY a few blocks from Fraunces Tavern. Elizabeth (Dally) Fraunces was able to read and write, manage the books for the restaurants and was an excellent cook in her own right. She taught all their children well and they became successful professionals. Now Sam's secret had to come out. He had been passing for white although Sam was of mixed race. It is believed that he had an English father and a mulatto mother. Sam usually wore a powdered wig, probably to hide his curly hair. The descriptions of him in contemporary writings noted he was *'from the West Indies'*, social code at the time for a person of mixed race and referred to him as *'Black Sam'*. Elizabeth accepted Sam and they were married on November 30th, 1757, in Trinity Church.[5]

Interracial marriages, while unusual, were not unheard of at the time. Anne Fairfax, sister-in-law to George Washington, and her brother George, sister Sarah and brother Thomas were children of the very wealthy William Fairfax (1691-1757) born in England. He was stationed in New Providence Islands, Bahamas where he met and married Sarah Walker (1700-1731) in 1724. Sarah's deceased father had been the Chief Justice of the Bahama Islands. Her mother was Sarah Alice, a free mulatto woman. Sarah and William Fairfax had 2 sons before he was named Customs Collector in Massachusetts Bay Colony and the young couple moved there in 1727. In Salem they had Ann and Sarah. Sadly, Sarah Walker Fairfax died giving birth to Sarah in 1731. William soon remarried to Deborah Clark of Salem, Massachusetts. William moved to Virginia in 1733 where he became manager of vast properties owned by Lord Thomas Fairfax. With their white stepmother, the light skinned children passed as white but his family in England knew their parentage. Son George studied in England where his wealthy relatives were concerned that he might turn black at puberty! He returned to marry Sarah Cary. Thomas was killed serving in the Royal Navy. At the age of 15, Anne married Lawrence Washington, half-brother of George Washington and renovator of his father's house which he renamed Mt. Vernon. Sarah 'Sally' Fairfax married John Carlyle, a well-known merchant in Alexandria. The Fairfax children's race became a subject of gossip when Anne's husband, Lawrence Washington, accused Reverend Charles Green of sexually assaulting Anne when she was a child and asked that he be assigned elsewhere. Green refused to be moved and filed suit against Lawrence Washington for slander. At the trial it came out that Green had begun molesting Anne when she was 9 and attempted to rape her at 14. Green's defense was to destroy her reputation. The governor intervened and arranged a settlement before the closing arguments. Rev. Green kept his role as Rector of Truro Parish. Anne's own deposition records are the only records from the trial that did not survive. Since the trial was held in the church it is supposed that Green or perhaps her prominent father destroyed them. Sadly, all 4 of Anne and Lawrence's children died young. After Lawrence died in in 1752 and her daughter died in 1754, Anne inherited Mt. Vernon. She had remarried to George Lee who collected the rents on Mt. Vernon. That estate passed to George Washington when Anne died in 1761 at the age of 33.

  With almost no white women in the West Indies, intercourse between the younger white, aristocratic plantation owners, and far more numerous black and mulatto women happened so regularly that it became socially acceptable there. Women often had no choice in the matter, but some were able, through these liaisons, to create an economically stable and elevated social position, offering the possibility of freedom for themselves and their children. Black or mulatto mistress '*housekeepers*' took a visible, socially accepted place in the public life of their white lovers, who occasionally freed and even married them. A man who fathered children with a slave he didn't own had no claim to his children. Many men didn't care, and those women and children remained slaves. Other men bought their slave mistresses, so their children were raised at his home but remained slaves, as did Thomas Jefferson. A few men created alternatives, buying a woman at the start of a relationship, and manumitting her, so their children were born free, as William Fairfax did. Manumission was a long and expensive undertaking, done only by those wealthier men who genuinely cared for their women.

Because of the growing number of free interracial children inheriting great wealth in the early 1700's, prejudice grew in the British West Indies against free people of color. This territory included Jamaica and its dependencies (Caymans and Turks Caicos and British Honduras (now Belize). The Leeward Islands of Christopher-Nevis-Anguilla plus Antigua-Barbuda-Montserrat were governed separately. Some aristocratic English planters deeply resented other's mulatto sons inheriting large plantations to become their financial and social equals. Poor and middle class whites resented the less wealthy but well educated mulatto sons as competition for severely limited professional opportunities. This animosity was soon formalized into laws. Beginning in 1711, Jamaica barred all mulattos (anyone less than 4 generations removed from an African ancestor) from employment in public offices. By 1733, mulattos lost the right to vote and, in 1743, the Assembly revoked their right to testify against whites in court. Schools

11

on the island were for whites only. The children of color, many of whom looked entirely white with blond hair and blue eyes, didn't fit into either culture.

It soon became clear that, to be successful, mixed race sons needed to leave the Islands. Wealthier families bequeathed their plantations and sometimes large holdings in England to these boys. Middle class families struggled to send their mixed race children to England, Scotland, or France to be educated and apprenticed. This was so prevalent that as many as 75% of the planters in Jamaica with mixed race sons sent them abroad to be educated in England and Scotland.[6] This occurred on other islands as well. George Fairfax of Nevis was sent to family in England for his education at the young age of 7.[7] It was expensive to do this, considering passage, tuition, room and board, books, and clothing to support a child overseas for 10 years or more. Sadly, many children were not well received by their European relations, jealous that family land and titles would go to a mixed race child. Many were disinherited, cheated, or sued out of their family fortunes.[8] It was a difficult life for them.

Samuel Fraunces was undoubtedly one of these children. He was possibly the son of Edward Fraunces, originally of London, who had a plantation in Vere, Jamaica and who returned to London before his death. Edward made lifetime bequests in his will of 20 shillings per year to negro servants Madge and Mary. His brother James Fraunces, an apothecary in London, inherited his estate, which then went to his Jaquelin cousins in America when James died without issue. He was a cousin of Elizabeth Jaquelin Ambler, Martha Jaquelin and Mary Jaquelin Smith of Virginia.

Samuel registered in NY as an English citizen, so we know he was likely born in the English owned West Indies. We can assume he probably went to England with his father who soon died. We must also assume that he did not have a large inheritance, so after completing his education, he was probably apprenticed, likely with a large wealthy household or hotel to the house steward, chef, or butler, maybe in France, then the height of fashion. In either country he would have been taught proper dress and decorum, elaborate table settings, presentation and how to manage staff. He learned about fine wines and mastered remarkable cooking skills. It is said that he spoke fluent French and functioned as a translator to Washington on several occasions. This child, cut off from all family at a young age, became a compassionate man with a lifelong commitment to helping the poor and oppressed. We will never know what prompted him to leave his early adult life in Europe to begin a new life in Colonial America. Perhaps he was rejected in love and hoped for a place with less prejudice.

In the 1700s spelling was phonetic. The name Fraunces was spelled Frances, Francis, Fronces, or Fraunces used interchangeably. When Sam first arrived in America, he used the name Francis but later used Fraunces. His descendants used many spelling variations. Fraunces will be used throughout for clarity.

13

1756 – Friends

Between 1756 and 1762, Sam and Elizabeth built a loyal clientele, and their Mason's Arms tavern became known for its fine food and wines. They began a catering service for wealthy clients who often entertained with large parties. Sam also developed a strong following for 'take away' meals for travelers. In 1759 he advertised: "*portable soups, catchup, bottled gooseberries, pickled walnuts, pickled or fryed oysters fit to go to the West Indies, pickled mushroom, large assortment of sweetmeats such as currant jelly, marmalade, quince, grape, strawberry and sundry other sorts.*"[9]

Sam and Elizabeth had their first son, Andrew Gautier Fraunces in 1759, named for their close friend, Andrew Gautier, a well-known carpenter. Andrew became such a close friend that Sam trusted Andrew enough to give him 'Power of Attorney' in his business affairs when he later moved to Philadelphia, calling him "*my trusty and well beloved friend, Andrew Gautier, House Carpenter in New York City*". Unfortunately, Andrew was later found to be a Loyalist spy, while Samuel was a strong Patriot.

Andrew Gautier, son of a French Huguenot, was born in New York in 1720. He became famous when Trinity Church caught fire in February 1749. Andrew climbed the steeple and put out the fire, saving the church. He is believed to have designed and built St. Paul's Chapel and to have carved the beautiful woodwork in it. Completed in 1766, it was in a field outside the palisade wall. It was the tallest building in New York City for many years and is today the oldest building in continuous use in Manhattan. George Washington had his own pew here when New York was the first Capitol.[10] Andrew was a well-known retailer of Windsor chairs and he and Sam had probably met when Andrew sold Sam chairs for the Mason's Arms. As New York City grew, Andrew Gautier became more influential, becoming Assistant Alderman from the Dock Ward from 1765 to 1767 and Alderman there from 1768 to 1783.

Sam and Elizabeth's other influential friends included Gifford Dally, probably a younger brother of Elizabeth's. The successful young couple had their 2nd child, a daughter named Margaret Amelia in 1761

.

Etching of Fraunces Tavern 1776

By Samuel Hollyer

1762 – Queen's Head

Sam and Elizabeth saw a wonderful opportunity when the De Lancey Mansion went up for sale in 1762. The lot on which the famous Fraunces Tavern now stands was originally under water. In an early expansion of Manhattan Island, the city filled in the Grand Dock area along Pearl Street creating a new block of property protecting City Hall from flooding. The Fraunces Tavern lot was originally number 49 Grand Dock Street. Owners of the old waterfront lots paid for the bulkheads creating the new lots so most, including the then Mayor of New York, Stephanus Van Cortlandt, purchased the new lots. When Van Cortlandt retired to his manor up the Hudson River in 1700, he gave the lot to his son-in-law, Etienne 'Stephen' De Lancey, who built an elegant new house, completed in 1720. The three and a half story tall De Lancey Mansion had a red brick front, with a side façade of small yellow bricks, imported from the Dutch Republic. The hipped lead and tile roof held a 3 room attic, and the building was as fireproof as possible. The Mansion was the finest home in the best part of town and the De Lancey family lived in the house until about 1735. It descended to Stephen's grandson, Oliver who already had a fine house uptown in a wealthier neighborhood. He rented it to his business partner, Colonel Robinson, who hosted George Washington at the home in February 1756. After Robinson's death in 1757, the building was occupied by the De Lancey and Robinson Company who moved their store into the former dwelling. De Lancey and Robinson and Company, was made up of Oliver and Philia Robinson, Beverley and Susannah Robinson and James Parker, and they used it as headquarters for their importing business. They advertised that they had moved their store *"to the house formerly occupied by the late Col. Joseph Robinson, being the corner house next to the Royal Exchange where they continue to sell all sorts of European and East India goods, Shoes, Stockings, and Shirts, white and checked, fit for the Army with a variety of other goods."[11]* By this time, the neighborhood had become more commercial and wealthy residents were moving uptown. The Robinsons decided to sell the building in 1761 just as Sam and Elizabeth were looking for an upscale location for their flourishing tavern business.

As Sam and Elizabeth walked up the short flight of marble steps from Broad Street and through the ornate front door, the scuffed wide plank floors glowed in the sunlight streaming in through the many dusty windows. Of course, it needed cleaning from years of use as a shop, but the elegance was there, waiting to be brought back to life. Undoubtedly, their excitement grew as they walked through the nine public rooms, marveling at the 14 grand fireplaces. The Long Room on the 2nd floor was bright and sunny with windows on 2 sides, easily warmed by its two fireplaces, perfect for hosting larger groups. The large kitchen, with a pump of remarkable fine water in it, delighted Sam, and there was a large dry cellar divided into 3 sections for wine and supplies. It had a small yard with another pump and room for chickens, and best of all, offered 5 bedchambers for lodgers and 3 more in the attic for their small family.[12]

The De Lancey Mansion was in a perfect location for a tavern, at the corner of Great Dock and Broad Street, a neighborhood of financial and legal firms and city offices. It was a block to the fort, main garrison for the top military officers of the British Army and Navy, surrounded by wealthy merchants. It was 3 blocks to the harbor, supplying a steady stream of clients for Sam's growing take-away food business and visitors who needed lodgings. The Customs House and the Exchange were very close.

It was fine enough to make the elegant impression Sam needed to attract wealthy guests. So, Sam and Elizabeth mortgaged their Mason's Arms tavern to Walter Rutherford for L400 plus interest, payable in 1 year, and used the cash and other funds to buy the De Lancey Mansion for L2000 on January 15, 1762. It is not clear where the other L1600 came from. Perhaps Sam still had some of his original money, or possibly it was savings from 7 profitable years at the Mason's Arms. Immediately after the purchase, Sam mortgaged it to his good friend Andrew Gautier, providing Sam and Elizabeth with cash to buy elegant new furnishings and stock the tavern-inn.[13] Sam was 40 and Elizabeth was 22. They now had 2 children, a successful business, and a prestigious new location. They named their new venture the Sign of Queen Charlotte.

King George III had recently married his 17 year old German wife, Queen Charlotte, who was rumored to be distantly related to a black Moorish ancestor. Several of her official portraits, by Sir Allen Ramsey

21

and others, do appear to show her with somewhat Negroid features. Sam probably felt her to be an especially fitting namesake. The name was soon shortened to the Queen's Head Tavern for the portrait on his sign. The Queen's Head became internationally known for its excellent food, gracious hospitality, and fine Madeira. Its larger meeting rooms soon attracted the top events in town. On July 26th, 1762, the Court of New York held a trial for its Debtor's Division at the new Queen's Head Tavern. Many other clubs were soon holding their meetings and dinners there. New York Provincial Government and City Courts met there regularly and from 1762-1775 members of the influential Social Club considered it their headquarters.

Sam and Elizabeth attracted the best of New York society, and Sam was becoming well-known as a caterer. Sam and Elizabeth paid off the mortgage on the Mason's Arms tavern and the one on the Queen's Head as well. He placed many ads in local newspapers advertising an "*Ordinary with Dinner every day at half after one at the Queen's Head Tavern*".[14] Other ads mentioned that he delivered catered meals and sold preserved items including soups, ketchup, nuts, pickled vegetables, oysters, jelly, and marmalades.

John Jones, Sam's friend, and well-known tavern keeper bought the Mason's Arms tavern on Feb 3rd, 1762, and Sam held the mortgage which was paid off on Jan 14th, 1765.[15] Jones advertised that he was opening his new tavern in the location "*formerly kept by Samuel Francis at the sign of the Mason's Arms*". He kept the name and sign and counted on Sam's excellent reputation to draw clients.[16] Jones got a new 63 year land-lease on the Trinity Church Farm property.[17] Sam used the mortgage payoff to buy property farther out of town and establish the Vauxhall Gardens Resort.

All was not smooth sailing in New York. From 1756 to 1763 the British were fighting the French and Indian War. The French in Canada and their Indian allies, moved into the Ohio River Valley, onto land already claimed by several states. Spain, whose colonies included Florida, Cuba, and islands in the West Indies, allied with France and fought against the British colonies in the south. The fighting was far from New York and offered business opportunities for supplying the forces but supporting the British Army and Navy, based in New York City, was a strain on the NY Colony's budget.

Great Britain (England, Ireland, and Scotland) had built professional military forces since 1661. During the French and Indian War, England's Parliament decreed that even the most senior Colonial Officers, who fought with the British troops, were to be subordinate to the most junior officers of the British Army. British Officers were generally wealthy aristocrats who had purchased their commissions and made the military their career. These Army and Navy officers were openly contemptuous of the 'Provincials', who were generally not career military, whom the most junior officers now officially outranked, despite their youth or lack of experience. Their daily condescension and rudeness created great resentment among Colonials that festered for years.

23

1763 – Restaurants

Samuel Fraunces was not just a successful tavern owner. He operated a well-known inn, supplying room and board to merchants and ship captains. By 1770, Sam's catering business was offering dinners to be delivered to those who lived at convenient distance from the Queen's Head Tavern. He made items like jellies, pickled fruits for relishes and desserts for purchase at the Queen's Head, like today's specialty grocers do. He also offered preserved meats, fish, and pickled items as 'Take-Away' food for long voyages.

Most importantly, Sam was a *'restauranteur'*, one of the earliest to adopt a new way of doing business. Restaurants allow you to order and pay for only what you want, at any time, brought to your table by a server. In the middle of the 1700's there were no true restaurants in Europe or the Colonies. Coffee houses offered hot and cold drinks, including alcohol, and pastry or snacks while patrons shared ideas in a quieter atmosphere than most taverns. Taverns served hearty but mediocre meals, during fixed hours, from communal pots on buffet tables. They were often crowded and noisy. Patrons paid a fixed price for the whole meal and served themselves.

The first true *'restaurants'* are, of course, believed to have originated in Paris. The word *'restaurant'* originally referred to a rich, highly flavored, meat based soup said to restore energy. A Monsieur Mathurin Roze de Chantoiseau was credited with opening the first *'restaurant'* on Rue des Poulies (which no longer exists) near the

Louvre in Paris in 1765. It ran between Rue de Rivoli and Rue Saint Honore and disappeared when Rue du Louvre opened. Chantoiseau became well known for selling meat based broths flavored with onions, herbs, and vegetables. A 'bouillon restaurant" means restorative broth. When he paid 1600 livres for the title of "cook caterer following the Court' Chantoiseau's bouillons became quite a fad as *restoratives fit for the gods.'*[18] The broth was intended to assist the asthmatic, tubercular, those with stomach ailments and other sickly city dwellers. This was the first establishment where people came primarily to eat rather than to drink coffee or spirits and where they could order by the dish at any hour of the day rather than pay a fixed price for a large buffet at specific hours of the day. It later moved to the Hotel d'Aligre. He also served chicken and eggs in individual portions, the first to do so.

Larousse Gastronomique claims the first Parisian restaurant worthy of the name was opened by Antoine Beauvilliers who opened the La Grande Taverne Anglais in 1782, at the Rue de Richelieu in the Palais Royale district. Antoine had been the chef to the Compte de Provence, brother of the King and was the first private cook to leave his master and set up his own business. He had a beautifully decorated, elegant dining room with linen tablecloths, well trained waiters, a fine wine cellar and impeccable food. He introduced the novelty of listing dishes on a menu (la carte), serving them on beautiful plates with the finest wines in crystal glasses. This allowed his customers to eat as if they were at Versailles, with prices to match! And so, the pleasure of eating and gastronomy developed.

26

Despite all this, in the 11th and 12 centuries during the Song Dynasty in China, there were establishments that set up a selection of demonstration plates showing food options and diners (usually traveling merchants) could select what they preferred. Waiters would take their orders and deliver to the tables. This was in 1126.

In 1793, the "first" 'Restaurant' opened in Boston. Jean Baptiste Gilbert Julien named his restaurant 'Julien's Restorator' and noted it as *"a resort where the infirm could obtain suitable nourishment"*. He had previously been a private chef to Monsieur Letombe, Consul of the French Republic. He too offered menus, charging by the dish. His menus included pastry, beef bacon, poultry, wines, oysters, and green turtle soup. He was nicknamed the 'Prince of Soups'. He was very successful, moving from Leverett's Lane to Milk Street until his early death in 1805. His widow, Hannah, ran the restaurant for 10 years before selling it to another Frenchman.

But, in 1763, in 'provincial' New York, Samuel Fraunces was already making restaurant history. His Queen's Head Tavern was famous for its fine food and wine cellar. Sam's guests were individually served by respectful waiters, at times convenient to them and charged for only what they ordered. This was a centerpiece of Sam's service over 20 years before Julien's Restorator opened in Boston! In 1772 Vauxhall advertised that food was available for large or small parties at shortest notice any time of day. In 1773 he advertised that the Queen's Head Tavern offered *"at any time of day or evening, beef stakes, mutton or pork chops, veal stakes or cutlets, fry'd oyster etc., served in the neatest manner to one or more persons, as may be*

27

required, with every other necessary requisite to give general satisfaction, particularly the best attendance, and the most respectful behavior."[19] Samuel Fraunces owned the first true restaurant in the Colonies. His fine food and wine cellar and his new way of doing business made him famous long before Paris started *'restaurants'*.

In American political matters, Tory and Whig, the same two political parties as in England, existed. New York had the largest Tory party of all the colonies, made up primarily of wealthy merchants with ties to England. This powerful group was led by Stephen De Lancey and included about 60% of the wealthy men in Manhattan. The Whig party included many of the landed, agriculture based, wealthy of New York. This group included the Livingstons, Schuylers, and the Jays. Both groups objected to British taxation and decisions made by Parliament without Colonial representation but were, for the most part, moderates. The Sons of Liberty faction, which soon formed from the Whig party, was made up of newly wealthy self-made men, including privateers and 'mechanics' (workers), who represented a more democratic point of view than the two main factions who had been in power for many years.

In 1763 the French and Indian War Peace Treaty was finally signed. On the losing side, France ceded control of Canada to England and gave Louisiana to its ally Spain. Spain gave up Florida to Great Britain. Britain now controlled the American coast from Canada to Florida, but the war had nearly doubled their national debt. As a result,

28

Parliament passed a series of new laws – and they were not well received in the Colonies.

Elizabeth and Sam kept an elegant establishment but one day in 1763 they watched in shock as the Queen's Head erupted. Pewter tankards were thumping the wooden tables in exasperation and men were shouting to be heard. Someone had read the newspaper aloud, and everyone was outraged over laws that Parliament had just passed.

Parliament had issued a Land Proclamation giving land grants to every British combatant in the recently ended French and Indian War. Field Officers got 5000 acres; Captains got 3000 acres; Staff officers got 2000 acres; non-commissioned officers got 200 acres and every common soldier was granted 50 acres. The same grants were given to all members of the Navy and several Indian Tribes who had fought on the British side. Not one acre went to the American Colonists who had fought beside them! Most of these English grants were in territory already legally claimed by Colonies, with American settlers living and working there. Most galling of all, the Proclamation prohibited American colonists from moving to the new territories, even though the colonist had fought beside them to win it!

Tories supported the Crown's right to award the land because English military forces had won them from France and Spain and therefore owned it all, but many had invested in land in those areas and were concerned about losses. Whigs felt that the laws of ownership, based on Colony charters and English common law, were being trampled because Parliament was giving away lands legally claimed by

Colonial legislatures. In the first real act of defiance, Colonists in the disputed areas refused to leave, and many more immediately moved to the territories.

Parliament then announced their plans to set up a permanent standing Royal Army in the Colonies. Prior to the 7 year French and Indian war, there had been no permanent Army on American soil. Parliament now ordered the Colonists to financially support a standing Army indefinitely. England had doubled their national debt to win these lands from France and Spain for these 'provincial' colonists, who could never have done it alone. They believed the colonies should be *grateful for their continuing protection* against possible future attacks. The Colonists, on the other hand, had expected the British forces to be recalled to England when the war ended, relieving the financial burden of housing, feeding, and provisioning them. The situation was viewed by the Colonies akin to a large wealthy family coming visit a poor relation, then refusing to go home, expecting the poor host to work harder to support them while they idly paraded around in fine clothes without working. Many Colonists felt there was no further need for an armed force now that England controlled all the land. The more suspicious among them believed Britain wanted the army to watch and control them.

Taxes became another sore point when Parliament imposed an import tax on products coming to the colonies to raise funds to support the Army. In fairness, colonial taxes were far lower than taxes paid by residents in England and covered only 1/3 of the Army's cost.

But the biggest issue was that the Colonies had no representatives in Parliament. This lack of representation was counter to English Common Law and against their rights as English subjects. If they were English subjects, they had a right to representation in Parliament. If they were not subjects, then Parliament had no right to impose taxes on them. Tempers ran high in the Queen's Head that day and arguments continued for weeks over these issues. Discussions continued for years as other laws were imposed.

1764 – Tension

Sam and Elizabeth were doing so well at the Queen's Head that they decided to expand. They bought an uptown property called Spring Gardens, moving their growing family to the large house and gardens, land-leased from Trinity Church. This let them rent out additional rooms at the Queen's Head. Sam soon advertised "that he had completely fitted up his house and Long Room at Spring Gardens Vauxhall",20 named after a famous London resort, to use as "a pleasure garden" where patrons could escape the heat and dust of the city. Elisabeth and the children lived at Vauxhall, and she managed this property while Sam managed the Queen's Head. It was a timely idea and Vauxhall Resort soon became 'the' place to be, but England was making American financial success difficult.

The American economy depended on merchants shipping tobacco, lumber, furs, fish, and other exports to England. They were paid for their cargo in English currency, which they would immediately spend in England, buying items to bring back to sell in the colonies like tea, coffee, glass, iron, fabrics, sugar, and spices. Since the British currency all stayed in England, there was a shortage of British money in the colonies, so each colony began printing Bills of Credit to use instead. Because these fluctuated in value, merchants were reluctant to accept them. To appease British merchants, Parliament passed a Currency Act suddenly making all Bills of Credit illegal and requiring purchases to be made only with British currency. But there wasn't enough British currency circulating in America to sustain the economy and this law soon created hardship and chaos.

Typically, farmers selling their crops were paid in Bills of Credit representing their entire year's income. They would normally spend that money locally to pay bills, buy more seed, perhaps a cow, a plow or clothing and other necessities to tide their family over until the next crop was reaped and sold. Merchants paid for large cargos of lumber or iron with the Bills of Credit, which were used everywhere in the Colonies. Suddenly all this money was declared worthless. Everyone who held Bills of Credit faced bankruptcy. Shopkeepers could not sell their products because no one had British currency to buy them. They could not buy replacement products from England since they couldn't move their stock. There was an immediate slowdown in the economy and trade, creating a downward economic spiral and creating great inflation as materials became scarce.

Parliament then mandated a monopoly, decreeing that the Colonies could now trade only with England and its colonies. This at once ended the thriving trade the colonies had developed with the West Indies, Azores, South America, and other European countries, which had also brought some British currency into circulation. Colonial merchants, now a captive market, were forced by English merchants to accept lower prices for their exports to England but had to pay higher prices plus taxes on imports they were bringing back. Colonial merchants and shopkeepers raised prices to cover these new costs and inflation soon made it almost impossible for an average person to buy necessities.

This hardship caused great resentment against England and a lot of smuggling. Many NY merchants were privateers, so smuggling was nothing new for them. Lots of the smuggling was in untaxed molasses from the French West Indies. This hurt the British West Indies but certainly helped the market for rum, which Colonists made in great quantities and exported. To end these losses, England then established the Sugar Act, reducing the import tax on sugar and molasses, but adding many new taxable items, including wines, coffee, pimiento, cambric, and printed calico. They also issued further restrictions on the export of lumber and iron from the Colonies. The new regulations caused an immediate drop in the production of rum, the most popular drink in the colonies. Sam and other tavern keepers felt the sting of this law. He was now paying much more for his imported wines, porter and tea and the ever popular rum doubled in price. Everyone resented the higher prices on their favorite drinks and there was a lot of muttering at the bar.

The lack of British currency, the sudden sharp decline in trade and high prices caused severe economic depression in the Colonies. The Merchants of NY wrote to Parliament that the *"suppression of trade.... must necessarily end....in the impoverishment of.... Northern Colonies and destruction of their Navigation.... in grievous detriment.... of the British Manufacturers and great diminution of the Trade, Power Wealth and Naval Strength of Great Britain. The incapacity of making good our payments.... must sink our credit and gradually decrease our Imports from Great Britain.... numbers of Manufactures will remain without employ and be obliged to transport themselves....to foreign parts for subsistence.*" Merchants and manufacturers, unable to pay rent, went bankrupt, cancelling contracts for indentured servants, which left them unemployed and homeless. Sam's wealthy clients could weather most downturns and visiting merchants could absorb Sam's higher prices, but many taverns closed, including Sam's old partner, James Taggart.

Parliament, now trying to stop the smuggling, set up a Customs Service which issued Writs of Assistance (general search warrants) to British captains, allowing them to confiscate any ship '*suspected*' of smuggling and sell its cargo, no proof needed! They increased the bounties offered for each arrest; no conviction required. A Super Vice Admiral, the Earl of Northumberland, based in Halifax, Nova Scotia, became the only authority who could hold trials and convict or release those arrested for smuggling. His juryless court outranked all the existing Colonial court systems. In the Halifax court, people were considered guilty until proven innocent, and failure to appear in distant Nova Scotia was an automatic guilty verdict. Colonists believed this was an illegal usurpation of their rights as Englishmen which, since the 12th century, had included the right to judgement by their peers.

Sam's wealthy merchant clients were finally affected too and incurred huge losses when their cargos, already taxed and paid for in England, and transported legally, were illegally confiscated. The ships, in which wealthy merchants had ownership, were confiscated, and sold for the benefit of English bounty hunters, ruining many merchants. They did not go quietly. Newspapers were full of stories about illegal seizures, resulting in many heated discussions in the Queen's Head tavern. Many of the merchants and ship owners held a meeting there and created a NY Committee of Correspondence. A newspaper announcement said, *"The Merchants of this City are earnestly requested to meet at the Queen's Head, near the Exchange, on Wednesday next on business of Great Importance to Trade."*[21]

Other actions were also taken. On Dec 3rd a newspaper ad informed people about a new organization, *"that, on account of the present deplorable State of our Trade, a Society for the Promotion of Arts, Agriculture and Economy in the Province of NY has been formed to promote the true interest of this colony, both public and private, and extended an invitation to every real Friend to become a member thereof and to meet the present members at the House of Mr. Samuel Francis at 6 o'clock in the evening of this day where the plan of the said society will be more fully explained."* [22] The Society was part of an effort by colonial manufacturers to produce clothing and furniture locally. They taught spinning, planting of flax, sheep-raising and other ways to reduce reliance on Europe and supply local employment for the many unemployed.

Other Colonies also created Committees of Correspondence. Each addressed petitions to the King, believing that if they only had a voice in Parliament, these onerous laws would not be passed. They firmly believed that benevolent King George was hearing only one side of the situation and would correct these issues if he was properly informed.

1765 – Riots

Sam and Elizabeth suddenly moved to Philadelphia in 1765. It is not clear why. They did not have any known relations there, but Philadelphia was then the largest city in America. Perhaps they hoped the pacifist Quakers would be less volatile than their New York clients. Philadelphia's economy was stronger than New York's and Quaker merchants were less willing to rock the boat or jeopardize their financial success. But Pennsylvania in 1765 was still a slave state with harsh regulations against blacks. Free blacks could be sold into indentured servitude for infractions including unpaid fines and free blacks, like Sam, who married whites were sold into slavery for life.

Sam leased out the Queen's Head tavern in New York to John Jones, friend, and proprietor of his old Mason's Arms tavern. He also leased out Spring Gardens-Vauxhall to a British Major James as a residence. It was at this time that Sam gave his old friend, Andrew Gautier, his '*Power of Attorney*' to transact all his business in New York. Shortly after arriving in Philadelphia, Sam and Elizabeth had another child they named Elizabeth on Dec 26th, 1765. She was baptized at Christ Church in Philadelphia on 27 Jan 1766.[23] Their first tavern in Philadelphia was situated on Front Street and called the Sign of Queen Charlotte Inn, Sam's favorite name. Most Philadelphians were pacifist Quakers, but there was growing anger there too at the

British Acts. Things became more heated, and the 1765 Stamp Act was the breeze that blew the smoldering kindling of discontent into flame.

The American economy was already in a major depression. People were suffering and everyone blamed the British. Then Parliament imposed the Stamp Act, the first direct tax on the colonies. This Act decreed that every document in the Colonies had to be printed or written on paper having a revenue stamp, including all deeds, wills, contracts including marriages, bills of sale, even playing cards and newspapers. And the tax had to be paid in British currency, still unavailable to almost everyone.

In response, Massachusetts Sons of Liberty faction of the Whig party, issued a circular letter sent to all the states that promoted the idea that that a unified front would persuade Parliament to repeal the Stamp Act. They proposed a meeting of all the Colonies, a Stamp Act Congress, to address these issues. This Congress meeting had representatives from 9 of the 13 colonies, and met from October 7th to 25th, 1765 at New York's City Hall (now Federal Hall). The Royal Governors of the other 4 colonies prevented their delegates from attending. This Congress issued the Stamp Act Resolves and a Declaration of Rights claiming that England's Parliament had no legal right to impose taxes because the Colonies had no representation in Parliament. They also signed a Petition to the King, protesting the lack of representation, unfairness of the Stamp Act, and restrictions on their trade rights.

New York was a hotbed of resentment against the British Army headquartered there. The city was in an ugly mood and several violent

40

brawls occurred between soldiers and citizens. As newspaper editorials and tavern talk became more heated over the Stamp Act, Governor Colden and General Gage, military commander of the British Army took refuge in downtown Fort George. General Gage infuriated the city by moving a regiment from Crown Point into the fort and training the fort's guns on the town. How dare the British Army threaten to fire on unarmed English civilians in their own city?

When the ship bearing the hated stamps arrived in New York harbor on October 23rd, 1765, accompanied by British warships, the Colonial ships in the harbor all lowered their flags to half-mast and muffled mourning bells tolled throughout the city. Angry men gathered in the streets, muttering about the situation, and that night placards were posted, threatening that the first man to distribute or make use of the stamped paper *"let him take care of his house, person and effects"*. James McEvers, appointed Stamp Distributer for New York City, refused to accept the stamps and resigned his position. Governor Colden defiantly marched the stamps under guard to the Fort.

Meanwhile in Philadelphia, on October 25th, a majority of the usually conservative merchants agreed to sign the Philadelphia Non-Importation Agreement. John and Sam Adams worked hard to influence their more moderate neighbors. The signers included men and women, Anglicans and Quakers, Jews, Presbyterians, and Lutherans. There were lawyers, clergymen, doctors, shopkeepers, and members of all economic classes. Sam did not sign it. Apparently, he was still trying to remain neutral and perhaps feared a racially

41

prejudiced backlash as a newcomer to the city. The Sons of Liberty proposed that if all Colonies refused to import anything from England until the Stamp Act was repealed, that show of unity and loss of revenue would have a huge economic impact in England and would be an effective, non-confrontational way of refusing to pay taxes. The passive resistance of the non-Importation idea became immensely popular, building support for the Sons of Liberty in every colony. News articles inflamed the general population about attempts by Parliament to tax everything. Even people who were not politically inclined became agitated and finally, even the more conservative merchants were convinced that something had to be done. In New York, 200 of the largest merchants drafted a New York Non-Importation Agreement on Oct 31st, 1765, which they sent as a Circular Letter to all the colonies. Merchants in other colonies soon signed it.

Nov 1st was widely publicized as a day of public demonstration in all the colonies. From north to south the tolling of muffled bells and flags flying at half-mast in each colony brought men to gather on streets and commons to discuss taxation. Sailors rowed in from their ships and farmers drove their wagons into town. Men in taverns and on the streets were in an angry mood. Loud shouts, clanging bells and firing cannons literally shook New York City. As dark fell, a large crowd, led by some Sons of Liberty, gathered at the Fort, demanding release of the hated stamps. When Gov. Colden and Gen. Gage refused and threatened to fire on the crowd, the crowd marched up Broadway to the Commons and hung Colden in effigy. There the crowd grew larger and soon became a loud and unruly, but unarmed, mob. Carrying flaming torches to light the dark, they marched back down Broadway to the Fort again. This time they built a large bonfire on the Bowling Green, broke into the Governor's stable and threw his carriage into the bonfire, and hung another effigy of Governor Coldon. With angry taunts coming from both sides, including Sam's tenant Major James, General Gage barely prevented his hot-headed troops from firing on the crowd.

As the frustrated torch-lit mob stormed back uptown, shouts from the crowd led them to the expensive home of Major James. This was the beautiful Spring Gardens Vauxhall, which had leased from Samuel. Major James was particularly unpopular with the crowd because he had called them *'a filthy rabble'* and threatened to shoot the unarmed demonstrators. Within a few moments of arriving, the furious crowd broke in to ransack the house, filling the night with shouts and the sound of smashing glass and cracking wood. The mob carried off all the silverware and anything else of value, leaving the house in ruins. A letter written at the time of this event noted that: *"Maj James ordered 15 artillery soldiers at his command to his house, near the coledge where a black fam. formerly dwelled, and the rest of the soldiers he kept at the fort...then the mob went to Maj James house and drove the soldiers out the back way, then with one consent they began upon the house and in less than 10 minutes had the windows and dores, the looking glasses, mahogany tables, silk curtains, a library of books, all the china and furniture, the feather beds they cut and threw about the streets and burnt broke and tore the garden, drank 3 or 4 pipes of wine, destroyed the beef, throo the butter about and at last burnt the whole*

43

only one red silk curtain they kept for a colour…"[24] This letter, written in 1765, noted that Sam was *"black"*.

After the riots had gone on for several days, the Mayor and City Aldermen, trying to prevent further looting and damage, met with the elderly, outgoing Governor Colden requesting that he turn over the stamps to them. Colden decided to let the incoming Governor deal with it and gave them the stamps. As soon as the Stamps were brought to City Hall, the Mayor announced that the stamps would not be distributed. The night of November 5th rang with the joyful sound of church bells and cannons firing salutes. The crowd, having prevailed over the hated British, gave many mighty cheers before eventually drifting home.

The New York City Stamp Act Riot lasted 4 days and involved between 3000-4000 people. There were injuries but no deaths. British soldiers were furious at New Yorkers' refusal to abide by British law and the city remained on edge for the rest of the year. The NY Colonial Assembly indemnified those who incurred damages, paying Major James *L*1745 for his losses, while Andrew Gautier, as Sam's agent, received *L*404.6 as compensation in 1766. It seems hardly enough to replace all the windows and doors, repair the fire damage, and re-plant the extensive gardens.

As a result of the rising tensions, General Gage called in more troops from the frontiers, and sent them to fortify New York and Boston, creating an obligation for those unwilling cities to supply food and housing for them. Parliament passed a Quartering Act, requiring that, if there were insufficient barracks for them, troops were to be quartered in "*inns, ale houses, victualling houses and houses of sellers of wine*". This was not well received in either city. Sam was undoubtedly relieved to be in Philadelphia rather than New York. At least there, his inn would not be requisitioned for troops. In Boston, the soldiers pitched tents on the Boston Common.

1766 – Repeal

Loss of trade from the Non-Importation agreements soon led English merchants to appeal to Parliament, which finally gave up and repealed the Stamp Act on March 20th, 1766. The Sons of Liberty sponsored exuberant celebrations in every colony. Their non-violent protest against England had forced Parliament to back down and repeal the hated law! The New York City celebrations started at Howard's Hotel and moved uptown to the Commons. A 21 gun salute was fired, an ox was roasted, and 25 barrels of beer and a hogshead of rum were consumed by the joyful crowd. A Liberty Pole was installed a few days later, on the western side of the Commons between Murray and Warren Streets to commemorate the happy event. Its top flag was inscribed "*to his gracious majesty, George III, Mr. Pitt and Liberty*". The frustrations and celebrations over the Stamp Act eventually died down, and people went back to their normal lives.

Sam and Elizabeth had opened their first Philadelphia tavern on Front Street but advertised on June 12th that they had moved the Queen Charlotte Inn, from Front Street to Water Street a little above Market. They offered food in their Ordinary from 1-4, staying open for coffee and tea in the afternoons and supplying desserts from Sam's Confectionery Shop. He had begun specializing in pastries and cakes advertising that he would make wedding cakes and desserts for Wedding Suppers, presumably catering them as well. Advertisements noted a *"universal assortment of sweetmeats, grapes, cherries, currant jellies, strawberries, raspberries, yellow and green peaches, gooseberries in bottles, ketchup and home-made pickles among which are mangoes, peppers, cucumbers, kidney beans, mushrooms as well as pickled oysters in kegs or by the hundred for shipping"*. Opening a restaurant and bakery in Philadelphia, a sophisticated town of about 30,000 mostly Quaker inhabitants, then the largest city in the country, was a difficult undertaking and was certainly harder because Sam was a stranger and because of the prejudice there. Philadelphia was also suffering economically and by 1767 most Philadelphia merchants were in economic difficulty. Business was slow but real estate in Philadelphia was booming and rents kept rising.

After the additional soldiers were brought in, the NY Legislature refused to requisition supplies for them as required by the British Quartering Act. They agreed to support the Virginia Agreements in which all colonies asserted *"no taxation without representation"*, refusing to pay the Quartering Act taxes. This was defying English law and caused financial difficulties for the soldiers, which they, of course, resented. Meanwhile, the Sons of Liberty encouraged NY tavern keepers and merchants to shun soldiers and not hire them when off duty (which had supplied a necessary part of their income). The soldiers, feeling the hatred and economic pain, were spoiling for a fight which soon led to the Liberty Pole riots.

When the Stamp Act was first repealed in March 1766, the Sons of Liberty sponsored huge celebrations in all the Colonies. A permanent Liberty Pole was erected in New York City on June 6th, 1766. It stood at the western side of the Commons on the North side of Chambers Street, across from the block containing Sam's old Mason's Arms tavern and another tavern called Montaignes. Barracks stood nearby on the north side of the Commons and the young soldiers viewed the Liberty Pole as a symbol of all their frustrations. On August 10[th,] a group of soldiers from the 28th Regiment cut down the 1st pole. When a group of unarmed citizens gathered the following day to put up another pole, soldiers fired on them, inflicting severe wounds. British commanding officers declared the ensuing citizen complaints false and refused to punish the soldiers.

A 2nd pole was erected by the Sons of Liberty but stood only a few days before the same soldiers again cut it down on September 23rd, 1766.

A 3rd pole was erected and this time the newly appointed Royal Governor Moore restrained the soldiers. But on the night of March 18th, 1767, after watching the citizen's annual celebration of the Stamp Act Repeal, angry soldiers again cut down the pole.

A 4th pole was erected the next day, with iron bands around it. It withstood one attempt to cut it down and another attempt to blow it up before the Sons of Liberty set up a nightly guard, fighting off 3 more attempts by soldiers to destroy it. Governor Moore again ordered the soldiers to desist, and that 4th pole stood undisturbed for 3 more years.

In November, a group of 240 New York merchants signed another petition to Parliament, complaining about the continuing monopoly and explaining again *"why the West Indies trade was vital to the city's long term prosperity and should not be sacrificed for the short term purpose of raising revenue."*[25] Once again, their petition was ignored.

1767 – Taxes

Sam was still in Philadelphia when newspapers announced that the Townshend Declaratory Act passed in Parliament. This Act declared that Parliament could legally "bind the colonies in all cases whatsoever" reasserting Britain's total control. Townshend persuaded Parliament to tax even more items such as glass, paper, lead and tea. Most importantly, he convinced Parliament to suspend the New York Colony's Legislature for "failing to provide adequate support for British troops stationed in New York City". New York had resisted paying for the added troops, but suspension of their Legislature was retaliation way out of proportion. NY was furious over dismissal of their voting rights as English citizens. \

John Jones still owned Sam's original Mason's Arms uptown building and had unsuccessfully offered it for sale in May. When he didn't find a purchaser, he mortgaged the building to Roger Morris on 12 June, 1766 for 2000 milled Spanish pieces of eight, to obtain the funds for his new Ranelagh Gardens venue.[26] Shortly thereafter Richard Howard leased the building and became the tavern-keeper of the Mason's Arms Tavern,[27] noting that it *"was the house formerly kept by Samuel Francis on the west side of Broadway, on the Great Square"*. Interestingly, Howard referred to Sam in his ad, and not John Jones, who had kept the tavern for the prior 3 years. Howard was succeeded by Alexander Smith in Oct 1766 and the following year, Smith and a partner Murray, announced they had "*entered into a partnership for carrying on the business of Vintners and Victuallers at the Masons-Arms Tavern in the fields, lately kept by Smith alone.*" Jones finally sold the Mason's Arms at a public auction on Jan 25th, 1768, noting that it rented for *L*80 per annum. It was bought by Roger Morris, the mortgage holder, who hired Sam's best friend, Andrew Gautier to find a new tavern-keeper. Alexander Smith leased it again, and it was then sold to the Sons of Liberty in 1770 when Bicker became their tavern-keeper and renamed it Hampden Hall. It was almost directly across from the Liberty Pole on the Commons, in the same block as Montaigne's tavern. In May 1772, John Cox became tavern-keeper, succeeded in 1774 by Edward Bardin. When Bardin left to open a house and garden on Beekman Street, Samuel Fraunces, back in NY, and his partner, T.C. Campbell bought the building again, keeping the name, Hampden Hall.[28]

John Jones had been running the Queen's Head Tavern. To open another venue called Ranelagh Gardens, he resigned his position at the Queen's Head and leased property from Anthony Rutgers in July 1767 with 18 acres and a new house to be built.[29] Management of the Queen's Head was taken over in January 1767 by Bolton and Sigell who advertised breakfast, dinners, and public entertainment at the house of Samuel Fraunces, still calling it the Queen's Head tavern. From the frequent use of his name in advertisements, it was clear that Sam had a wonderful reputation. He still owned the Queen's Head

Tavern building and was receiving lease payments and possibly a percentage of the income for use of his name.

John Jones Ranelagh Gardens, with a large new house and pleasure garden was on a hill not far from Vauxhall Gardens, which Sam was now commuting from Philadelphia to repair after the mob had destroyed the gardens and much of the interior. Travel by stage between Philadelphia and New York was a three day journey each way in good weather, so Sam remained in NY for extended periods while he restored the Vauxhall property. Elizabeth managed the Queen Charlotte Inn in Philadelphia on her own, while pregnant, with 3 children under 8. During this period, Sam sent a note to a *"dear friend"*, merchant Thomas Clifford of Philadelphia, accompanied by a gift of 6 lobsters and a promise to see him again in 6 weeks indicating the usual length of his stay was at least that long. Thomas Clifford, though largely apolitical, had signed the earlier Philadelphia Non-Importation agreement.

Later that year, Elizabeth and Sam offered a *L*3 reward in Philadelphia for 2 run-away indentured servants, George Waller from Ireland (18) and Joseph King from England who had a red carbuncle on his face.[30]

1768 – Vauxhall

Sam and Elizabeth started 1768 in Philadelphia with the birth of another daughter named Catherine on January 26, 1768.[31] They returned to New York City four months later, moving back into Vauxhall in May. Sam undoubtedly thought it more advantageous to operate Vauxhall and the Queen's Head locations that he owned outright, to renting in Philadelphia. That June of 1768, Sam announced that Vauxhall Gardens had been completely renovated and was open for the summer. He noted that *"since his absence it had been occupied by Major James, but it was now in good order and prepared to serve the finest wines and other liquors, and relishes at all times. He offered large or small entertainments in the most genteel manner on shortest notice. Dinners, Suppers etc. could be dressed at Gentlemen's own houses and the utmost care would be taken on all occasions. Breakfasting, Tea, Coffee etc. Mead, Cakes, Tarts, Jellies, Sillibubs all at the lowest rates."[32]* The summer resort again became a popular spot.

The sound of quiet laughter and the sweet smell of flowers floated through Vauxhall Gardens. Cool breezes blew off the broad Hudson River, sparkling at the base of the small hill, cooling off the humid summer days as elegantly dressed people wandered under the shady trees in the gardens, watching stately ships sail up and down the river. When darkness fell, it became enchanting with flickering torches and candlelight. Vauxhall had 2 large gardens, and a dining hall building

56' long and 26' wide with a kitchen below, frequently rented for private balls. In addition to the gracious 12 room family home, there was a coach house, stables and staff to care for visitor's carriages and a good well. The upper garden offered flowering trees, manicured fragrant flower gardens and blossoming shrubs. The lower garden was devoted to vegetables and fruit trees, supplying enough produce for Sam's restaurants and market. Admission was 4 shillings.

Business began to slow as the noisy city grew north so Sam added a new attraction, a waxworks display. Wax figures were all the rage in Europe, first appearing in the Colonies in 1749. Sam, always looking for a new opportunity, embraced this popular curiosity providing *"genteel entertainment suitable for the entire family"*, and his exhibit became wildly popular. In this time before photographs, movies or magazines, only drawings, paintings or sculptures could show what a Queen or King really looked like. At Sam's Vauxhall Gardens, for a small fee, you could walk among life size figures whose faces were accurate sculptures of famous living people. You could see the sumptuous dresses, sparkling rings and shining crowns of your King and Queen. Was she really '*black looking*'? In the flickering torchlight, the figures seemed to come alive. What an experience!

Wax figures appeared in the colonies in 1749 when James Wyatt, apparently the first to do so, advertised an exhibit. Three years later in 1752, Richard Brickell advertised the same figures in a traveling exhibit in Philadelphia[33] for a fee of two shillings, 6 pence. By 1768, almost 20 years after Wyatt's original exhibition, wax figures were a popular pastime, and Sam began advertising a group of 10 figures at

Vauxhall Gardens, *"rich and elegantly dressed according to the ancient Roman and present mode."* One scene represented *"the great Roman General Publius Scipio who conquered the City of Carthage, standing by his tent, pitched in a grove of trees (among which are some of different fruits, very natural) attended by his guards; with the King, the young Prince and Princess, and other great Personages brought before the General who were taken prisoners in the city. Also, there are several very masterly pieces of Grotto-Work and Flowers, composed of various shells etc. The whole affording a very agreeable entertainment and are declared by those who have traveled and seen figures of the like kind, much admired in London and Paris, to be no way inferior."* [34]

In 1772 Sam added King George III and Queen Charlotte to his display: *"large as life, dressed in the newest and most elegant manner. Representing their present Majesties, King George and Queen Charlotte, sitting on the throne with their usual attendants, several of the nobility, all properly disposed in a large apartment genteelly fitted for the purpose and proper persons to show the same, from eight in the morning till ten in the evening."* Sam's exhibit continued to grow. He soon announced new additions *"To the Encouragers of Ingenuity and the Public in general: At Vaux-Hall in this City, there are to be seen at any Hour of the Day, a very great Variety of Wax Figures as large as Life, also entirely new dressed, and that in the most elegant as well as genteel Taste. Amongst other curious Representations, one Room contains that of the Banquet in Macbeth, with the Appearance of Banquo's Ghost, and a large Gallery filled with Spectators. Also,*

Harlequin and Columbine, are finished in a very pleasing Manner, and have attracted much Notice; in fine, no Representation of the like Kind has ever been in this City, by any Means equal to the Grandeur and agreeable Entertainment of the present, which have been compleated with very great Trouble and Expence." [35] Sam's life size figures were last mentioned and briefly exhibited at the Queen's Head Tavern after he sold Vauxhall Gardens in 1773. Sam's wax museum was considered equal to any then in existence.

One possible source for Sam's figures might have been two American Quaker sisters, Patience (Lovell) Wright and her sister Rachel Lovell who became successful enough at sculpting life size wax figures that they opened a Waxworks House in Philadelphia and another in New York City, in 1770. After a fire destroyed their Manhattan location on Queen Street, Patience moved to London where she sculpted many members of the nobility, including King George and Queen Charlotte. She also worked as a spy early in the American Revolution, sending information, hidden in her wax busts, to Benjamin Franklin. In 1780 she moved to Paris but, by then, miniature wax figures were more popular. She returned to London in 1782 and was preparing to return to the Colonies when she died in 1786. She was buried in an unmarked grave in London. Her sister Rachel continued sculpting and exhibited a talking figure in 1788 who would answer questions for a half dollar.

Philippe Curtius, popular at the French court, began showing his wax figures at fairs in France about 1770. By 1780 he had set up 2 exhibition spaces at the Palais Royal and Blvd du Temple in Paris. He bequeathed his wax figures to Madame Marie (Grosholtz) Tussaud, his illegitimate daughter and talented protégé. She continued to tour with Curtius's Cabinet of Curiosities in England until 1808. She later set up Madame Tussaud's in 1835 in Baker Street, London, still in existence today.

Advertisements for Vauxhall noted that there were also "*a collection of 70 miniature waxwork pieces including the Queen of Sheba bringing presents to King Solomon with a view of his palace courtyard and gardens*"[36]. A contemporary of Sam's noted that Vauxhall offered "*several masterly pieces of grotto work and flowers, composed of various shells etc., the whole thing affording a very agreeable entertainment*".[37] In 1773, shortly after Sam had sold Vauxhall, a newspaper ad appeared, offering a miniature *"Wax and Shell work.—This is to inform the Public, That at the House of Mr. M'Neill, at the Corner of Chapel-Street, opposite the new Brick Meeting-House, is to be seen, gratis, and disposed of publickly, by the 20th of May next; a most elegant Piece of Wax and Shell Work; the Scheme taken from Homer's Illiad. The Scene Hector and Andromache, with several other beautiful Figures, at the City Gate; the whole judged to be completely finished. The proprietors of this Work, beg leave to acquaint the Ladies, that as they intend continuing in New-York for a few Months they propose teaching, on the most reasonable Terms; the Wax and Shell in all its different Branches; and any Ladies inclining to be taught, by applying speedily, may have Time to be perfectly instructed, before their Departure from this Place. N.B. Ladies from the Country may be accommodated with Board at a moderate Price."*[38]

This ad would have aroused little interest except that, 10 years later, Sam made a gift to Martha Washington of a miniature shell work of this same famous scene.

Sam's note to President Washington said, *"I most earnestly beg your Excellency will order about the carriage of a small piece of Shell-Work which I have lately completed for Mrs. Washington purposely – whose acceptance of it will confer the greatest honor on me – the field is Hector and Andromache adorned with Shell-Flowers, the collections of a number of years."* Sam's gift to Martha was the same scene of Hector parting from his wife Andromache and their infant son, dressed in elaborate silk costumes with silver and gold threads, in a temple grotto with domestic animals and flowers made of wax, shells, fabrics and mica. They were enclosed in a hand built box of pine with a mahogany veneer and glass panes on the front and sides.

While this was a popular scene from mythology, it seems oddly coincidental that an almost identical tableau was advertised for sale at the house of Mr. McNeill on Chapel Street in 1773, blocks from recently sold Vauxhall. There are several possible explanations for this coincidence. The work advertised for sale may have been one of the miniatures on display at Vauxhall. Sam, who was an inspired wedding cake decorator may have made the original and offered it for sale, deciding to keep it when it didn't sell. Another possibility was that Sam may have seen this original and decided to emulate it for his gift ten years later. Or, perhaps, he bought the original tableau, updated it and constructed the display case for his gift to Mrs. Washington. His note indicated *"he had completed it purposely for Mrs. Washington"* and it

60

was the "*collection of a number of years*". This gift still exists. It is the only waxwork believed to have been made by a man. It took 15 months to transport this delicate gift from New York to Mount Vernon. Martha cherished his gift placing it in the bedroom she shared with George, where it remained until her death. The waxwork tableau and the chest on which it stood then went to Tudor Place, home of Martha (Custis) Peter, Martha Washington's granddaughter, where it is still displayed. In 2012, Samuel's gift was restored by Tudor Place at a cost of $37,400.

Frustrations continued growing over Townshend's taxes. In February, Samuel Adams of Massachusetts wrote another Circular Letter, supporting the idea of "*No Taxation Without Representation*", calling on all the colonies to unite in supporting non-importation agreements. England, determined not to back down, pressured the Royal Governors to force their Legislatures to repeal the Non Importation Agreements.

When the Massachusetts Legislature refused to repeal it, Parliament suspended the Massachusetts' Legislature, as they had New York's. Then, in September, Gen. Gage, Military Commander in the colonies, ordered two regiments to occupy Boston, including the 29th Regiment of Foot. This group's well-deserved reputation for poor discipline had already caused brawls in New York. Massachusetts Colonial officials were appalled at the suspension of their legally elected Legislature and a military occupation in response to their non-violent communications with Parliament and their King. They still considered themselves English citizens and entitled to their rights as such. Non-political citizens in Massachusetts and New York fumed over suspension of their Legislatures, which put a military occupying force in charge of each colony, although the elected officials in each city kept their positions. There were many small fights between soldiers and civilians which ultimately culminated two years later in the Battle of Golden Hill in New York and the Boston Massacre.

1769 – Choices

Opposition to the Townsend Acts was now in its 2nd year. In March 1769, a group of New York Merchants met at Sam's Queen's Head Tavern and established a Committee of Inspection to enforce their Non-Importation Agreement.

Samuel was 47 in 1769, at the height of his success. He owned 2 of the most famous restaurants and the finest resort in America. He was financially well off, and had overcome racial prejudice with his genial personality, excellent hospitality, fine food and well known generosity. What made him risk all that and alienate many of his clients for the Patriot cause? Sam and Elizabeth were of the prosperous self-made class, as were Elizabeth's Dally family and the Sons of Liberty. Another deciding factor was probably political distaste. Sam knew members of the New York Provincial legislature well because they met at his tavern. This Tory dominated body had first voted to support the Virginia Resolves, in solidarity with other colonies, opposing Parliament's rights to tax the colonies. Parliament had disbanded the NY Legislature but a new one, dominated by Tories was elected several years later. Then a new Governor arrived in NY and this Legislature abruptly held another secret vote. The Tory group, led by De Lancey, voted to comply with the Quartering Act. They provided £2000 to provision the troops that General Gates had moved to New York after the Stamp Act Riots, which NY had been refusing to support since 1759. All soldiers were now to be given adequate housing and provisions at the colony's expense. There was strong opposition from the Livingston faction (Whigs), who believed this decision was a complete repudiation of their principles. Alexander McDougall wrote a broadside, published in the New York papers, called "*To the Betrayed Inhabitants of the City and County of New York*" implying that the Royal Governor had promised the De Lancey group high ranking positions in exchange for their vote. They had McDougal arrested and jailed. This betrayal of the Virginia Resolves infuriated many New Yorkers and led to a complete separation of the political factions between the Tory De Lancey group, "*gentlemen class Friends of Liberty and Trade*" who ultimately became Loyalists, and the "*lower sorts*" Livingston-McDougall Whigs and their Sons of Liberty faction who became Patriots. Perhaps Sam simply didn't like or trust the De Lancey crowd. As the wealthiest merchants from aristocratic families, they were also the most class conscious and prejudiced. Another consideration might have been the rhetoric that the Whigs were using, referencing freedom from tyranny and slavery. A natural desire to oppose slavery in any form would have swayed Sam towards the Patriot side, although Patriots in NY certainly did not support freeing any real slaves at this point.

1770 – Massacres

This year started with everyone on edge. Citizens, agitated by news articles written by the Sons of Liberty were becoming unwilling to wait for peaceful solutions that weren't happening because Parliament ignored all communications from the Colonies, who still had no representation. British soldiers were becoming more unruly, and their officers increasingly unwilling to control them. These soldiers passionately hated the Sons of Liberty, considering them traitors. The Liberty Pole, erected and guarded by the Sons of Liberty, became a symbol to them of everything they hated. Above all, they believed these socially inferior provincial bumpkins should obey their masters, Britain, and its Army.

On Jan 13th, 1770, a party of soldiers from the 16th Regiment tried to blow up the 4th Liberty Pole. They were interrupted by several citizens and, furious at being thwarted, attacked the unarmed men in front of Montaigne's tavern. The civilians scrambled inside and barricaded the doors, but the soldiers smashed all the windows and broke down the door, entering with swords drawn and destroyed the tavern. They stabbed one man with a bayonet and badly beat another, leaving only when their commanding officers finally arrived and ordered them back to their barracks. The soldiers tried again to destroy the Liberty Pole and finally, on the 3rd night, they managed to cut it down and saw it up, dumping the pieces in front of Montaigne's Tavern, as a direct provocation to the Sons of Liberty.

The Liberty boys responded by circulating handbills calling for a public meeting the night of January 17th on the Commons. Over 3000 angry citizens showed up at the stump of the Liberty Pole. The elected civil authorities, moderate Law and Order Tories, passed strong resolutions against the daily vandalism and brawling by soldiers. They agreed not to employ any soldiers and threatened to arrest soldiers found outside barracks after roll call as enemies of the city, asserting that civilian rule was pre-eminent, as it was in all Colonies. The soldiers took that as a direct challenge to British authority. The next day two soldiers from the 16th Regiment were arrested while posting handbills insulting McDougal, the Sons of Liberty and insisting the military was supreme even in civilian matters. They were brought to the mayor's office to be held for a civilian trial.

About 20 soldiers rushed to the mayor's office, pulled their bayonets, and stormed the building to release them. The mayor and a group of Aldermen refused to release the men and ordered the soldiers back to their barracks. The angry soldiers refused the mayor's orders, but did eventually move up the street, bayonets still drawn. Aldermen and others followed to prevent vandalism. As the angry soldiers reached the top of Golden Hill, near John and William Streets, they were joined by a larger group from the barracks on the Commons, agitated about the arrests. At this point, an officer ordered them to draw their bayonets and cut their way through and they turned and charged into the unarmed crowd. A few men at the front had sticks and were able to briefly hold off the soldiers. Another group of soldiers from the downtown Fort, seeing a brawl and fearing their brother soldiers were under attack, charged up from the bottom of the hill, attacking the civilians from the rear. The noisy, bloody brawl was eventually dispersed before anyone was killed, though several unarmed civilians were seriously injured.

Angry soldiers spent the night fuming over the impending civil trial of the two soldiers, and the outraged citizens of all parties vented their fury in the taverns over the soldiers' behavior and unprovoked attacks on unarmed civilians. The next morning, a group of soldiers accosted and assaulted a woman on her way home from market, wounding her slightly before a group of men came to her rescue. Around noon, a group of civilian sailors brawled with soldiers and a sailor was believed mortally injured by a soldier's bayonet. The soldiers again ignored the mayor's order to disperse. Since their commanding officers were nowhere to be found, a large group of civilians, Tory and Whig, gathered to enforce the mayor's order. This was a true riot and the furious citizens fought and routed the soldiers, who were driven back to barracks. Word spread through the city like wildfire that soldiers had again attacked unarmed citizens and several hundred men, including the city leaders, again gathered on the Commons to discuss the deteriorating situation.

A group of 20 soldiers, diverted from the direct route to their barracks, and marched right into the middle of this town hall meeting. The civilians, refusing to be provoked, quietly separated to let them pass, until one older man made a taunting comment. A soldier broke

67

ranks and grabbed the man's cane, trying to beat him with it. This set off another brawl in which the furious New Yorkers were again victorious. These 2 days of street fighting were called the 'Battle of Golden Hill'. These large riots, 6 weeks before the Boston Massacre, were the first blood spilled in the Revolution, although no one died. People realized the hated and unwanted English Army they had been forced to pay for, had turned on them.

People read incredulously about the Battle of Golden Hill. With the military refusing to control or punish their soldiers, there was tremendous concern. If these soldiers could attack unarmed colonists including women and the Tory Mayor of the 2nd largest city in the Colonies with impunity, what was next? Civilians and soldiers were all itching for a fight after years of hostility, and anger was rising to the boiling point. In this tense atmosphere, the NY Sons of Liberty requested permission to re-erect a 5th Liberty Pole on the Commons and the Council, trying to keep order, refused. So, the Sons of Liberty bought a private piece of property 11 feet wide and 100 feet long near the original site and erected a new pole on Feb 6th, 1770. This pole was seated 12' deep and encased for most of its height with iron bands riveted together. It bore the inscription, *"Liberty and Property"* – the phrase *"to his gracious majesty, George III"* was left off this one.

Another attempt was made on the new Liberty Pole on April 21st and citizens trying to stop it were forced to retreat to Hampden Hall which the British soldiers surrounded and threatened to burn. Bickers and his family sent someone out the back way to sound the alarm bells, bringing rescue in time. The pole then remained undisturbed until 1775 when a British Sgt. Cunningham tried to assault some men around the pole and was severely beaten. In retaliation, one of his first orders when the British occupied the city in 1775 was to remove the Liberty Pole.

In the middle of this street brawling Sam re-opened Queen's Head Tavern. On Sept 3rd, 1770, he placed a large ad noting: '*On Thursday the 20th will be opened the Queen's Head Tavern, near the Exchange, for many years kept by the Subscriber (late by Bolton and Sigell) is now fitting up in the most genteel and convenient manner for the Reception and Entertainment of those Gentlemen, Ladies and others who may please to favor him with their company. As the best Clubs, and the greatest entertainments in this city were at the above Tavern, in the time of the Subscriber, he flatters himself the public are so well satisfied of his ability to serve them as to render the swelling of an advertisement useless, other than to assure his former friends and the public in general that every endeavor will be used to give them the highest satisfaction and the utmost respect on all occasions, as shown by their already much obliged and very obedient servant, Samuel Francis*

N.B. Dinners and suppers dressed to send out for lodgers and others who live at a convenient distance, also cakes, tarts, jellies, whip syllybubs, Blaumange, Sweetmeats etc. in any quantity; cold meat in small quantities, Beef stakes etc. at any house; pickled oysters for the West Indies or elsewhere. The house at the Gardens will be duly attended as usual. [39] He also advertised that the tavern was open *"For the Polite and Rational Amusement of Philosophical Lectures"*. For the next several years Sam and Elizabeth ran both the Queen's Head Tavern and Vauxhall Gardens. Elizabeth managed the uptown Gardens. It was their home, quieter and with room for their 4 children aged 3-12, while Sam managed the downtown Queen's Head Tavern. Elizabeth oversaw schooling their children. She could read, write and do sums, something few women of the time knew how to do. She taught them well and the boys all became successful businessmen.

Each year, Abraham de la Montaigne held, in his tavern garden across from the Commons, an annual celebration for Stamp Act Repeal. But in 1770, Montaigne's tavern was reserved by the De Lancey Tory faction for the annual celebration. Since this group had just repudiated the Virginia Resolves, the moderate Livingstone Whig faction and more volatile Sons of Liberty refused to join them and decided to buy their own tavern. A notice was placed in the NY Gazette, notifying the Sons of Liberty in the city of their intent to buy the *"Corner House on Broad Way near the Liberty Pole, lately kept by Edward Smith"*. The Sons of Liberty bought Smith's Tavern on the corner of Warren and Broadway and named it Hampden Hall, installing Henry Bicker as the tavern manager. They celebrated the 1770 Stamp Act anniversary in their new tavern and garden. Hampden Hall was Sam's original Mason's Arms building and Sons of Liberty continued to congregate there until shortly before the English occupied Manhattan.[40] The new tavern set off a competition with Montaigne's Tavern, in the same block, over how large their respective celebrations had been. Henry Bicker attested under oath that over 300 men had paid for the celebration dinner at Hampden Hall. The De Lancey group at Montaigne's was considerably smaller and apparently a number of his guests had never actually paid. A newspaper ad placed, by the Widow Montaigne Sept 17th, 1780, in English occupied Manhattan, requested the past due payments for that celebration, threatening to list debtors' names in the paper.[41]

Boston was also a powder keg. Much as the Liberty Pole was a lightning rod for disaffected soldiers in New York, Boston's Custom's House and its employees were a symbol of England's hated taxes. In February, Ebenezer Richardson, a Boston Customs employee, threatened a group of boys throwing stones at his house. When a stone broke a window, striking his wife, he angrily fired a rifle into the crowd, hitting 11 year old Christopher Seider, who died later that night. This child was the first person killed in the Revolution. His funeral became the largest held in Boston and over 2000 people attended. Richardson was convicted of murder in civilian courts but at once received a Royal pardon and a new job with the Customs Service. England was making it plain that they would overrule civilian laws despite English laws to the contrary. A few weeks later, on March 5th, 1770, a few boys were harassing a sentry, Pvt. Hugh White, outside the Custom House on King Street. A wigmaker's apprentice, named Garrick, taunted a passing Officer, Capt. John Goldfinch, claiming that he had not paid his wigmaker's bill. Goldfinch, having paid the bill the prior day, ignored the insult but Pvt. White left his post and knocked Garrick out with a blow to the side of his head from his musket butt for being *"disrespectful"* to a British officer. Of course, civilians had no legal obligation to be respectful to an Army officer. A friend of Garrick's angrily confronted Pct. White about the assault, and the furious Pvt. White threatened to shoot both men. As the dispute escalated, church bells rang an alarm, bringing more people out. Pvt. White, now surrounded by about 50 men and boys, yelling and throwing snowballs at him, sent for support and 7 additional soldiers arrived and stood in a rough semicircle on the steps of the Customs House, facing the crowd. The angry civilian crowd grew to 350 people who began throwing snowballs at the soldiers, yelling taunts and daring them to fire. One soldier was hit in the head by an icy snowball and fell, dropping his weapon. Embarrassed and furious at the jeers, he picked up his rifle and fired into the crowd. There was a shocked moment of silence, then, although no order to fire was given, the 8 members of the 29th Grenadier Company, fired into the crowd in a ragged volley, hitting 11 men. Three died instantly, including Crispus Attucks, a 47 year old sailor of Indian and black descent; Samuel Gray a rope maker; and mariner James Caldwell. Samuel Maverick a 17 year old apprentice and Patrick Carr, an Irish immigrant, both died later of their wounds. Six others were injured in the incident which became known as the 'Boston Massacre'. Paul Revere, a Boston silversmith and a Sons of Liberty member, engraved a propaganda piece, widely printed throughout the colonies, depicting a solid line of Royal troops firing point blank into a crowd, although there were actually only 8 soldiers involved. The soldiers claimed self-defense against the large, threatening crowd. When they were brought to court-martial in October, six of the soldiers were

acquitted outright. The other two were found guilty of manslaughter and their only punishment was to be branded on their thumbs.

In April, due to pressure from English merchants suffering from the Non-Importation Agreements, Parliament gave in again and repealed the Townshend Acts, as they had done with the Stamp Act, removing taxes on most imports except tea. The passive resistance of the Non-Importation Agreements had worked again. They also decided not to renew the much resented Quartering Act, hoping to defuse the rising anger. But it was far too little, and far too late.

1771 – Quiet

After repeal of the Townsend Acts things were relatively quiet. In January Sam and Elizabeth offered Vauxhall Gardens for sale. The city had grown out around it and Vauxhall was no longer the peaceful retreat it had been. With no offers, Sam kept both venues going and introduced the Wax Works exhibit to encourage clients to come. The city built a retaining wall to protect his foundation which had been damaged when streets were widened.

In June, an incident in the NY newspapers showed just how aggressive soldiers had gotten against citizens. It told of two visitors from Brookhaven, LI who had checked into Mr. Milner's Inn downtown and walked into Exchange Plaza. They were followed by 3 soldiers who suddenly attacked them without provocation. The British sentry in the plaza did not help, and the men, beaten and badly injured, were dragged to the guard house and accused of throwing stones at the sentry. Despite their protests, they were held for several hours and only released upon payment of 45s, paid under duress as one feared bleeding to death. The following day the men complained to the British Commanding Officer and were advised to request a Court Martial, which they did. They brought witnesses who testified that they had just arrived, were respectable businessmen and had not thrown stones. Four soldiers appeared as defense witnesses and perjured themselves, insisted they had seen the men throw stones at the sentry and claiming that the money was not extorted, but was a bribe paid to obtain release without further inquiry. The soldiers were cleared of all charges by their officers. The civilians were then informed that, having had a Court Martial, they could not bring a civil suit for damages. Unfair incidents like incensed the population.

The NY Provincial Council met at Sam's Queen's Head Tavern to plan a welcome dinner for the new Gov. Tryon. In August, Sam was paid L48.16.4 for this entertainment by the Board. Sam's was still the finest place in town.

1772 – Unity

By 1772 the Sons of Liberty were active in every colony. Most citizens supported the Non-Importation Agreements, refusing to buy any taxed imports, including sugar and tea. In November, Samuel Adams called a meeting in Boston to form a Massachusetts Committee of Correspondence. They wrote a 3 part <u>Boston Pamphlet</u> and distributed it to every town in Massachusetts and to leaders of the other colonies. The first part outlined the rights of British American Colonists as English citizens; the second noted how the recent British policies violated those rights; and the third was a Letter of Correspondence addressed to towns in the Massachusetts Colony urging unified action against. The Boston meeting was prompted by news that the salaries of Royal Governors, Lt. Governors and Judges, previously paid by each Colony, were now to be paid by Parliament, making these officials dependent on Parliament and removing the only tool the colonies had of withholding their pay to induce cooperation.

The issue of self-rule, and independence from Britain, was now openly being discussed. All the colonies, whether dominated by Whigs or Tories, promptly passed similar resolves and agreed to act with unity.

1773 – Tea

This was another year of bubbling agitation. Most Colonies now had Committees of Correspondence. The economy was still depressed and a lack of English currency and support for non-Importation policies led to many shortages.

In September 1773, Sam and Elizabeth sold Vauxhall Gardens. Their land-lease was L40 per year for 27½ lots with 61 years remaining on the lease.[42] In the past 5 years the noisy city had surrounded Vauxhall and the neighborhood had deteriorated. Vauxhall Gardens was bought by Erasmus Williams who re-named it Mount Pleasant and advertised the large structure as a lodging house. It was noted as being *"near the college and the hospital now under construction"* (that hospital was on Jones' former Ranelagh Gardens property which had also closed) and located so *"within 15-20 minutes a moderate walker could be anywhere"*. A variety of resorts using the name Vauxhall Gardens operated in later years in different locations, leapfrogging development, but Sam was not involved with any of them.

Sam now 51, and Elizabeth 33, moved back into the Queen's Head Tavern on Pearl Street downtown. Their family had grown to include newborn Sarah, 5 year old Catherine, 8 year old Elizabeth, 12 year old Margaret, and 14 year old Andrew. The 3 attic rooms at the Queen's Head were certainly crowded. Sam and Elizabeth now publicly supported non-Importation and advertised that they offered: "*fine ale of this country, equal to any imported draft and porter from London, many wines of different sorts, punch and other liquors.*"

The Colonies still had no representation in Parliament and in May 1773, tone deaf Parliament again provoked outrage when they passed the Tea Act.

The East India Trading Company had existed for almost 100 years and made its shareholders extremely wealthy, socially, and politically influential. So, when the Company, deeply in debt, appealed to Parliament for help, they did. The Company owned 18 million pounds of unsold tea so Parliament decreed that the East India Trading Company would become the sole supplier of tea to the Colonies. This perhaps could have been acceptable, but Parliament then exempted the Company from paying tea taxes and authorized them to sell directly to consumers through their own paid agents.

Newspapers were inflamed by this new outrage and taverns were again full of shouting and table thumping fury. This decree put American merchants in direct competition with a company who already owned tea they had been selling to them, didn't have to pay taxes on it and could undercut any price by selling through their own employees. This arrangement threatened all merchants who soon realized they could be cut out as middlemen on other products as well, since England had a monopoly on trade. This act thoroughly provoked the previously moderate merchants who were trying to mediate. Angry consumers chose to drink more expensive smuggled tea or coffee, believing the taxes set a precedent since they still had no representation.

In September 1773, the East India Trading Company shipped its first 500,000 pounds of tea to its designated *'tea agents'* in the Colonies. American sentiment was almost unanimous that any tea should be shipped back or thrown overboard in a widely publicized *"Return or Ruin"* policy. When the first tea ships arrived in Philadelphia in October, the tea agents there were pressured to resign, and the ships returned to England without offloading. In Charleston, the tea was offloaded and promptly dumped into the river. A second shipment to Philadelphia was also unsuccessful when that captain, threatened with tar and feathering, left without putting into port. Newspapers published all these events and angry citizens vowed not to drink any tea. In Lexington, Massachusetts every bit of tea in town was donated and burned in a great protest bonfire. Coffee became the patriotic beverage of choice.

Boston unsuccessfully tried to get their tea agents to resign. When 3 ships carrying tea arrived in Boston Harbor the Massachusetts Royal Governor refused to let the ships sail out of the harbor until the taxes were paid. Boston citizens put the *'Return or Ruin'* agreement into action. One cold December night, a number of men disguised as Indians boarded the 3 ships and threw 342 chests of tea overboard. Even though armed British warships surrounded them, not one shot was fired, and no one was ever arrested, although many knew the men involved in the Boston Tea Party.

81

This act was a huge provocation to England. The cost to the East India Company for 92,000 pounds (46 tons) of lost tea on Dec 16th, 1773, was over $1,725,000 in present day money. Most Boston citizens cheered the men of Boston Tea Party, but England was not amused, and Parliament vowed that someone was going to pay.

1774 – Intolerable

In 1774, Sam and Elizabeth celebrated the birth of their second son, named Samuel M. in New York City. Samuel M. was the first of their children to have much darker skin and throughout his life he and his descendants were identified as Negro. This child and his descendants conclusively prove that Sam was of mixed race. The Queen's Head tavern was now the de facto headquarters of activity against the Tea Act. Sam's empathy for the underdog matched the mood of the Patriots far better than the Tory Loyalists. Sam valued his freedom more than most and was not about to let England 'enslave' him, financially or politically. The New York Tea Party was planned in April 1774 at Sam's Tavern. It began when a Sons of Liberty group took control of the *HMS Nancy* at Sandy Hook on April 22nd. They prevented the crew from disembarking and escorted her Captain Lockyear into New York City to Sam's Tavern. The NY Committee persuaded the consignees to refuse the shipment and Capt. Lockyear agreed not to offload his 698 chests of tea.

While Capt. Lockyear prepared to return to England, the *London* arrived. Her Captain Chambers had sailed from Charleston and intelligence from there informed the New York Committee that Chambers had tea on board. He too was interrogated at Sam's tavern by the Committee, and finally admitted he had 18 tea chests aboard, smuggled for his own profit. A group stormed his ship, dumped his tea in the river and used the tea chests to start bonfires in the streets. The NY Tea Party took place on April 22nd, 1774. Again, no arrests were made. Gen. Gage vowed punishment. He drafted a series of punitive measures that were passed by Parliament. These became known as the Intolerable Acts and led both sides inexorably closer to war.

The first Intolerable Act, the Massachusetts Government Act, was passed on May 20th when Parliament revoked the charter creating the Massachusetts Colony and declared the Colony an occupied military protectorate of England. Every elected official was replaced by appointees of Gen. Gage who occupied Boston with four regiments. This act went far beyond the earlier disbanding of the Colony's Legislature. This was an outright military occupation and suspension of all civilian rule. The Massachusetts Colony no longer existed.

Parliament then issued the Boston Port Act, in retaliation for the Boston Tea Party, which closed Boston's port on June 1st, 1774, throwing thousands of Bostonians out of work. Other colonies had to send food overland prevent starvation.

Gage, acting independently, then declared any meeting of more than 3 men to be treason and ordered his appointed officers to arrest anyone at such a gathering. At this, real fury erupted throughout all the colonies. Assembly was not a treasonable offence under English law. Only Parliament could alter the Treason Act of 1537 and they had not done so. Even Loyalists knew Gage had totally overstepped his authority and warned Gage and Parliament that the colonies would never accept this usurpation of their English constitutional rights and enforcing this would result in retaliation. Their letters were ignored.

The majority of the American population now believed that England intended to ruin them financially to force subjugation. Rhetoric equated this tyranny with slavery. Moderates of both parties kept trying to obtain representation in Parliament, feeling that war could still be averted if they had a political voice, but could not gain enough support in Parliament to force a vote.

As the new leaves of spring sprouted in 1774, so did public agitation. A Continental Convention was to be held in Philadelphia to discuss these matters. A meeting was called in June at "Black Sam's" Tavern to create a committee to elect delegates for the Continental Convention. That meeting created the original NY Committee of 51, dominated by members of De Lancey's Tory faction. When the non-politically connected people of Manhattan heard the Tories controlled this group, they held an immense mass meeting on the Commons on July 6th which made clear that the majority stood with the Hampden Hall, Patriot Whig, Sons of Liberty faction and the Tory controlled Committee of 51 was disbanded. Another meeting at 'Mr. Fraunces Tavern' then appointed the delegates who attended the First Continental Congress. It was evenly split between factions, but the Tory Provincial Congress instructed them to seek resolution with Britain.[43] Massachusetts delegates, traveling to the Continental Congress, were entertained by the New York delegates at Fraunces Tavern. The diary of John Adams notes it as: *"the most splendid dinner I ever saw; a profusion of rich dishes, etc."*

From Sept 5th to October 26th, 1774, this First Continental Congress met at Carpenter's Hall in Philadelphia. All the colonies, except Georgia, sent elected delegates. Virginia's Peyton Randolph was quickly elected president of the body which produced a Declaration, asserting colonial rights to *"Life, Liberty and Property"* and a series of Resolves, opposing the Intolerable Acts. Among the resolves was a prohibition on the slave trade. This decreed that no additional slaves could be imported and sold into the Colonies, even though NY was the center of the slave trade. Slavery quickly became contentious between the more industrial north and the agricultural south. This First Continental Congress also created The Association to support Non-Importation Agreements. Congress sent copies of the Declaration and Resolves to Britain and published them throughout the Colonies. Delegates agreed to stay active and to meet again the following year if their grievances were not addressed by Parliament. The New York Committee continued meeting at *"Black Sam's"* where, in November, a bill was paid for their expenses for: *"L4.14.6 for "Madeira 35, Punch 5, Sangary 3, Porter 16 and Spruce 1/6."*[44]

Newspapers carried conflicting descriptions of all this, depending on their editors. People were in a constant state of tension and, whenever a ship arrived in port, taverns filled with men wanting to hear and discuss the latest news from England. Sam did well in the busy port of NY.

In December, Paul Revere's Patriot Underground spies in Boston learned King George had issued a proclamation prohibiting export of arms and ammunition to the colonies and ordered the Army in America to *"secure their weapons"*.

At this time, America had no large scale gun manufacturers, so weapons were bought abroad. The American long rifle was made one at a time, making then expensive and scarce. European gun-makers had an assembly line process where specialists made one or two parts, like a barrel or trigger that were sent to a central assembly location. This enabled low cost, high volume production and the large standing armies of Europe supported a strong market. Many Americans now believed war was coming and knew weapons and ammunition would be critical. The poorly guarded Fort William and Mary, in the mouth of Portsmouth Harbor, New Hampshire was selected as a target.

The Boston Committee of Correspondence sent Paul Revere on a dangerous 55 mile horseback ride on icy, rutted roads to warn Portsmouth that Gage was sending reinforcements to the fort. When Revere arrived with the news, Samuel Cutt sent word to the Portsmouth Committee of Correspondence who at once organized 200 men to seize the gunpowder from the fort. Camouflaged in a blinding snowstorm, they rowed to the fort with 200 more men from neighboring towns. Despite being shot at by the soldiers, the unarmed group broke in, looting the fort of its 16 cannons, 60 muskets and all its ammunition. This was the first organized assault on the King's property, considered the *"first victory of the American Revolution",* and led to Gage's later decision to confiscate the Patriot arms at Concord.

87

NY and Brooklyn in 1776

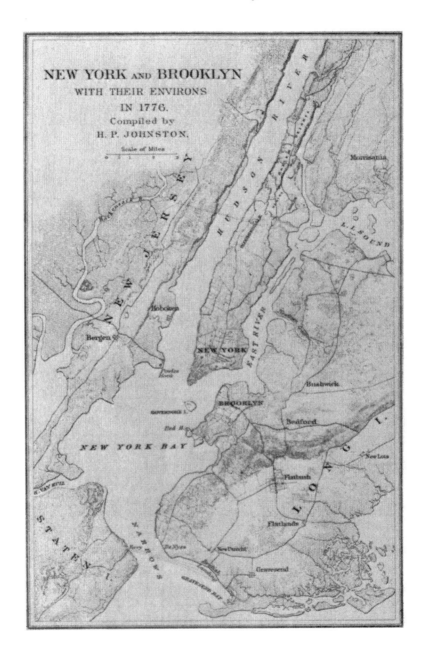

The War Years

1775 – War

After Gage disbanded the Massachusetts Colony legislature, former members of the Legislature secretly formed the Massachusetts Provincial Congress. Led by John Hancock and Samuel Adams, they called for local armed militias to be created throughout Massachusetts and encouraged all colonies to prepare for armed conflict. When Parliament heard they were advocating armed resistance, they declared Massachusetts in an *"open state of rebellion"* and retaliated by ordering all the Massachusetts ports, not just Boston, closed and blockaded. Gage was ordered to suppress this *"rebellion"*, even though there had been no armed resistance at this point. On March 23rd, Patrick Henry delivered his speech, swearing he would never be 'enslaved', and declared *"Give me Liberty or Give me Death!"*

Parliament issued another Intolerable Act on March 30th. The Restraining Act banned the New England Provinces from fishing in the North Atlantic and closed all ports. Only New York, Delaware, North Carolina and Georgia ports remained open. New York was suddenly crowded with diverted ships and Sam's tavern became the center of all the news from Europe.

This blockade crippled New England's economy, as intended. Their ship-building facilities and fishing fleets had become the economic engine for the region. Fish supplied 35% of New England's total export income, which shipped 85% of all fish caught in the colonies, employing thousands of men.[45] Fishing of cod for food and whales for lamp oil, involved 8% of the adult male population, almost 10,000 men.[46] Even small towns like Gloucester had a fleet of over 100 vessels. Now they were out of work. The blockade kept food and goods out of New England. Shops closed and starvation was avoided only when other colonies again sent food overland. Then the British Navy began forcibly impressing seamen. Resentment increased even more.

Samuel and Elizabeth listed the Queen's Head tavern for sale, hoping to buy Hampden Hall. New York was benefitting financially from the problems in New England but, with the looming threat of war, the Queen's Head didn't sell. Why would Sam and Elizabeth want to sell the best known, most elegant restaurant in the Colonies, with a built in clientele from the nearby busy harbor? Hampden Hall (their original Mason's Arms) had been their first married home. It offered more bedrooms for their growing family now that they no longer owned Vauxhall Gardens. It had a large garden and was located across from the Commons where the children could play. They now had 6 children from 1 to 16 and the Queen's Head was too crowded. Hampden Hall was on the busiest most fashionable street in uptown. But, perhaps most compelling, British were expected to shell the city, and the Queen's Head was located dangerously close to the harbor. The uptown location would certainly be safer. When the Queen's Head didn't immediately sell, Sam quickly reassured his clients that he was still in business and instead took on a partner, Mr. T.C. Campbell. Together they bought the old Mason's Arms-Hampden Hall tavern and announced that they had:

"opened the large commodious house lately occupied by Edward Bardin, corner of Warren Street, in the road to the Water Works where coffee, hot rolls, mead, cakes and every other genteel entertainment would be provided. NB: The Queen's Head tavern near the Exchange is kept by Francis and Campbell as usual."[47] Elizabeth and Campbell probably ran Hampden Hall while Sam ran the downtown Queen's Head, now with more rooms for lodgers.

Samuel's new partner was Thomas Charles Campbell, a dealer in linen, china, and glass. This was apparently his only venture into tavern keeping, and he may not have been personally involved, only lending funds. There is no evidence that he was a Loyalist and much to show he was not. Hampden Hall was closed shortly before Washington's Army occupied Manhattan when Sam sent Elizabeth and the children out of town for safety. When the English occupied the city, Hampden Hall was used for housing English soldiers. The Queen's Head was also used for housing early in the British Occupation until 1778, when it was reopened by Loyalist tavern operators, John and William Smith.[48] In another indication that TC Campbell was a Patriot, he returned to the linen business in NY City after the war. Loyalists were not welcomed and most moved back to England or to Nova Scotia. An older widower with adult children, he married Samuel's 16 year old daughter, Sarah, in 1789. That November he advertised his linen shop on Maiden Lane. Their only child, Marie, was born in New York City in 1804.

Gage then decided to make a secret raid with 700 British soldiers to seize Patriot munitions stored at Concord. Colonial spies learned his plans and removed most of the arms and ammunition. Because Revere, Dawes and Prescott warned the countryside of the raid in their famous midnight ride, militia gathered at Lexington and Concord to confront the British, who had to go through Lexington to reach Concord. That dawn on April 19th, 1775, about 70 militiamen stood face to face on Lexington Green with the British advance guard. It was later determined from witnesses including the British, that the British had fired *"the shot heard 'round the world"* beginning the battle, which left 8 Colonials dead and 10 wounded. The British finally reached Concord, destroying the remaining colonial supplies, but the militia and local farmers forced the Redcoats into a running retreat along the entire route to Boston, killing 250 soldiers. The Lexington and Concord militias offered the first armed resistance against England.

New York City was electrified when they heard the news. A group of NY Patriots immediately seized 530 weapons at the arsenal. The Customs House and all public stores were seized and the whole city was *"one continued scene of riot, tumult and confusion."*[49] Loyalists on the NY Provincial Council proposed to *"read them the riot act"* and imprison the ringleaders, but cooler heads among them noted that the *"ferment was general and not confined to a few"* and declined to provoke a confrontation. The city then learned that England was sending 14 more regiments to New York. Angry men began parading around Manhattan carrying guns. Over 3000 men attended a great meeting on the Commons to form Militia companies and the NY

Provincial Congress created a Committee of Safety of 100 men to run the city. This Committee shut the port of NY, intercepted and read mail, and moved cannons from the Battery to Kings Bridge to prevent British troops from entering Manhattan Island by land. They sent out a resolution that "*every inhabitant be provided with arms, accoutrements and ammunition.*"[50] New York City, filled with British soldiers and a port full of English Naval ships, began preparing for war.

The Massachusetts Provincial Congress met on April 23rd and agreed to go to war over the British occupation of Boston. They ordered 13,600 men to be mobilized into 26 militia company regiments. New Hampshire, Rhode Island, and Connecticut raised smaller forces and volunteers from all over New England marched to Boston, establishing militia camps around the occupied city.

The Colonies organized a 2nd Continental Congress in Philadelphia. On May 6th, John Adams and John Hancock, Massachusetts delegates to the 2nd Continental Congress, arrived at Kings Bridge, Manhattan, on their way to Philadelphia. There they met up with delegates from Connecticut, and all were escorted into Manhattan by nearly 1000 armed men. Thousands of clapping, cheering citizens of Manhattan lined the road and the city bells rang. The crowds went with the delegates to Sam's where the delegates had dinner at the Queen's Head with important local leaders. Several delegates stayed at Sam's and others lodged at Capt. Sears' house before continuing their trip.[51]

The 2nd Continental Congress met in Philadelphia from May 10th to December 12th of 1775 at the Pennsylvania State House. They elected John Hancock President. Congress realized that war was inevitable and recommended that all the colonies prepare.

On June 14th Continental Congress created the first Continental Army selecting wealthy Col. George Washington of the Virginia Militia as Commander in Chief. Washington accepted his commission on June 16th, offering to serve without pay, asking only that his expenses be covered after the war. His Army consisted of the 22,000 militia troops now massed around Boston and 5000 militia men in New York. Militia men typically enlisted for only 3 months.

Congress also decided that 10 additional companies of Continental Army troops were to be raised by each colony for one year enlistments. They then created some structure to run a country made up of diverse Colonies. On July 26th they created a Postal Service with Benjamin Franklin the Postmaster General. They authorized the printing of money, in defiance of the English Currency Act of 1764. On Nov 10th, they approved the Continental Marine Corps and on November 28th the Continental Navy was established. They appointed a secret committee to seek help from Europe. Most of this was widely reported and the British were infuriated.

On June 17th, 1775, the Battle of Bunker Hill (actually Breed's Hill) took place on Charlestown Peninsula overlooking Boston Harbor. William Prescott's Militia of 1200 men holding the high ground, was attacked by over 2000 British soldiers who charged up the hill in organized rows. The Colonial militia, with little ammunition and no bayonets, was famously ordered not to fire: "*until you see the whites of their eyes*". Their first volley mowed down the Redcoats, who retreated. The 2nd charge was also mowed down forcing another retreat, but the 3rd charge was successful when the militia ran out of ammunition. The British lost over 1000 men, many of them command officers, and over 800 more were wounded. The Colonists lost about 140 men with 300 wounded, but most were able to escape. Although the Colonists lost that battle, they performed with great bravery, inflicting massive casualties on the British. Washington learned of the battle as he started riding from Philadelphia to Boston, and he made sure the newspapers praised the militia's heroic acts. Even the British commended the bravery of the Militia men. Word of the battle reached New York on June 22nd. War had officially begun.

On June 25th, Washington arrived in New York on his way to Boston, the same day that New York's Royal Gov. Tryon returned from a visit to England. The city received General Washington with great joy at 4 pm. Then at 9 pm Tryon arrived and was amazed to hear bells ringing, great cheering and drums beating. He delightedly asked, "*Is all this for me?*" but was mortified to see Gen. Washington pass by on Broadway, attended by beating drums and cheering crowds, on his way to fight the British in Boston.[52]

On June 27th, Generals Wooster, Schuyler and other officers of the Connecticut forces dined at Mr. Samuel Fraunces in the Fields

(Hampden Hall) *"where elegant entertainment was provided by the New York Military Club. The Day was spent in utmost Harmony, everything conspiring to please, being all of one Mind and one Heart."*[53]

In Philadelphia, the 2nd Continental Congress, in one last effort to avoid war, sent an Olive Branch Petition to Britain in July. This was a direct appeal to King George, asking him to mediate between Tory and Whig factions in Parliament. However, before the delegation could present their petition, the King issued a Proclamation for Suppressing Rebellion and Sedition. His unwillingness to hear the Olive Branch Petition, or act as a mediator, doomed the moderate position.

The 2nd Continental Congress issued a written response to the King and Parliament stating that they had always been loyal to the King, but they believed Parliament had no legitimate authority over them because the Colonies were not represented in Parliament. They said that it was their duty as loyal Englishmen to continue resisting this violation of the British Constitution. King George retaliated by declaring all the Colonies to be in an Open State of Rebellion and issued a Proclamation closing all colonies to commerce and trade. With the British monopoly, this was intended to force capitulation.

There were good men on both sides of this issue. Most people in America believed they deserved representation in Parliament and their rights as citizens were being ignored. Moderates believed the problems were essentially political and could be resolved. But there were also underlying loyalties that led people to choose sides. Religious communities had undergone several years of a 'Great Awakening'. Those who held to the old order had strong ties to their mother countries (England or Amsterdam) and distain for all things American. The larger group who followed the new, more personal and democratic Dutch Reformed Church became Whigs. The Dutch Reformed Church was heavily influenced by Presbyterians and Congregationalists who had been formed in opposition to the Anglican Church. Catholics came primarily from Spain and France, traditional enemies of England. Preachers on both sides preached that God favored their position. All had a strong belief in democratic representation, which England appeared to be dismissing. As the war progressed, neutral and even Tory farmers and small merchants suffered most from the British and Loyalist units who indiscriminately confiscated crops and stock, not just for their own needs, but to prevent possible use by the Continentals. The Americans foraged on a much smaller scale and often left scrip in payment. Loyalist units often performed violent retaliatory raids on individual homes and churches, creating animosity which drove many to become Patriots. Patriots were fighting against a system of politics, economics and religion controlled by the wealthy. The Tory system of England had led to their poverty and exclusion, and they had fled to the Colonies to escape it. They didn't want to see that control exerted here.

Older wealthier men felt great loyalty to England with extended family and business connections there. They were generally conservative law and order types, believing that Patriots were young, rabble-rousing troublemakers. Some felt that war against the greatest Army in the world simply could not be won. Britain had a huge, trained army and navy in the Colonies and a solid tax base in England to supply funds to support their troops. They felt it would be madness to go to war when the Colonies had no Army or Navy, no weapons and no way to pay and equip them.

People tried to remain neutral as long as possible, but eventually everyone had to choose a side. The mentality of, "*if you are not for us, you are against us*" evolved into "*join or die*" used by both sides. Patriots tried to win the support of the population. The English and Loyalists took a more punitive approach. This truly became a civil war with Americans fighting each other as much as the British.

But the Colonies were not prepared for war. George Washington, in Cambridge supervising the siege of Boston, was stunned to learn that the total store of colonial gunpowder was less than 10,000 pounds, about 9 shots per man. Washington had 10,000 3 month militia men when he arrived in Cambridge. Only 2,500 re-enlisted to stay past the end of the year. British warships filled Manhattan's harbor and anchored in the rivers. In August, the NY Militia Bill was passed authorizing every NY municipality to create at least one company of 83 able bodied men willing to serve for at least 3 months. Every man between 16 and 60 was to provide themselves with a good musket or rifle and bayonet, 23 rounds of cartridges, 12 flints, and a knapsack, and meet on the first Monday of each month to train. Sam and his oldest son Andrew, of course, complied. Then the war came to Manhattan.

On the night of August 23rd, under orders from the NY Provincial Congress, John Lamb and 60 of his NY militiamen began dismantling and moving the cannons from the Battery up Broadway to the Commons, where they were arranged around the Liberty Pole. The *HMS Asia*, anchored in the harbor, sent a barge in to see what was going on, which fired on Lamb's men. They fired back, killing a man on the barge. At that, the *Asia*, a 64 gun warship, fired on the town. The shelling lasted from midnight until 3 in the morning, killing one person and wounding 3 others.

For 3 long hours fireworks from the gunship lit the sky and the whistle and crash of falling cannonballs shook awake the city while bells tolled the alarm. Elizabeth and the children were at Hampden Hall, far enough from the harbor to be safe. The Queens Head Tavern was near the harbor in the direct line of fire, and Sam quickly moved his guests to the lowest floors. Suddenly they heard a huge crash and the house shuddered with the sound of breaking tiles and glass. An 18 pound cannonball had crashed through the roof of the Queen's Head Tavern. A poem written shortly after this event by Philip Freneau contained the couplet: *"At first we supposed it was only a sham, till he drove a round ball thro the roof of Black Sam."*[54] The shelling of the city caused great panic and, the next day, frightened residents began to evacuate the city. It created the first traffic jam in NY as almost 9000 inhabitants, mostly women and children in carts and carriages and walking with bags of possessions, moved out of Manhattan.

1776 – Assassination

On January 9th Thomas Paine's 50 page <u>Common Sense</u> was published in Philadelphia. People were impressed by it, one of the first publications to openly advocate Independence from England. His words still resonate: *"We have it in our power to begin the world anew. America shall make a stand, not for herself alone, but for the world."*

Washington was struggling with his army. Militiamen had excitedly arrived in bitterly cold Cambridge with no uniforms, a variety of different guns and little discipline for a 3 month stint. Boston, several miles away and situated on a peninsula surrounded by deep water, had been occupied and under martial-law for 8 years by the British Army and Navy. In 1774, King George had established the Boston Port Act, in response to the Boston Tea Party. This act prohibited all shipping or landing to offload goods in the Harbor of Boston until restitution was made to the King's Treasury and the East India Company for lost tea damages. This Port Act closed the Boston Port to all ships. By January 1776, the harbor hosted many British Naval vessels sent to enforce the blockade. Boston was kept alive by other colonies defiantly transporting food by land.

In the Continental Army in Cambridge, the bickering soon started. Long standing grudges between colony's militias soon broke out in fights. The northern colonies elected their leaders by popular vote while the southern colonies appointed the most experienced soldiers to lead. Neither would accept orders from ranking officers of the other. Militias didn't want to submit to the authority of a central Army. The private militias wouldn't follow Washington's orders unless their leader received a high paid rank in the new Army, something completely out of Washington's control as the Continental Congress made those decisions. To make things worse, the militia regiments often just left to go home when their 3 month enlistments were up.

Continental soldiers enlisted for one year (later extended to 3 years), but the colonies were seriously delinquent in their contributions, so soldiers weren't getting paid, they had no clothes, and suffered from rotting food and little ammunition. The desertion rate was appallingly high. Washington wrote every day to Congress that he needed guns and ammunition and money to pay the men. At one point he had only enough ammunition for 3 shots per man.

The Continental Congress expected Washington to conquer the large well trained, fed and warmly clothed British Army with undisciplined, untrained forces, little ammunition, and no cannons. On the brink of disaster, Col. Knox pulled off an amazing feat which led to the end of the siege. Facing months of stalemate, the 25 year old former bookseller, Henry Knox, with no experience in war but lots of knowledge obtained by reading, proposed to Gen. Washington that he could bring large cannons recently captured from Fort Ticonderoga and Fort Crown Point in upstate NY overland to Boston. Desperate, Washington told him to go ahead and try.

To the disbelief of everyone, Knox performed the unbelievable feat of bringing 59 cannons weighing 60 tons from Fort Ticonderoga and Fort Crown Point to Boston, over 300 snowy miles in 58 days. He and his men built barges to float them across icy rivers and sledges pulled by ox teams to get them through deep snow in rural NY. They slogged through swamps and over the steep Berkshire Mountains. The cannons were stealthily placed on Dorchester Heights one night, under cover of darkness, movements hidden behind walls of hay-bales. The next morning, the British occupiers in Boston woke to the fact that the Colonial Army was now in a superior firepower position and could decimate their fleet as well as the city. When the British cannons could not reach the Dorchester Heights emplacement, they were forced to surrender. Washington negotiated to let them leave peacefully if they agreed to not destroy the city of Boston. After loading as many Loyalists as possible on their ships, the English sailed out of Boston Harbor on March 17th, 1776. They went to Nova Scotia to disembark the civilians and wait for reinforcements from England. This ended an 8 year British occupation of Boston and was the first win for the Colonial Army. Everyone was euphoric!

Gen. Washington could not celebrate. He quickly realized that there were many traitors in the ranks and that the troops were too easily infiltrated, so he directed the formation of a corps of sober, intelligent, and dependable men, detailed from the various regiments of infantry then assembled at Cambridge, to be known as the Commander in Chief's Guard. He specified the men should be between 5'8" and 5'10" tall, well drilled, handsome, and well built. They were to guard the General and his baggage which contained all orders for the army, all communication between Washington and the Continental Congress, all Washington's correspondence from his officers regarding their plans, need for ammunition and equipment, what maneuvers were being ordered and most importantly, to guard the meagre funds upon which the entire Army relied. Four men were selected from each regiment from every state's militia to be considered. Washington personally selected his men, and the Guard was formally organized at noon on 12 March 1776 with about 80 men. On the morning of 13 March, Caleb Gibbs of Massachusetts was commissioned as Captain-Commander and George Lewis, Washington's nephew from Virginia, was commissioned Lieutenant of the group, commonly known as the Life Guards. Each man took an oath to protect the life of Gen. Washington, Commander in Chief of the Army, his Official Papers, and the cash of the Continental Army. Their motto was Conquer or Die. It was considered a great honor to be selected and Washington ensured that soldiers of each of the 13 colonies were represented. They pledged their lives to this task and remained constantly in attendance on Washington and his leading officers, much as today's Secret Service details are. It was just 3 months later that some turned traitor.

Knowing that New York City was next in the British crosshairs. Washington sent General Lee with 300 men to fortify Manhattan. The Provincial Assembly of New York was controlled by Loyalists and was the only Provincial legislature that had refused to ratify the resolutions of the First Continental Congress. A flash point in loyalties was reached on 16 Sept 1775 when the decision was made to confiscate the arms of anyone who would not sign a General Association Pledge of support for the American cause. This order created an uproar! Loyalists violently disagreed with the Colony taking away their guns because they would not support a rebellion against their lawful King. Many hid their guns and ammunition and many men, who had not embraced either side, took the Tory side over this as a matter of principle. In the face of this furious resistance, the NY Provincial Congress abrogated the measure but the following March of 1776, in great need of guns and ammunition, the Continental Congress recommended to all colonies to disarm the Tories. As this was done, resentment grew and festered.

When Gen. Lee and his Colonial Army troops arrived in NY to begin fortifying the city against the expected English attack, the Loyalist controlled Committee of Safety, would not let them enter. They finally agreed but only if Gen. Lee put himself under the authority of the Provincial Government, claiming they were afraid his rash actions could provoke the British ships into shelling the city. A delegation from the Continental Congress intervened and made clear that Gen. Lee was to remain under direct orders and control of Gen Washington and the Continental Army, the Committee of Safety reluctantly relented and let Lee enter the city on 4 Feb with a regiment of Connecticut soldiers. Washington soon sent 6 more regiments to dig trenches in the unpaved streets and erect wooden barricades. Knowing that Manhattan Island would be surrounded by ships and unable to hold out for long, they determined to make street fighting as difficult as possible.

When Lee and his troops arrived in the city, British Governor Tryon escaped to a British ship in the harbor to avoid capture and confiscation of his papers and money. He was still very influential in stoking the fires of Loyalists in the city and setting up plots to help the British win the war. On 16 Feb 1776, Gen. Lee wrote to the NY Committee of Safety that Gov. Tryon was trying to buy guns from gunsmiths in the city and issued an order prohibiting all communication with the British ships. He requested that the NY Committee of Safety approve and support his orders. This would have cut off all supplies and communications between Gov. Tryon and his Tory supporters. The Tory controlled Committee protested that this could provoke the British to retaliate and stop necessary food supply shipments from New Jersey and Long Island and refused to comply. Many of the City Watch were secret Loyalists who sabotaged the cannons they were guarding. The American Army conscripted all white males in the city to work building fortifications every other day. Black slaves worked every day.

Washington and his troops left Cambridge on April 4th, marching across 4 states, over 300 cold, frozen, muddy miles in 9 days (over 33 miles a day), arriving in Manhattan on April 13th. New Yorkers lined the streets to cheer the arriving soldiers. Used to spit-shined, well trained British troops marching in formation, they were horrified to see this stinking rag-tag army. The Continental soldiers were exhausted from the long hard march; unshaven, unbathed, and wearing filthy unmatched clothing, few had uniforms. They didn't march in formation, they all had different weapons and appeared totally disorganized. The remaining Loyalists in Manhattan laughed at Washington's Army, believing the war would be over in days. Washington had fewer than 9,000 untrained, poorly armed men, and only 7000 were well enough to fight, against 30,000 English and Hessian professional forces, with reinforcements arriving daily.

Loyalists fled as Continental soldiers arrived. The NY Committee of 100 compiled a list of all licensed dispensers of liquor. Hampden Hall was not listed, indicating that Elizabeth, pregnant with daughter Sophia and her 6 children and their partner, Thomas C Campbell, had probably left the city, but Sam was still running his Queen's Head Tavern.[55]

On April 9th, an informant sent a letter to the British describing Patriot defenses around the city. Among them were 6 cannons *"above Black Sam's Hill on Greenwich Road facing the North River in a Half Moon configuration. In the total Column, the half-moon Battery of Black Sam's Hill will contain about 400 men; this battery is open on the side next to the New Hospital as the Hospital Covers it."*[56] This Half Moon Battery was on the hill of Sam's former Vauxhall Gardens Resort.

In New York that April through July, the chief officers of the Continental Army were Commander in Chief Gen. Washington; Gen. Israel Putnam, 2nd in charge; Gen. Henry Knox; Gen. Nathanial Greene;

111

Gen. William Alexander; Gen. Gates; Col. Alexander McDougall; Col William Smallwood and Maj. Gen. Adam Stephen, among others. Gen. Lee, 3rd in command of the Army, had been sent south and was not in NY. And Generals Schuyler, Arnold and Sullivan were in the Northern Provinces near Canada. Washington's military 'family' included six members in constant attendance including: Secretary Adj. Gen of all the Continental Army, Col. Joseph Reed; and Aides de Camp Lt. Col. George Baylor; Lt. Col. Robert Hanson Harrison; Lt. Col. Richard Carey; Lt. Col. Samuel B Webb and Lt. Col. Alex Contee Harrison. Capt. Caleb Gibbs and Lt. George Lewis were commanders of the Life Guards.

Reed and the Aides de Camp lived with the General and Mrs. Washington at the Mortier House, and worked at the Kennedy House Headquarters each day, tasked with writing the multiple daily letters to the Continental Congress, making copies, and delivering all General Orders to each military post, creating maps, and managing all of Washington's voluminous correspondence. Several of the Generals lived at Kennedy House Headquarters and everyone worked at Headquarters daily and ate at Fraunces Tavern for their large midday dinner meal. Samuel Fraunces also delivered the light evening supper at Mortier House on Richmond Hill as Washington remained at work until late and did not partake of this meal.

Washington set up his headquarters at the Kennedy House at 1 Broadway and promptly began to patronize Sam's Queen's Head Tavern. On April 16th, he issued General Orders for a *"General Court*

Martial at Mr. Fraunces Tavern at 10 o'clock. All Evidences and Persons concerned to attend the court." Continental soldiers were now billeted in vacant buildings including Sam's uptown Hampden Hall with Officers among them to prevent vandalism. All the New York papers were full of ads for Loyalist merchants that had "*removed from the City*" requesting creditors to make payments. Many houses and stores were offered at low prices for sale or lease. New York was suddenly full of 10,000 young men mostly from rural villages seeing the big city for the first time. The frequent courts-martial attested to the rampant drinking, whoring, and lack of discipline, to abstemious Gen. Washington's great displeasure.

The first suggestion of a secret plot occurred on 13 May 1776 when Washington received a package from the King's District Committee of Correspondence in Albany County, warning him of a plan by NY Loyalists to rise up in arms against the Colonial forces when the British fleet arrived. They enclosed depositions from 2 unidentified men who said the plot included the majority of the NY Provincial Congress and implicated General Schuyler, who was a "*true man for the King who held a British Commission.*" This was the first news of a widespread plot. Washington, who luckily had perfect confidence in Gen. Schuyler, forwarded the letter to him so he would know what the Loyalists were saying. This was an early case of using disinformation to cause dissention in the ranks.

Meanwhile also on 13 May, a group of prominent Loyalists throughout New York *"established a secret society pledging themselves to one another on everything holy to espouse the cause of their King, and seize every opportunity to dissolve the councils of NY Provincial Council and defeat what they termed the 'insidious machinations of an ambitious faction…and to diligently and faithfully restore the constitutional government and the happy connection that once existed between Great Britain and America."* The copy of this agreement, found in Gilbert Forbes papers, also *"swore never to reveal the other conspirators even under penalty of death"*. It was this group who was instrumental in the plot that was unfolding locally in NY.

Out on Long Island, Loyalists Israel Youngs and his brother Isaac Youngs of Cold Spring, in Suffolk County and Henry Dawkins (a silversmith and engraver recently released from prison) decided to make some counterfeit money. This was easy to do because each colony printed different money and the printing process was poorly controlled. In fact, currency was often so badly printed that counterfeiters had to make deliberate errors so that their money didn't look too good. The only security the colonies used for printing money was a special rag paper, manufactured in Philadelphia, restricted only to Colonial representatives. Dawkins had already been approached by Gov. Tryon who asked him to engrave some plates because Tryon intended to print counterfeit money on board. Instead, Dawkins apparently decided to go into business on his own and convinced the Youngs brothers to join him. The Youngs paid for Dawkins to buy a printing press and engraving tools which they hid in their attic. Dawkins moved into the Youngs' attic and engraved plates for Massachusetts and Connecticut currency. They were now ready to start printing but didn't have the necessary special paper. They contacted a neighbor and cousin of the Youngs who was going to Philadelphia to sell some horses and asked that he buy some paper for them and gave him a sample. So, Isaac Ketchum went to Philadelphia but was not able to find anyone who would sell him the paper. He soon realized he was raising suspicion with his enquiries and that even if he did find the paper, the large sheets would not fit in his saddlebags. He decided it was too risky to go ahead with the scheme and returned home.

A Patriot resident of Long Island named Charles Friend, of Westbury, reported to the NY Committee of Safety that he had visited a friend in Cold Spring named Thomas Henderson who confided that Henry Dawkins, living at the Isaac Youngs house was counterfeiting money. Henderson told him there was a chest of tools and that one of the Youngs brothers had inquired about buying paper. Henderson also said that Youngs was bragging that he would pay all his debts later that summer with Colonial money. Col. Malcolm arrested Henry Dawkins, Israel and Isaac Youngs, Isaac Ketchum and John Henderson and brought them before the NY Committee of Safety. Since incriminating evidence, including some fake notes and the printing plates and press, were located at the Youngs house, the men were all held for trial. Loudly proclaiming their innocence, they were placed in a cell in the basement Jail of City Hall with many other Loyalists arrested on a variety of charges. Angry cursing, boasting, and bragging filled the cells. On 8 June, Ketcham, who had not wanted to be involved in the counterfeiting in the first place, thought he might get a lighter sentence if he informed on the others. He sent a letter to the head of the Intelligence committee, John Jay, stating that Israel Youngs had discovered a plan that must be guarded against but was not willing to explain it to anyone else but Jay. There was no apparent response to this letter and Ketchum remained in his cell but kept listening.

The 3rd NY Provincial Congress met every day at Sam Fraunces' Tavern for 6 weeks from May 18th to June 30th, 1776. This NY Provincial Congress had originally been controlled by De Lancey Tory Loyalists but the Patriot Whig faction, by June 17th, had enough votes to elect a Patriot majority. At their next vote, New York Province voted to join the other Colonies in supporting the Declaration of Independence.

Shortly after Washington's return, from a trip to Philadelphia to confer with the Continental Congress, on Tuesday June 18th, 1776, an *"elegant entertainment"* was given by the 3rd Provincial Congress of NY for General Washington and his Command Staff at Sam's tavern to celebrate. The bill was:

Entertainment (food)	*L 45.00.00*
6 Dozn & 6 bottles of Madeira	*L 23.08.00*
2 (ditto) & 6 bottles of Port	*L 9.00.00*
Porter 23/-Cyder 37/-Spruce 4/6	*L 4.09.06*
Sangary 66/-Cyder 18/-Punch 12/	*L 4.16.00*
Madeira 12/-Bitters 3/	*L 0.15.00*

Lights 8/ - Wine Glasses Broken 16/	*L 1.04.06*
4 Wine Decanters 8/2 Water Decanters 14/	*L 1.02.00*
A Chainie Pudding Dish 12/-tumblers 14/	*L 1.06.00*
This account was paid June 25, 1776,	*L 91.01.00*

They gave 31 toasts which might explain the broken items.

Meanwhile, Loyalist Mayor of Manhattan David Mathews and many Loyalist merchants in the city were still going back and forth to the 4 British ships in the harbor ships and holding planning meetings with Gov. Tryon and English naval officers. Tryon was sitting like a spider spinning out his web to recruit more Loyalists to their plot. Loyalist merchants were openly provisioning the British ships until Washington published a proclamation that they *"would be considered enemies to the Colonies and if apprehended, would be treated as such."* The new Patriot majority 3rd NY Congress finally supported Washington's order.

Part of the English plot was to destabilize the many different colonial currencies that were now being printed. Gov. Tryon had Dawkins, a known counterfeiter, brought on board to engrave plates from which he could print counterfeit money. The counterfeit bills that Hickey and Lynch were accused of distributing had probably been printed by Rivington, owner of the NY Gazetteer, a Tory newspaper, who openly advertised that *"Person's going to other colonies may be supplied with any number of counterfeit Congress notes…so neatly and exactly executed…it being almost impossible to discover that they are*

117

not genuine." Tryon paid Loyalists to bribe the unpaid Continental soldiers to join British soldiers to rise up to take over Manhattan when the fleet arrived. Many soldiers, believing that the Continental Army would inevitably be defeated, hedged their bets by agreeing and giving their names, enticed by the promise of 10 shillings a month and land grants after the war. They believed that their names being registered with the British would keep them safe if the British won. It isn't hard to understand their motivation when they were unpaid, poorly fed, inexperienced, and so greatly outnumbered.

Governor Tryon, also decided to arm as many Loyalists as possible. Since many Loyalists guns had been confiscated, Tryon was meeting with gunsmiths and purchasing guns for the Tories, some of whom also had hidden their guns and refused to give them up during the earlier confiscation. The widespread plot involved many Loyalists in Manhattan, Long Island, Staten Island and New Jersey, Upper NY state, Connecticut, even as far as Cape Cod, Massachusetts.

In New York, Gov. Tryon crafted plans to blow up Kings Bridge at the upper end of the island to cut off any means of escape so the British forces could surround Colonial troops. The British tried to convert Colonial Artillery men because they had the necessary access to the gunpowder magazines in the city, which Loyalists planned to blow up and to the cannon emplacements, where cannons were to be spiked to be inoperable. It isn't hard to understand their motivation when they were unpaid, inexperienced, and surrounded by the huge British Army and Navy.

Tryon then added another more dangerous twist to the plot. He arranged for Gen. Washington and his staff to be kidnapped or murdered, knowing this would effectively end the infant Revolution. For this, he decided to specifically recruit some of Washington's Life Guards.

Since 1776 there has been a persistent legend about Thomas Hickey, the first man executed by the United States and the Plot of the Poison Peas. One version of the story has Hickey adding arsenic to a bowl of peas to be served to General Washington and his top Generals. His plot was supposedly discovered by his lover, Phoebe Fraunces, daughter of Samuel Fraunces who was the housekeeper at Mortier House. She testified against Hickey at his trial and grieved over him when he was hung. This myth has been perpetuated in respected sources as early as 1804 and in multiple books. Others claimed that the entire assassination plot was fake and never happened. They acknowledged that Hickey was hung, but not for trying to poison Gen Washington. Both versions are wrong, but there are threads of truth that, when traced, do unravel the mystery. Here is the true story of the Poison Peas Plot and it is almost stranger than fiction.

On 15 June, 21 year old Thomas Hickey and Michael Lynch, two of Washington's Life Guards, were arrested and held in New York's City Hall Jail for passing counterfeit Colonial Bills. The bills were probably provided by Gilbert Forbes from those printed by Rivington, the newspaper publisher, from plates made by Dawkins. The 2 Life

Guards were put into the cells at City Hall with the other disaffected Tories there, including Dawkins, the Youngs and Isaac Ketchum among others. Hickey and Lynch remained in the City Jail awaiting a military court-martial. Since the men were all Loyalists being held for counterfeiting, they soon began bragging of their exploits. Their first day in jail, Hickey and Lynch were overheard by Hiram Ketchum, boasting about Tryon's plans. Ketchum figured he could use the information to lighten his sentence so the following day, 16 June, he wrote to the NY Committee of Safety saying he had important information. Finally, someone listened to Ketchum.

To hear Ketchum's testimony, a Secret Committee was formed of 3 discrete men; Philip Livingston, John Jay and Gouverneur Morris to ensure everything was kept confidential. Ketchum was brought before this Secret Committee the following day, 17 June. The Committee agreed to dismiss charges against him if he would be an informant. Ketchum agreed and reported back to the Secret Committee 2 days later that: *"There were near 700 men enlisted for the King…The fleet was soon expected, and a number of others were in a band to turn against American Army when the King's troops arrived."* Ketchum explained that Hickey and Lynch had been recruited by Gilbert "Forbush", (actually Forbes) a well-known gunsmith who owned the 'Sign of the Sportsman' shop on Broadway. The recruits were promised 5 guineas bounty, 200 acres per man, 100 acres for his wife and 50 acres per child if they would enlist in His Majesty's Service. Forbes was to get paid a bounty for each man he recruited. The conspirators met at several well-known taverns including Corbie's which was located near the Mortier House and being closest to Barracks for the Life Guards, was their primary gathering place. Communication was made with Tryon on board the ship by Corbie's servant *"a mulatto colored negro dressed in blue clothes."* An old, retired soldier of the Royal Artillery, a Sgt. Graham, had been employed *"to survey the works about the city and on Long Island and based on his information a plan of operations had been concerted."* Washington was informed of this information that day.

More revelations soon came. William Collier, a waiter at the Sergeant's Arms Tavern of Alexander Sinclair, told his friend, Joseph Smith, about a group of men acting suspiciously at the tavern. Collier hid in an adjacent room and overheard them talking about a plot and identified Forbes as a leader of the group. Worried about retaliation, and loss of his job, Collier asked Smith to pass on the information. Smith brought this information to Jay's Committee on the 19th. This confirmed Ketchum's information. Based on the information the Secret Committee was providing, George Washington rode out to Kings Bridge and increased the defenses around it.

The same day that Ketchum and Smith appeared before the Committee, William Leary, a prominent Patriot businessman from Orange County, NY, also reported to Jay's Committee that he was in the city, looking for a runaway indentured servant, and had met a former employee named James Mason, who had tried to recruit him into a Tory plot.

Examination of William Leary:

William Leary says that he came hither last Monday, about ten o' clock, in pursuit of William Benjamin, a workman of a Mr. Erskine, who had run away from Bigwood Ironworks. He found the said Benjamin at the house of one Forbes, at the Sign of Robin Hood. Forbes ran and got a pistol for Benjamin to defend himself, and Leary took hold of Benjamin and prevented him from using the said pistol. Leary carried Benjamin to Paulus-Hook Ferry, who was there rescued by Sergeant Cornet, of Captain Roosevelt's Company, and by the said Captain inlisted. Leary then met James Mason, a workman of Mr. Erskine, who had been discharged. James Mason asked Leary if he did not want to see James Ramsay, Christopher Wyley, and George Gammel. Leary said yes. James Mason said Leary might see them if he would take an oath that he did not come to take them up which Leary refused saying he would, nevertheless, be glad to see them. Mason asked Leary if he had run away, who answered in the affirmative. Mason then asked what Leary would do with himself, and whether he would do as he and the rest of them had done. Leary asked what that was. Mason said he must go and be qualified, and then he would tell him. Leary agreed to be qualified; but asked on what foundation? Mason told him he was to swear before a gentleman in this town to go on board of the man-of-war; that he (Mason) and his companions had so sworn and were to receive wages and provisions until they should be able to get there. Leary asked who the gentleman was that swore them. Mason replied it was a gentleman employed by the Mayor or Governor of the town; but Leary thinks it was the Mayor who swore

122

them and found provisions for them until they had an opportunity to get on board the man-of-war. Mason then conducted Leary to the house where George Gammel, James Ramsay, and Christopher Wyley lived. This house is a Scotchman's, just below the Jews' Synagogue, a private house; does not know the man's name. When Leary came in, George Gammel asked him if he was in pursuit of them; Leary answered in the negative. George Gammel then said, 'Did you come away in the same manner as we did?' Leary said 'yes'. Gammel then said, 'we will have a drink together'. Gammel said he would divulge his mind to Leary if Leary would be true to him. Leary answered, 'I will be as true to you as you are to me.' Gammel then took Leary aside and asked when he would go on board of the man-of-war. Leary said he did not know but would take the first good opportunity. Asked Leary if he wanted a pass. Leary said he had a pass sufficient for him to go as far as he wanted. Gammel brought Leary a person to give him a pass, whom Leary does not know, but believes he should know him again if he were to see him. Leary said he wanted to see the New-England encampment, to see one Amos Hutchins, a Captain; intending to decoy them thither, and have them apprehended. When Leary had got about half way up the Broadway, they discovered his pistols, and would have fled, thinking, as Leary supposes, that he meant to take them up. James Ramsay and Christopher Wyley ran off. Leary pursued and caught James Ramsay. They then gathered together, and asked Leary why he carried pistols, who replied that they were for his defense, until with them he could get on board of the man-of-war. They being then suspicious, turned back; but Leary first asked George Gammel when he intended to go on board of the man-of-war, and how. Gammel answered, 'I intend to leave town this night, and go to Long-Island, and get from thence to the man-of-war;' but whether to get a person to put him on board, or to steal a boat or canoe. Gammel then said the gentleman who was employed by the Mayor had desired them not to be seen more than two together. The gentleman had further told him the Riflemen were so thick on Long-Island as to prevent him from getting on board until a more convenient opportunity; and perhaps they might not get on board until General Howe arrived with his fleet. They expected a large body of men to join them from Goshen, and they were to get on board with the utmost dispatch after General Howe's arrival.

William Leary

Examined by, and sworn the 20th of June 1776, before us:

John Jay

Gouverneur Morris

The Committee at once arrested James Mason and interrogated him as well, on June 20th.

Examination of James Mason:

About two weeks and a half ago a man took his qualification that he would not divulge anything about the business he was then upon. When he went up to Goshen from Kingswood, about five weeks ago, to look for a place as a miller, he saw a man who had been four days on board the man-of-war, by name William Forbes, a tanner and currier by trade; that as you go up the Broadway you come to the street in which is the Oswego market, opposite to the south side of which, four doors from the corner of the Broadway, lives one Lowrie, a tavern-keeper, a fat man, who wears a blue coat, and that he hath frequently met the said William Forbes in that house; that he told Mason he never lodged twice in the same house, being afraid; Mason asked where he did lodge, Forbes would not tell him; that Forbes hath a house of his own, five miles from Goshen, at which he saw him when Mason was looking for a place. Forbes told Mason he had been four days on board the man-of-war last April, when the ship Savage fired on Staten-Island; that Gov. Tryon would give five guineas bounty and two hundred acres of land for each man, one hundred for his wife, and fifty for each child, upon condition they would inlist in his Majesty's service. Mason bore Forbes's expenses to town, Forbes undertaking to repay him in hard cash when they got on board; that Forbes was to have a bounty from the Governour for every man he could get, and had been sent home for that purpose; that the Governour had desired him to go up and get as many men as he could; that the recruits were to assist the King's troops when they came; that recruits were not to go on board, because they could do more good on shore, and besides they were on short allowance in the ship and crowded, as Forbes had told Mason. Forbes and Mason came to New-York by way of Elizabethtown, and on their way, at Warwick, Forbes enticed William Benjamin to go along with him, and at Elizabethtown, Forbes inquired at Deacon Ogden's, where he used to work, and told Mason, after the inquiry, that they could not get on board from Bergen-Point or Staten-Island, as there were Riflemen stationed there, but must go to New-York, for there was a man there, one McLean, a shoemaker, near the Royal Exchange, who was

125

employed by the Governour to carry recruits on board; that Forbes and Mason came to New-York in an Elizabethtown boat, and went first to Thomas Mason's, at the corner of Beaver street and Broadway, at the Sign of the Highlander, where they left their baggage, and William Benjamin to take care of it, and went thence to McLean's, to inquire for a passage; that McLean and Forbes whispered together, and then Forbes told Mason that McLean said there was no opportunity of getting on board in two or three nights; that McLean recommended them to one James Houlding, a tavern-keeper in Tryon Row, opposite the gate of the upper barracks, for lodging; that they went up to Houlding's, leaving Benjamin still at Mason's, and, after dusk, Mason went for Benjamin, and he and Benjamin carried the baggage up, and all three lodged at Houlding's that night, telling Houlding Mr. McLean had sent and recommended them there as a safe house; next morning Forbes went to see for an opportunity to get on board, and did the like for two or three days; Forbes and Benjamin staid at Houlding's one week without being able to get on board of the man-of-war; William Benjamin agreed to go on board of the man-of-war also, and accept the Governour's bounty; after the first week, as they could not get on board, Houlding observed that they ought to be spread about, for that keeping them together would occasion suspicion in his house; that one Corbie, who lives near General Washington's, used to resort to the house of Houlding, where he was introduced to Forbes, and Mason also got acquainted with Corbie; that many Tories resorted to Houlding's, amongst whom were two brothers, of the name of Fortune, the one a tanner, living in the Swamp, and the other a saddler, whom

126

he hath seen working at Cook's, in the Broadway; also, one Fueter, a silversmith, who was ridden about town for a Tory, and another of the same name, whom he takes to be his brother; also, a man without an arm, whom he believes to be an old pensioner, and Gilbert Forbes, a gunsmith, living opposite to Mr. Hull's tavern, a short thick man who wears a white coat; that these persons, as he believes, knew of Mason's intention, but did not care to trust him, as he had not taken his qualification; that Mason was qualified before the said Gilbert Forbes and the said William Forbes, at the house of the said Corbie; that William Forbes gave him the book, and that they made him swear not to divulge anything of what Mason now tells; that when Mason was at Houlding's, Gilbert Forbes, William Forbes, and Corbie, advised Mason to go to Corbie's house and work a little in the garden to prevent suspicion. Gilbert Forbes promised Mason ten shillings per week subsistence money, of which Mason hath, at different times, received twenty-six shillings and eight pence; that Mason complained ten shillings was too little; Forbes said he could not help it, but he would write to the Governour to try to get it increased to twelve; that he afterwards told Mason he could not get an answer because a boat coming from the Governour was near being taken, and had thrown the letters overboard; that William Benjamin and William Forbes have also received money from the said Gilbert; that, according to the advice of the Forbeses and Corbie, went to Corbie's, and continued there until last Saturday; that while Mason lived at Houlding's, Corbie came there between nine and ten o'clock at night, and brought with him a mulatto-coloured negro, dressed in blue clothes, about five feet eight inches high, well-set, but knows not his name or to whom he belongs, but is informed that he hath since been taken up and put in jail; when Corbie and the negro came in there was a great deal of whispering round between Corbie, William Forbes, the negro, and another man who had been waiting to get on board and did go on board that evening; that afterwards Mason and William Forbes had some conversation about the negro; Forbes told him the negro was going on board the man-of-war with that man and two or three more, but the craft was so small it would not carry them all for fear of discovery, wherefore he, Benjamin, and William Forbes, were obliged to stay behind; that when Mason was qualified, there was present one Clarke, who had been a school-master about eight or nine miles from Goshen, and with whom the said William Forbes was acquainted; that the said Clarke said in the examinant's hearing that he had inlisted about sixty men, of whom he had a list, and who were ready to assist when the troops came; that Mason believes the list was given to Gilbert Forbes to be, sent to the Governour, for that the name of Mason, William Forbes, and William Benjamin, were taken down by the said Gilbert, as Mason supposes, to be sent to the Governour; that one Hickey, of the General's Guards, he believes to be concerned, who is now in confinement; that one Green, of the General's Guards, a drummer, is concerned, for that Mason saw Gilbert Forbes in conversation with said Greene, but could not hear them, and since that time Greene hath administered an oath to this Hickey and some other soldiers of the General's Guards, and, as Mason is informed, is to have one dollar per man from Forbes for every man he shall inlist; one Barnes, of the General's Guards, one Johnson, a fifer of the Guards, who, as well as Greene and Hickey, have been in the regular service, are qualified for the same purpose; that William Benjamin told Mason he heard Gilbert Forbes say that he would go to the Mayor and get one hundred pounds which he must have; that Mason and William Forbes, in their way from William Forbes' s house, came to a fine house; that examinant asked what fine house that was; that Forbes said it belonged to the brother of the Mayor of New-York; that he knew him very well, and had been there several times and must go there now to tell him what he was going about, to know if he had any word to send to his brother, and that the Mason must walk on slowly and he would overtake him; that at the door of the house Mason saw an old, short, thick, fat man; that Forbes stayed there about a quarter of an hour, and then followed and overtook Mason who asked Forbes if the Mayor' s brother had given him any letter; Forbes said no, he had only desired him to tell his brother that he was well; that the Mayor' s brother asked who Mason was, and Forbes told him it was a young man going upon the same errand that he was. Mason believes Gilbert Forbes is at the head here, and the Mayor and the Governour.

James Mason

Examined the 20th of June 1776, by us:

John Jay

Gouverneur Morris

James Mason's testimony confirmed that Gilbert Forbes was tasked with recruiting men to the plot and those other conspirators included Thomas Hickey (Life Guard), William Green (Life Guard drummer),

129

James Johnson (Life Guard fifer) and William Barnes (Life Guard). He confirmed that Gilbert Forbes, the gunsmith, was paymaster for the plot, Mayor Matthews had contributed L100 to the plot, and he named 3 taverns where the conspirators regularly met: the Sign of the Highlander, Lowrie's and Corbie's Taverns and named additional conspirators Upon hearing all this, the committee halted the hearings, issued arrest warrants for the named conspirators including Mayor David Mathews, and went to warn Washington. It was now early evening, and the Committee didn't know that, without an earlier intervention, all would have been lost.

The city had been awash in rumors for weeks about the British fleet coming and Loyalist plots. Sam Fraunces, of course, heard all the gossip. When the fleet arrived, the British would almost certainly land additional troops, including Hessian mercenaries, to join British troops and Loyalists on Long Island and Staten Island and launch a land invasion covered by Naval gunships shelling the city. Rumors swirled about who were Loyalists and how many men might really fight for the British when the fleet arrived. Despite all these rumors, there was no hint of killing George Washington. Assassination was against all rules of war, and the British were big on honor and rules, so no-one remotely expected such a thing.

June 21, 1776, was a Friday. Sam Fraunces' ground floor rooms were noisy with his usual lunch crowd. His staff was busy keeping the buffet tables well stocked, filling wine glasses and beer tankards. Sam was cheerfully greeting and seating guests as they arrived, taking payments, and overseeing the kitchen and waitstaff between chats with his regular customers. That day, General Washington's group arrived as usual, each officer entering with a hello to Sam, giving him their drink orders and making their way up to their regular spot in the 2nd floor Long Room, where they could eat and talk in private. Sam brought up their drinks and supervised laying out the buffet for Washington and his men.

"Sir, can you stay a moment?" Sam quietly murmured to General Washington as he and his staff rose to leave the Long Room after lunch. As Washington stood impatiently waiting, Sam removed the bowl of fresh spring peas. Washington, who loved peas, asked Sam why he hadn't served them at lunch. He sat suddenly, stunned, as Sam explained that he had seen a Life Guard add something to the bowl and feared they might have been poisoned. In disbelief, Washington called in a physician, who quickly determined that the peas had, in fact, been laced with arsenic. To prove this, they probably fed some to one of the chickens or house cats which immediately died. Due to Sam's quick thinking, no one had eaten any of the poisoned peas.

Arsenic is an odorless and tasteless poison readily available as rat poison. It would take about 4 teaspoons to be fatal to a man. Considering the large bowl was to be shared, the dose of arsenic was probably designed to create the symptoms of food poisoning, immediate severe abdominal pain, nausea, vomiting and bloody watery diarrhea. With these experienced fighting men disabled and expecting support from the trusted Guards, they could have been easily 'helped'

131

out of the restaurant. Whether they were to be killed or taken by boat from the back yard of Kennedy house and taken to England to be tried for treason, has never been decided. It was determined however through later testimony, that Washington was to be stabbed by Life Guard Greene. It was believed that his death would demoralize the Patriots and the loss of leadership would doom the revolution. This was the Poison Peas Plot and yes, despite the many incorrect stories about it, the incident really did happen, and Samuel Fraunces foiled it.

That afternoon, when John Jay and Gouverneur Morris arrived at Kennedy House Headquarters to brief Washington about the plot of Tories to rise-up and fight with the British, Washington told the Committee and his horrified command staff about the attempted assassination and their very close call. Washington realized that the plans to take the city had now been set in motion and the arrival of the British fleet must be imminent. He at once took his trusted Captain Gibbs and a small number of men out to arrest 40 men, including Drummer William Green, Fifer James Johnson, Private John Barnes and five or six more members of his Life Guard and several the named civilian Loyalists from the information Jay's group had provided.

Washington sent instructions to General Nathanial Greene, camped near Flatbush, Long Island, to arrest Mayor Matthews there that night at exactly 1 a.m. on June 22nd. Washington didn't want Matthews to hear of the arrests and destroy incriminating documents. Col. James Clinton arrested Fletcher Mathews, brother of Mayor David

Mathews, in Orange County, confiscated all his papers and brought him to City Hall for examination about the plot.

Gilbert Forbes and Mary Smith, Washington's housekeeper at Mortier House, were also arrested on the evening of the 22nd. Forbes was interrogated by the Secret Committee headed by John Jay and held for further questioning. Mary was interrogated by Jay's Committee but released later that night since there was no direct evidence against her …yet.

Washington had received letters of warning, in the days before the assassination attempt, that his housekeeper, Mary Smith, was a well-known Loyalist. She was the well-connected widow of Edward Smith and owned a prosperous boardinghouse in Great Dock Street near the Royal Exchange, close to Fraunces Tavern. She was an attractive woman about 33 years old, a staunch supporter of the King, and often passed on letters and information to the British and Loyalists.

When Gen. Lee and his troops began arriving in New York, Colonial soldiers were quartered at her boardinghouse. Mary, refusing to care for the enemy, moved herself and her son, Horatio, 3 slaves and all her furniture into the large, vacant Richmond Hill home of a Loyalist friend named Abraham Mortier. He was paymaster of the British Army in NY Colony and had returned to England. His gracious house was located on Richmond Hill outside the city limits and just south west of Greenwich Village. It was an unwelcome surprise to Mary Smith when Mortier House was, several months later, occupied by none other than General and Mrs. Washington and his aides. Having nowhere else to go, Mary stayed to spy for the British. Unlike most women at the time, Mary could read and write and do sums and she continued supplying information to the British.

Mary's niece, Lorenda, also was at the Mortier house. Lorenda was born in America and had lived for many years with the family of merchant Jacob Walton at his Bellevue House at Hoorne's Hook. Jacob Walton was a wealthy merchant from a well-known loyalist family. Jacob was born in 1733 on Staten Island to Jacob Walton Sr. and his wife Maria Beekman. He was a member of the NY Provincial Assembly and founder of the NY Chamber of Commerce. He had married Mary 'Polly' Cruger in 1760 and they had 5 children of whom 2 lived to adulthood. Mary was the daughter of the Hon. Henry Cruger Esq. Jacob and Mary (Cruger) Walton moved to Long Island when General Lee commandeered their home for his troops in April 1776. At this time Lorenda moved to Mortier House with her aunt. Both Waltons died in 1782 in Flatbush, Long Island. They are buried at Trinity Church Cemetery on Manhattan. Mary was only 38. Their beautiful home at Bellevue was shelled by the British and burned to the ground.

Lorenda was a pretty, vivacious, and passionate Loyalist of 16 or 17 in 1776. She wanted to support the Loyalist cause, so she carried information between Loyalists and Capt. Vanderput on his warship, Asia, by smuggling letters in her petticoats. She was almost captured in March 1776 returning with letters from the warship Asia. To deflect suspicion, she pretended to be, and was thereafter, widely reported in the newspapers, as a "girl of the town" visiting Capt. Vanderput. In early June, Lorenda delivered a letter from Tories to a Mr. Ryan, a

Loyalist leather goods dealer, with instructions for his quick escape and where he could find a Loyalist refuge. Ryan read the letter and at once fled, leaving Lorenda to care for his pregnant, bedridden wife. A Patriot mob stormed the Ryan house that afternoon and tore it apart looking for Ryan. The Committee of Safety, led by Capt. Gibbs, one of Washington's Life Guards, was furious that Ryan had escaped. He made Lorenda strip off her clothes so he could search them for letters. She had no letters on her but believing her to be a woman of ill repute as well as a Loyalist, he forced her to stand naked in a window in view of the mob of men.

As known Loyalists, Mary, Horatio and Lorenda's movements were restricted to Mortier House and they and her slaves, were able to go no further than the security perimeter established by the Life Guards. It is highly likely that this fervent Tory and attractive young woman had extensive conversations with the handsome young Life Guards during her time at the Mortier House. Lorenda was at Mortier House with Mary Smith and Horatio, the night of the Poison Peas assassination attempt on June 21. Her pension petition in England outlines the events that followed:

About 6 pm on Saturday the 22nd they all endured heavy questioning by Washington's aide Capt. Gibbs and an Indian Chief at the Mortier House. Mary Smith was taken downtown to be interrogated by Jay's committee, leaving Lorenda and Mary's son Horatio in confinement at the Mortier House. Jay's Committee didn't have any direct evidence against her yet, so Mary was released. When she returned to Mortier House about 10 pm, Washington and his military staff put a dish of peas on the table and Mary, Horatio and Lorenda were told to eat from it. They hesitated, believing it to be poisoned. This convinced Washington, who said he believed Mary guilty of treason and attempted murder but didn't have enough proof to hang her. He told the three to leave Mortier House at once. It was now after midnight. They quickly gathered their belongings, carried by Mary's slaves, and walked to a vacant house where they spent the night. Mary, Horatio and her 3 slaves were able to get passage to Long Island where they remained until the English returned to re-occupy Manhattan on September 15th. Lorenda made her way north to the Throgs Neck area.

Questioning about the plot continued. Along with 34 other arrested plotters, Mayor David Matthews was examined on June 23, 1776, by Philip Livingston, John Jay and Gouverneur Morris:

His testimony was that he had gone on board about 6 or 7 weeks ago to meet with Gov. Tryon. Had received money from Tryon to pay Gilbert Forbes for guns that Forbes had made. He claimed he held the payment for several days as he was afraid to get caught but finally paid Forbes. That one day a man in regimental uniforms came to his office and claimed he was a Life Guard for Washington but wanted to fight for the King and had enlisted 100 men to that cause. Matthews claimed he had nothing to do with enlisting men and sent him away… That Matthews does not know otherwise than by sight and has never spoken or written a line to Peter McLean, a shoemaker in the town, on any subject whatever.

David Matthews was examined in New-York, June 23, 1776, by Philip Livingston, John Jay and Gouverneur Morris. It is clear from later information that Matthews was much more involved, but he did not name others and tried to make his involvement as innocuous as possible in this interrogation.

On 24 June Washington Issued General Orders: *"to strengthen the guard on the prisoners at City Hall to 100 men with 40 being required from several brigades. The General Court Martial now sitting is to assemble at the house where the Provost is kept until further orders."* There were 28 prisoners in City Hall Jail at the time, most of them implicated in the conspiracy, including Mayor David Mathews, Gilbert Forbes, and several members of the Life Guards. The extra guards were the result of Ketchum passing on overheard bragging about planned escapes.

On 26th of June, accused counterfeiter Israel Youngs was deposed about what he had heard concerning the plot against the Army:

Youngs testified that he was in a room with Thomas Vernon, a hatter in New York city. Vernon told Youngs that he had been on the Dutchess of Gordon to meet Gov. Tryon and had seen Richard Hulet and Thomas Cornell there. Vernon told him Tryon was printing counterfeit money on board and was giving it out freely. That Rivington was on board to aid with the printing, and it looked real. Youngs said that Vernon told him about a Captain in the Colonial Army in Col. McDougall's Regiment had a commission from Governor Tryon and was actively recruiting others and had so far 100 men. Vernon also told Youngs that he had been engaged to bring counterfeiter Dawkins to the Dutchess of Gordon but had been afraid to do so. He knew Dawkings from a prior jail sentence. Youngs said that Thomas Hickey and Michael Lynch of the General's Guards were in the same room with him, and they swore they would never fight for America. They told him over 700 men had inlisted for the King and were to rise up the night the fleet arrived. They explained the fleet was to go up the East River and some up the North River to surround Manhattan Island. Hickey and Lynch were to go to King's Bridge and sabotage it and then board the English ships. Youngs said that when the plot was discovered, they became uneasy but comforted themselves that Lynch's name was aboard the Dutchess of Gordon so he could not be identified, and Hickey said he had never signed anything.

Israel Youngs

Sworn the 26th day of June 1776:

John Jay

Gouverneur Morris

Hickey was not among those who tried to poison Washington as he was already in prison before this attempt. Contrary to his belief that he and Lynch would not be accused, Life Guard Sgt. Thomas Hickey, had a speedy military court-martial on June 26th at Headquarters, Kennedy House at 1 Broadway. The Army decided to make him an example to deter further plots. There were only 4 witnesses at his court martial. None was a woman.

Proceedings of a General Court Martial of the Line, held at Head-Quarters, in the City of New York by warrant from his Excellency

George Washington, Esq`, General and Commander-in-Chief of the forces of the United American Colonies, for the trial of Thomas Hickey and others, June 26th, A` D. 1776.

Col` Samuel H` Parsons, President.

Lt` Col` William Sheppard,

Maj` Levi Wells,

Capt` Joseph Hoyt,

Capt` Abel Pettibone,

Capt` Samuel Warren,

Capt` James Mellin,

Capt` Warham Parks,

Capt` William Reed,

Capt` Joseph Pettingil,

Capt` David Lyon,

Capt` David Sill,

Capt` Timothy Purcival.

William Tudor, Judge Advocate.

The warrant being read, and the Court first duly sworn, proceeded to the trial of Thomas Hickey, a private sentinel in his Excellency the Commander-in-Chief's Guard, commanded by Major Gibbs, brought prisoner before the Court, and accused *"of exciting and joining in a mutiny and sedition, and of treacherously corresponding with, inlisting among, and receiving pay from the enemies of the United American Colonies."*

The prisoner being arraigned on the above charge, pleads not guilty.

William Green (Life Guard) sworn, deposes: *"That, about three weeks ago, I was in company with one Gilbert Forbes, a gunsmith, who lives in Broadway, and we fell into a conversation on politics. I found Forbes' s pulse beat high in the Tory scheme. I had repeated conversations with Forbes afterwards, and he was always introducing politics, and hinting at the impossibility of this country standing against the power of Great Britain. He invited me to dine with him one day; and a day or two after asked me if I would not inlist into the King's service. I asked him where the money was to come from to pay me for the service; Forbes replied the Mayor would furnish money. I was pleased with the notion of getting some money from the Tories, and agreed to the scheme, with a view to cheat the Tories, and detect their scheme. I mentioned the matter to several, and, among others, to Hickey, the prisoner. I told him the principle I went upon, and that we had a good opportunity of duping the Tories. Hickey agreed to the scheme, but did not receive any money, except two shillings which I gave him. Forbes left it with me to inlist and swear the men. Forbes swore me and one Clark on a Bible to fight for the King; but I swore Hickey to fight for America. After the prisoner was engaged, I proposed to him to reveal the plot to the General, but Hickey said we had better let it alone till we had made further discoveries. All that Forbes proposed to me was, that when the King's forces arrived, we should cut away King's Bridge, and then go on board a ship of war, which would be in the East River to receive us. I inlisted ten or a dozen* and told them *all my plan. The prisoner wrote his name upon a piece of paper with five others, which I gave to Forbes, and this was all the enlistment that I knew of the prisoner's signing."*

William Green was a Life Guard and was court martialed following Hickey. His testimony was trying to minimize both their actions and paint them as patriotic.

Gilbert Forbes (civilian): *"A night or two after General Washington arrived in New-York from Boston, Green fell into company where I was. We were drinking, and Green toasted the King's health, and I did so too. A day or two afterwards Green called upon me, and said, that as I had drank his Majesty's health, he supposed I was his friend, and immediately proposed to inlist some men into the King's service and told me he could procure considerable numbers to join him. I put him off and declined having any hand in the business. But in repeated applications from him, I at last fell into the scheme. Green was to inlist the men, in which I was not to be concerned, nor have my name mentioned. In a day or two Green gave me a list of men who had engaged, among whom was the prisoner, Hickey. Soon after which, Hickey asked me to give him half a dollar, which I did, and this was all the money Hickey ever received from me. Green received eighteen dollars and was to pay the men who inlisted one dollar apiece, and we were to allow them ten shillings per week subsistence money. I received upwards of a hundred pounds from Mr. Matthews, the Mayor, to pay those who should inlist into the King's service, who, after inlisting, were to go on board the King's ships, but if they could not get there, were to play their proper parts when the King's forces arrived."*

William Welch (civilian): *Between a fortnight and three weeks ago I met the prisoner in the street; he asked me to go with him to a grog-shop. When we got there, he told me he had something to tell me of importance but insisted on my being sworn before he would communicate it. I accordingly swore on the Bible to keep secret what he should tell me. He then said that this country was sold, that the enemy would soon arrive, and that it was best for us Old Countrymen to make our peace before they came, or they would kill us all. That we Old Countrymen should join together, and we would be known by a particular mark, and if I would agree to be one among them, he would carry me to a man who would let me have a dollar by way of encouragement. I did not relish the project, and we parted."*

Isaac Ketchum (civilian): *"Last Saturday week the prisoner was committed to jail, on suspicion of counterfeiting the Continental currency, and seeing me in jail, inquired the reason of it. I told him because I was a Tory. On this a conversation ensued upon politics. In different conversations he informed me that the Army was become damnably corrupted; that the fleet was soon expected; and that he and a number of others were in a band to turn against the American Army when the King's troops should arrive and asked me to be one of them. The plan, he told me, was, some were to be sick, and others were to hire men in their room. That eight of the General s Guard were concerned but mentioned only Green by name. He further told me that one Forbes, a tavern-keeper, was to be their Captain, but that the inferior officers were not yet appointed, lest the scheme should be discovered."*

The prisoner, Thomas Hickey, being here called upon to make his defense, produces no evidence; but says, *"he engaged in the scheme at first for the sake of cheating the Tories, and getting some money from them, and afterwards consented to have his name sent on board the man-of-war, in order that if the enemy should arrive and defeat the Army here, and he should be taken prisoner, he might be safe."*

The Court being cleared, after mature consideration, are unanimously of the opinion that the prisoner is guilty of the charge against him, and of a breach of the fifth and of the thirtieth articles of the Rules and Regulations for the government of the Continental Forces; and the court unanimously sentence and adjudge that the prisoner, Thomas Hickey, suffer death for said crimes by being hanged by the neck till he is dead.

Samuel H Parsons, President

By His Excellency George Washington, Esq, General and Commander of the Army of the United Colonies.

To the Provost-Marshal of the said Army:

"Whereas Thomas Hickey, a soldier inlisted in the service of the said United Colonies, has been duly convicted by a General Court-Martial of mutiny and sedition, and also of holding a treacherous correspondence with the enemies of said Colonies, contrary to the Rules and Regulations established for the government of the said

troops; and the said Thomas Hickey, being so convicted, has been sentenced to death, by being hanged by the neck till he shall be dead; which sentence, by the unanimous advice of the General Officers of the said Army, I have thought proper to confirm: These are, therefore, to will and require you to execute the said sentence upon the said Thomas Hickey this day, at eleven o' clock in the forenoon, upon the ground between the encampments of the Brigades of Brigadier-General Spencer and Lord Stirling; and for so doing this shall be your sufficient warrant. Given under my hand this twenty-eighth day of June, in the year of our Lord one thousand seven hundred and seventy-six."

George Washington

Head-Quarters, New-York, June 28, 1776.

New-York, June 28, 1776.

Hickey was certainly part of the plot to desert the American army and join the British. But he was in jail at the time of the attempted assassination. Hickey was a good looking, charming Irishman of about 5'8" who had come to the Colonies with the British Army. He fought under Maj. Gen. William Johnson, who commanded Iroquois and Colonial militia forces during the French and Indian War. Johnson died in 1774 which is probably when Hickey deserted the English army. Hickey then moved to Wethersfield, Connecticut where he *"bore a good character"*. There he enlisted with Knowlton's Connecticut Rangers and went to Cambridge for the siege of Boston. It was there that he was proposed as exemplary for the Commander in Chief's Guard. Assuming he had served at least 1 year under Johnson when he was 18, then lived 2 years in Wethersfield before enlisting for the militia, he would have been about 21 at the time of his selection to the Guards. Washington had personally selected Hickey and he was a favorite of Washington and the other Guards. Now Washington, feeling betrayed, wanted to make an example of him to quell others who might be thinking of turning traitor. All 20,000 off duty soldiers were ordered to assemble on the Commons on June 28th to witness his hanging. In addition to the Army, many civilians attended.

Surgeon William Eustis wrote to Dr. David Townsend that day, *"He appeared unaffected and obstinate to the last, except when the chaplain took him by the hand under the gallows and bade him adieu, a torrent of tears flowed over his face; but with an indignant scornful air he wiped them with his hand from his face, and assumed the confident look; with his last breath the fellow said that "unless Greene was very cautious the design would be executed upon him".*

He was hung at 11am. Washington then sent out a General Order to the troops: *"The unhappy fate of Thomas Hickey, executed this day for mutiny, sedition and treachery, the General hopes will be a warning to every soldier in the army to avoid these crimes and all others so disgraceful to the character of a soldier and pernicious to his country, whose pay he receives and bread he eats. And in order to avoid those crimes, the most certain method is to keep out of the temptation of them, and particularly to avoid lewd women, who, by the dying confession of this poor criminal, first led him into practices which ended in an untimely and ignominious death."*

145

And so, Thomas Hickey's was the first military execution in the United States. He was condemned for mutiny (criminal conspiracy to overthrow lawful authority), sedition (inciting rebellion) and of holding treacherous correspondence with enemies of the United American Colonies.

But who was the *"lewd woman"* Washington alluded to in his letter to the troops? What happened to Hickey's confession? The 'lewd woman' was almost certainly the Loyalist spy, Lorenda Holmes, Mary Smith's niece, who lived at Mortier House and knew the guards well. Lorenda expressed regret over the death of Thomas Hickey in her petition for a pension in the UK for her acts for the Crown during the Revolution. Whatever Hickey did confess was never revealed. His hanging was used as a message to potential traitors.

Details of the attempted assassination were kept out of the newspapers to avoid frightening supporters with how close to success the plot had come. With a large English fleet expected within days, the matter was kept very quiet, although surviving letters, written at the time by Washington and people close to him, confirmed the plot and its details.

One of Gen. Washington's aides, Samuel B Webb wrote in his personal journal on 22 June which he kept private: *"Some days past, the General received information that a most horrid plot was on foot by the vile Tories of this place and the adjacent towns and villages. Having taken the necessary precautions ... a number of officers & guards went to different places & took up many of their principals;*

among whom, was David Mathews Esq., Mayor of the city. To our great astonishment we found five or more of the General's Life Guard to be accomplices in this wicked plan; which was, at the proper time, to assassinate the person of his Excellency & the other General Officers, blow up the magazine, and spike the cannon. It was to be put in execution as soon as the enemy's fleet appeared, if no proper time offered before."

The same day, Brig. Gen William Heath also wrote in his private journal: *"This day a most horrid plot was discovered, in the city and camp. A plan has been laid to massacre the generals of the army on the first approach of the enemy, to blow up the magazines, [and] spike the cannons. A number both of citizens and soldiers are seized and secured among whom are the Mayor of the city. One Forbes, a gunsmith, who it is said is one of the principals, and several of the General's Guard are also in the plot."*

Despite thee attempts to keep the plot secret, word was getting around. A letter from Dr. Drowne on June 24th to his sister referenced the attempted assassination: *"A most infernal plot has lately been discovered here, which, had it been put into execution, would have made America tremble and been as fatal a stroke to us, this country, as gun powder treason would to England, had it succeeded. The hellish conspirators were a number of Tories (the Mayor if ye City among them) and three of General Washington's Life Guards. The plan was to kill Generals Washington and Putnam and as many other Commanding Officers as possible...to set the city on fire in nine several places. To spike up the cannon. Then to give a signal to the Asia and ships expected; and blow up the Magazine. The Drummer of ye Guards was to have stabbed the General. The pretty fellows are in safe custody."*

Another letter dated the same day, *"My last to you was by Friday's post, since which a most barbarous and infernal plot has been discovered among our Tories, the particulars of which I cannot give you, as the Committee of Examination consists of but three, who are sworn to secrecy. Two of Washington's guards are concerned, the third they tempted to join them made the first discovery. The general report of their design is as follows: Upon the arrival of the (English) troops they were to murder all the staff officers, blow up the magazines, and secure the passes of the town. Gilbert Forbes, gunsmith in the Broadway, was taken between two and three o' clock on Saturday morning, and carried before our Provincial Congress, who were then sitting, but refusing to make any discovery, he was sent to jail and put in irons. Young Mr. Livingston went to see him early in the morning and told him he was sorry to find he had been concerned, and, as his time was very short, not having above three days to live, advised him to prepare himself. This had the desired effect; he asked to be carried before the Congress again, and he would discover all he knew. Several have been since taken, (between twenty and thirty,) among them our Mayor, who are all now under confinement. It is said their party consisted of about five hundred. I have just heard the Mayor has confessed bringing money from Tryon to pay for rifle-guns that Forbes had made. (British General) Burgoyne is arrived at Quebeck with his fleet".*

148

24 June 1776: Letter from William Whipple to John Langdon, Philadelphia:

*"There has been a most hellish conspiracy at New-York. We have not the particulars of it yet; but, by the best information I can get, **the plan was to assassinate the General, blow up** the magazine, and spike the cannon. This was to be done on the arrival of the enemy, it is supposed; however, there is a full discovery of the whole plot, and a considerable number (say thirty or forty) of the infernal villains seized, and I hope justice will be done to them."*

25 June 1776: John Rodgers to Matthew Tilghman, President of Maryland Convention:

"A report prevails here, which is believed to be true, that a most diabolical plot to assassinate the General at York, blow up the magazine, and spike the cannon, has lately been discovered. Many people, it is said, have been thrown into prison, and some remain under guard; among the rest is the Mayor of the city. What with external and internal enemies, we fancy we shall very shortly have our hands full of business."

We are, sir, with great esteem, your most obedient servant,

J˙ RODGERS.

Finally, Washington confirmed all this in a letter to Congress on 28 June 1776.

Congress, I doubt not, will have heard of the plot that was forming among many disaffected persons in this city and Government for aiding the King's troops upon their arrival. No regular plan seems to have been digested, but several persons have inlisted and sworn to join them. The matter, I am in hopes, by a timely discovery, will be suppressed and put a stop to. Many citizens and others, among whom is the Mayor, are now in confinement. The matter has been traced up to Governour Tryon, and the Mayor appears to have been a principal agent, or go-between him and the persons concerned in it. The plot had been communicated to some of the Army, and part of my Guard engaged in it. Thomas Hickey, one of them, has been tried, and, by the unanimous opinion of a Court-Martial, is sentenced to die, having inlisted himself and engaged others. The sentence, by the advice of the whole Council of General Officers, will be put in execution to-day at eleven o' clock. The others are not yet tried. I am hopeful this example will produce many salutary consequences and deter others from entering into the like traitorous practices.

On 28 June 1776, a letter from Governor Trumbull to General Schuyler:

PS: Have just received intelligence that propitious Heaven hath revealed a most hellish plot to assassinate our General and destroy the magazine of ammunition at New-York. Such wickedness will never be suffered to go unpunished.

28 June 1776: letter from Dr. William Eustis, a surgeon to Dr. David Townsend outlined the plot: *"You will doubtless have heard of the Discovery of the greatest and vilest attempt ever made against our country I mean the plot, the infernal plot which has been contrived by our worst enemies and which was on the verge of execution; you will, I say, undoubtedly have heard of it but perhaps I may give you a better*

idea of it than you have yet obtained. The mayor of York with a number of villains who were possessed of fortunes and who formerly ranked with Gentlemen, had impiously dared an undertaking, big with fatal consequences to the virtuous army in York and which in all probability would have given the enemy possession of the city with little loss. Their design was, upon the first engagement which took place, to have murdered (with trembling I say it) the best man on earth: Gen. Washington was to have been the first subject of their unheard of SACRICIDE; our magazines which, as you know are very capacious, were to have been blown up: every General Officer and every other who was active in service his country in the field was to have been assassinated; our cannon were to be spiked up; and in the short the most accursed scheme was laid to give us into the hands of the enemy and to ruin us. They had plenty of money and gave large bounties and larger promises to those who were engaged to serve their hellish purposes. In order to execute their design upon our General, they had enlisted into their service one or two of his Excellencies Life Guard, who were to have assassinated him; knowing that no person could be admitted into the magazines or among the cannon but those who were of the artillery, they have found several in our regiment vile enough to be concerned in their diabolical designs – these were to have blown up the Magazines and spiked the cannons. (Tell Homans, one Rotch, a fellow he bled for me in Morton's company No 1 was taken up with his brother for being concerned.) ...We are hanging them as fast as we can find them out. I have just returned from the Execution of one of the General's Guard; he was the first that has been tried; yesterday at 11 o'clock he received sentence, today at 11 he was hung in the presence of the whole army. He is a Regular Deserter...he appeared unaffected and obstinate to the last, except that when the Chaplain took him by the hand under the gallows and bad him adieu, a torrent of tears flowed over his face, but with an indignant scornful air he wiped em with his hand from his face and assumed the confident look. You remember Gen. Greene commands at Long Island; with his last breath the fellow told the spectators that unless Greene was very cautious the design would as yet be executed on him. (note: Hickey was referring to Life Guard Green not General Green)

The trial will go on and I imagine they will be hung, gentle and simple as fast as the fact is proved upon them.

That any set of men could be so lost to every virtuous principle and so dead to the feelings of humanity as to conspire against the person of so great and good a man as Gen. Washington is surprising; few of our countrymen (as you may well imagine) are concerned; they are in general foreigners upwards of 30 who were concerned and tis said Gov. Tryon is at the bottom..."

29 June: The Constitutional Gazette (New York):

"Yesterday forenoon was executed in a field between the Colonels McDougall and Huntington's camp, near the Bowery-Lane, (in the presence of near 20,000 spectators) a soldier belonging to his Excellency General Washington's guards, for mutiny and conspiracy; being one of those, who formed, and was soon to be put in execution, that horrid plot of assassinating the Staff Officers, blowing up the magazines, and securing the passes of the town on the arrival of the

152

hungry ministerial myrmidons: It's hoped the remainder of those miscreants, (now in our possession,) will meet with a punishment adequate to their crimes."

Similar letters from others were published in the Hartford Courant on 1 July and the Continental Journal on 4 July in Boston. Washington Irving wrote at the time:

"The wildest reports were in circulation concerning it. Some of the Tories were to break down King's Bridge, others were to blow up the magazines, spike the guns and massacre all the field-officers. Washington was to have been killed or delivered up to the enemy. Some of his own bodyguards were said to be in the plot"

So, what happened to the other conspirators?

29 June: Gilbert Forbes, was again interrogated, and admitted his involvement claiming Matthews had given him L100 supplied by Tryon to bribe Continental soldiers.

Gilbert Forbes, being again examined, further saith: *"That he knows one ————- Silk; that he was left by Captain Aidey to wait upon his wife, who lives on Long-Island, somewhere near Hempstead; that he is often in town, frequently staying at Mrs. Oiry's and Mrs. Brandon's, has the air of a soldier, wears a short brown hunting coat and a double-breasted jacket of the same colour; that he used to wait on a Mr. Miller, who lives or lodges in Mr. Gouverneur's house on Rotten Row; that Sergeant Graham (an old soldier, discharged from the Royal Artillery) was employed by Governour Tryon to speak to Forbes about inlisting men for the King's service, and told Forbes from*

153

the Governour, that if Forbes exerted himself in that business and raised a number of men, he should have a company; that the said Sergeant also informed him that, at the request of the Governour, he had surveyed the ground and works about this city and on Long-Island, in consequence of which he had concerted a plan for an attack, which he had given to Governour Tryon, and of which the Governour approved, which was as follows, viz: that the man-of-war should cannonade the battery at Red Hook, and while that was doing a detachment of the Army, with some cannon, &c., should land below or about Red Hook, and march round so as to come upon the back of the batteries near Swedeland House; that a small part of the detachment should make a feint of marching up the road leading directly to the battery, but that the main body were to make a circuitous march so as to reach the battery while our attention was engaged by the feint aforesaid; that if they carried that battery, which they expected to take by storm, they were immediately to attack the battery on the hill near the ferry, which the Sergeant said would be easily done, as no embrasures were made or cannon fixed on the back side of it; that this latter battery, when in their possession, would command the works on Governour's Island, which they would keep between two fires, viz: the battery last mentioned on the one side, and the shipping on the other; that then the shipping, with the remainder of the Army, were to divide, one division was to run up the North River and land at or near about Clarke's farm, and march directly to Enclenbergh Hall, and fortify there; the other division was to run up the East River and land in such manner as to gain a footing on Jones's Hill, from whence they expected

154

to command and silence the battery on Bayard's Hill; that should they gain possession of the places above-mentioned, their next object would be the grounds adjacent to King's Bridge, where they intend to erect strong works, so as to cut off the communication between the city and country."

Gilbert Forbes, being further examined, saith: *"That some time before the man-of-war removed from the town to the Narrows, one Webb, a burr-millstone maker, told Forbes that if he had any rifles to sell he might get a good price for them by sending them on board the man-of-war, and that a young man who lived with James Rivington told him the same; that Forbes had then nine rifles which he made, but they were bad and would not shoot straight, and eleven smooth narrow-bored guns; that he sent some of them to one Mrs. Beck's, a tavern-keeper, near the Fly Market, with orders to send them on board, which she accordingly did, and that the said Webb carried the remainder; that the said Webb told Forbes that Governour Tryon would give him three guineas apiece for them; that at the time when an exchange of prisoners took place with the man-of-war, and Tiley was, among others, exchanged, the Mayor, viz: David Matthews, Esq', sent for Forbes and told him he was going on board the Governour's ship, and that he would get the money due from the Governour to Forbes for the rifles aforesaid; that on his return the Mayor told Forbes he would pay him in a few days; that Forbes never did receive any money from Matthews for the said fire-arms; Forbes told Charles Benson that he was about inlisting men, and that he told Forbes it would do."*

Gilbert Forbes

155

Examined by and before me, this 29th June 1776:

Philip Livingston

By 29 June most of the British fleet had arrived at Sandy Hook and there were well over 110 ships present. Note: Sandy Hook is a sandy peninsula off Monmouth, NJ in lower New York Bay. It is south of Staten Island and Brooklyn, then occupied by the British and Manhattan Island, then occupied by the American Army.

On 7 July 1776 Washington's General Orders noted that: "...*Serjt George Douglass, John Davis, John Cooper, Robt Sawyer and George Clarkson, all of Capt.Van Wycks Company, Col. McDougall's Regiment, tried at the same Court Martial for "Mutiny and Sedition": Serjt George Douglass is acquitted, the others severally found guilty and sentenced, Davis to be whipped Thirty-nine Lashes, Cooper, Thirty Lashes; Sawyer and Clarkson be whipped each Twenty Lashes, on their bare backs for said offence. The General approves of the foregoing Sentences & orders them put in execution at the usual time and place.*"

Oddly, these soldiers were tried for the same offense as Hickey but were not executed. It is not clear whether they were part of the assassination plans, but they were certainly part of the larger plot to side with the British.

There was an interesting event publicized on 9 July. Rev. John Marsh of Wethersfield, CT wrote: "*You have heard of the infernal plot that has been discovered. About ten days before any of the conspirators were taken up, a woman went to the general and desired a private audience....she let him know that his life was in danger and gave him*
156

such an account of the conspiracy as gained his confidence...Upon examination, one Forbes confessed that the plan was to assassinate the general and as many of the superior officers as they could and to blow up the magazine upon the appearance of the enemy's fleet and to go off in boats prepared for that purpose to join the enemy. Upon examination Forbes confessed that the plan was to assassinate the general and as many of the Superior Officers as they could, and to blow up the magazine upon the appearance of the enemy's fleet and go off in boats prepared for that purpose to join the enemy."

It is not known who this woman was or where she got her information.

The celebration was brief. The British fleet kept coming, a few ships each day, until on August 1st a huge fleet of 45 ships appeared in the harbor. Then 21 more arrived. Soon there were over 200 warships surrounding Manhattan Island. Over 32,000 British troops were stationed on Long Island and Staten Island, well trained military veterans with experienced officers to lead them plus 20,000 Hessians, considered the most accomplished, ruthless fighting machines in the world. Faced with this overwhelming force, more men deserted from the Continental army. Many who did stay were stricken with camp fever, too ill to fight or leave. Fighting was imminent.

The first combat between the Continental and British Army in New York was the Battle of Long Island, sometimes called the Battle of Brooklyn Heights, on 27 August 1776. Trying to protect New York City, Washington took the battle to the British on Long Island. Both

157

sides hoped that a large show of force would cause the other side to reconsider war, so each side sent in everything they had. It was the largest and bloodiest battle of the Revolution and ended in terrible defeat for Washington. Over 43,000 men fought for over 6 hours under a blazing hot sun. Washington's 11,000 men were badly outnumbered by over 32,000 Redcoats. He inexplicably left a pass undefended and local Loyalists guided a British commander through to outflank him. Realizing the battle was lost, survivors quietly retreated to the shore at twilight and stole away by boat to Manhattan. Washington lost over 1700 of his scarce men that day. He took the last boat while his decimated, demoralized troops rowed silently across the East River to Manhattan as foggy darkness and heavy rain drew a curtain across the terrible day. Washington and his men then marched north, crossed Kings Bridge and retreated up to White Plains. The English occupied Manhattan on 15 September 1776.

On 28 November 1776, a Declaration of Dependence was signed by 547 Loyalists from NY and the surrounding area. They were a mixed representation including merchants and freed slaves, pledging to remain loyal to the King. This signing ceremony took place in Samuel Fraunces Tavern.

While Washington was organizing defenses for New York City, other matters required his attention as well. After Loyalist housekeeper Mary Smith was evicted, Washington immediately wrote to General James Clinton that he was "entirely destitute of a housekeeper" and had heard good reports of Elizabeth Thompson from Clinton's neighborhood in Manhattan asking Clinton to pass on a letter to her.

Elizabeth Thompson was then a widow of 72. She arrived at Mortier House to replace Mary Smith on July 9th, 1776, the day the Declaration of Independence was read in NY. She was paid an annual salary of L50 *"New York money"*. One of Washington's aides managed the books for her as she could not read or write. The indomitable Elizabeth Thompson traveled for 7 years with the Washington family. That terrible winter in Valley Forge, Elizabeth, then 74, lived with the General and Mrs. Washington and 25 staff members in 5 small rooms in the Isaac Potts house. She remained Washington's housekeeper until she retired at the age of 79 in 1783. Washington offered her a permanent home at Mount Vernon, but she replied that her *"heap of ailments"* made travel from her home in New York City impossible. Washington remained in touch with her until her death. Elizabeth Thompson was a propertied widow before the war and lost several buildings in the Great NY Fire. The loss of income gave her great distress as she prided herself for self-sufficiency. In 1785 she finally received a retirement pension of $100 per year from the Continental Congress for her service.

William Green was interrogated, and Court Martialed after Hickey was hung. At his trial more information about the plot to kill Washington was revealed. He testified that he and Hickey were just trying to dupe the Tories, claiming he wanted to reveal the plot to the General, but Hickey thought they should learn more first. This story

159

was shown to be a lie when Green was named by others as the man who agreed to stab Washington. Green then confessed that Mary Smith, Washington's housekeeper at Mortier House, had supplied the arsenic for the assassination attempt. Unfortunately, his testimony was not taken until the day after Mary fled the city. Green and his men did not make their attempt to stab Washington that day because the bowl of peas that would have made everyone too ill to fight back was removed by Samuel Fraunces. Green was also Court Martialed and was probably quietly hung after testifying against Hickey.[57]

Gilbert Forbes, a civilian, confirmed at his hearing that Washington and his officers were to be killed. When he was arrested, all his papers were confiscated. Among these was a letter noting that *"they would be ready to act by Saturday"*, and naming James Clavering and his Negro man Cuff. William Collier, the waiter from the Sergeants Arms, testified against Forbes noting that Forbes was a very active member of the group. Forbes was sent to jail in Litchfield, CT and was still there as of May 19, 1777, when his mother Philander sent a petition asking, he be moved to a larger cell.[58] He was later released and was an executor of his father Gilbert's estate in 1790 with his mother Philander.

Isaac Ketchum, the Tory who originally reported the plot, testified at Hickey's court martial that Hickey claimed that eight members of the General's Life Guard were involved but had mentioned only Green by name. Ketchum was released after testifying against Hickey and all charges against him were dropped, as agreed. He moved to Long Island where he died in 1806. He and his wife, Freelove Carll, had 11 children.

It is assumed that the other Lifeguards, James Johnson, Michael Lynch and John Barnes were also Court Martialed and hung, although there is no specific confirmation. A contemporary letter mentioned that *"we are hanging them as fast as we can"* referring to the conspirators.[59]

David Matthews had been Mayor of NY since February 1776 and in addition to his home in the city, had a summer home in Flatbush, LI where he was arrested. After his hearing he was sent to the jail at Litchfield, CT with 12 other civilian conspirators, including Forbes. He was placed on house arrest at the home of Major Seymour, a relation of his wife but he violated parole, escaping on November 20th, 1776.[60] He returned to British occupied Manhattan and remained Mayor there until the Evacuation in 1783. During the war, he was a frequent visitor to the notorious British prisons and produced false affidavits, denying neglect by British officials and falsely swearing that the Colonial prisoners were well-fed and comfortable.[61] Matthews left Manhattan on Evacuation Day for Nova Scotia where he became president of the Council and Commander in Chief of the Island of Cape Breton.

On 4 July 1776 in Philadelphia, the 3rd Continental Congress 13 colonies formally voted to approve the Declaration of Independence. written by Thomas Jefferson, Benjamin Franklin, John Adams, Roger Livingstone, and Roger Sherman. Copies were sent to all thirteen colonies to be read to the public and published in newspapers on July 9th, 1776. The Declaration explained that Congress had *"dissolved the connection between this country and Great Britain"* and declared the *"United Colonies of North American to be free and independent States".* Then Jefferson's stirring words were read, explaining that *"...all men were created equal and endowed by their creator with the inalienable rights of life liberty and the pursuit of happiness."* Since George III had trampled on those rights, the people of the United States of American had the right to break the bands tying them to Great Britain and form a new government to rule themselves.[62] Word reached the steamy city of New York on 6 July in a letter from John Hancock with a copy of the Declaration. On 9 July Washington ordered all off duty soldiers to assemble on the Parade Grounds in Lower Manhattan. Here, at 6 pm, an officer read the Declaration of Independence to the troops and civilians who had gathered. When the reading concluded there was a moment of silence then a huge eruption of cheering. A group of excited soldiers ran downtown to the Bowling Green and toppled the statue of King George, which was melted to make bullets. The whole city was in jubilant tumult with cannons firing, guns shooting into the air, bells ringing and people cheering in the streets. This declaration also allowed the United States to make a formal alliance as a real country with France to supply money and soldiers to the war efforts. Samuel Fraunces had front row seats to this momentous event.

Jubilation didn't last long in Manhattan. The British fleet arrived, a few ships each day, until on August 1st a huge fleet of 45 ships appeared in the harbor. Then 21 more arrived. There were now over 100 sailing ships anchored in New York harbor, up and down the rivers around Manhattan. Over 32,000 British troops were stationed on Long Island and Staten Island, well trained military veterans with experienced officers to lead them plus 20,000 Hessians, considered the most accomplished, ruthless fighting machines in the world. Faced with this overwhelming force, more men deserted from the Continental army. Many who did stay were stricken with camp fever, too ill to fight or leave. Everyone knew a battle was coming at any moment.

The first combat between the Continental and British Army in New York was the Battle of Long Island, sometimes called the Battle of Brooklyn Heights, on August 27th, 1776. Trying to protect New York City, Washington took the battle to the British on Long Island. Both sides hoped that a large show of force would cause the other side to reconsider war, so each side sent in everything they had. It was the largest and bloodiest battle of the Revolution and ended in terrible defeat for Washington. Over 43,000 men fought for over 6 hours under a blazing hot sun. Washington's 11,000 men were badly outnumbered by over 32,000 Redcoats. He inexplicably left a pass undefended and local Loyalists guided a British commander through to outflank him. Realizing the battle was lost, survivors quietly retreated to the shore at twilight and stole away to Manhattan. Washington lost over 1700 of his scarce men that day. He took the last boat while his decimated, demoralized troops rowed silently across the East River to Manhattan as foggy darkness and heavy rain drew a curtain across the terrible day.

The British made the next move. The invasion of Manhattan Island began on Sunday morning, Sept 15th. Everyone knew it was coming but no one knew where it would start. Kip's Bay, at the foot of 34th street, along the East River was defended by about 500 Connecticut Militiamen, shopkeepers and famers, new untrained volunteers. Many had no muskets, and some were armed only with scythes. They spent a tense night, hunkered behind hastily built dirt walls. They woke at dawn to the horrifying sight of 5 huge gunships, moored just offshore end to end, looming over them. At 11 am the ships began a massive bombardment. The whistle of incoming cannonballs and the thunder of cannon fire deafened them. Concussion's half buried the men under dirt and sand along the shore. When the smoke and dust began to clear, the men saw the river covered with 80 flatboats carrying thousands of Redcoats and Hessian soldiers from Long Island, so many that, "when they came to the edge of the tide, they formed their boats in a line…until they appeared like a large field of clover in full bloom."[63] They ran.

General Washington arrived to find the men in chaotic retreat. He rode among them, shouting orders and furiously trying to bring order, even threatening to shoot some of the officers but, in their panic, they would not rally. Two thousand Continental reinforcements soon arrived but, seeing the large body of advancing Hessians, they too turned and ran, leaving the outraged and frustrated Washington riding alone within 80 yards of the enemy *muttering "Are these the men with which I am to defend this country?"*[64] Washington lost 400 more men in this engagement. He regrouped in Harlem Heights and the next day, Sept

16th, in Battle of Harlem Heights, Washington forced the Redcoats to retreat, finally giving some heart to his outnumbered, demoralized men. But Manhattan was now occupied by the British.

Sam Fraunces was now fully committed to the Patriot cause. He had been hosting Patriot meetings at his tavern although few knew about his help in foiling the assassination plot. Sam had sent his pregnant wife Elizabeth and the children away. Sophia, their 2nd child with dark skin was born in Elizabethtown, New Jersey that year. Sam and his oldest son Andrew were both in the New York City militia moving north with Washington as he retreated from Manhattan. When their 3 month militia enlistments ended, they joined Elizabeth in New Jersey.

Elizabeth and the children had gone to stay in Elizabethtown, New Jersey. Her mother was born in Perth Amboy and father in Middlesex where he owned a store. The Dally family attended the Dutch Reformed Church in NJ where her father was prominent in the congregation. It is not clear where she stayed during the occupation. Elizabeth's sister Catherine (Dally) Simmons and her husband, John William Simmons, tavern owners, left NY when the British occupation happened. Simmons enlisted and his family were in Orange, New Jersey. Her brother Gifford Dally enlisted with the Continental Army and his family moved to Philadelphia, where he and his wife later ran the City Tavern. Sister Mary Dally never married. She apparently moved to Philadelphia too as that is where she became a shopkeeper and died. There were probably family members with whom she could shelter during the war. It was from Elizabethtown, New Jersey that Sam was later captured. T.C. Campbell also apparently evacuated Manhattan before the British arrived. He was probably too old to be in the militia. That Campbell was not in NY was affirmed when his name was not on the Loyalist Pledge required of all residents when the English occupied New York.[65] Andrew Gautier, Sam's old friend, was a signer as were John and William Smith, who later managed the Queens Head Tavern in 1778.

Before Washington's retreat from Manhattan, several of his officers had recommended burning down the city. Almost 70% of the property in the City belonged to Loyalists. Washington brought the suggestion to the 3rd Continental Congress in Philadelphia, who flatly rejected it. There would be no burning down of New York City by the Americans. By the time the British entered Manhattan, there were only about 500 people, primarily Loyalists and slaves, left in the city. General Robertson was military commander of New York City and General Howe was military commander of all British troops.

The Great Fire of Manhattan broke out on Sept 21st, 1776, a few days after the English re-occupied the city. One eyewitness account by John Joseph Henry, an American prisoner aboard the HMS Pearse, said the fire began in the Fighting Cocks Tavern near Whitehall Slip. It appeared to start in several areas at once and was widely assumed to have been arson. The city soon became a chaotic vision of hell as the roaring fire rapidly advanced north and west. Sparks blown by strong winds started more fires, consuming everything in its path and the crash of collapsing houses and shouts of those trying to flee filled the air. The screams of terrified women looking for their children as their houses burst into flames and of people trapped in the fire added to the horror. Warning bells were silent - all the bells in the city had been melted down for cannons. The fire pumps did not work, and the buckets had been damaged by the retreating troops. The voracious monster leapt across Broadway near Beaver Street, devouring most of the city between Broadway and the Hudson River and north to Robinson Street. The inferno eventually died after 10 horrific hours when the wind suddenly changed direction at about 2 in the morning, blowing it back on the already burnt areas. It is estimated that between 800-1000 buildings burned – 30% of the buildings in Manhattan – including Old Trinity Church. It was widely assumed at the time, by both the British and the Patriots, that the New England Militia had started it. Some militia men were caught in the city and thrown into the fire in fury. Were they arsonists or defectors? No one was ever charged. Washington wrote privately to Cousin Lund Washington that: *"Providence, or some good honest fellow, has done more for us than we were disposed to do for ourselves."* Luckily, Sam's Queen's Head Tavern was spared although the fire came very close, stopping just across Broad Street. Its lead roof and brick construction protected it.

The British confiscated all buildings still standing, assigning them to British officers. Sam's Queen's Head and Hampden Hall taverns were used for housing. All churches, other than the Church of England, were converted into prisons, infirmaries, and barracks. A great number of Loyalists, who had left when Washington occupied the city, now rushed back to town, causing tremendous over-crowding. A tent city called Canvas Town was erected in the burnt ruins near Sam's Queen's Head, occupied mostly by black slaves to whom the British had promised freedom.

On November 16[th,] the British attacked recently built Fort Washington, the last American stronghold on Manhattan. Fort Washington and Fort Lee controlled high bluffs on opposite sides of the Hudson, intended to keep the British from using the river to move troops and supplies upstate. (The George Washington Bridge now spans the river at this point.) Washington had left 1200 men to hold this fort and soon sent 1800 reinforcements. Col. Robert Magaw, Commander of the fort, was convinced he could defend it, but he hadn't counted on William Demont, his adjunct, defecting. Based on Demont's information, the British surrounded the fort, forcing McGaw to surrender. Fifty nine Americans were killed, and the remaining 2837 men became Prisoners of War. Of the 230 officers and 2607 soldiers who surrendered, only 800 were still alive 18 months later.[66]

Howe then attacked the unfinished twin across the river, Fort Lee in New Jersey. On Nov 20th, 1776, 5000 British troops quietly ferried across the river in the dark. They landed undetected, slightly above the fort, and began climbing the steep bluffs in silence. They weren't seen until first light when they were halfway up the bluff. General Greene ordered his 2000 greatly outnumbered men to immediately abandon Fort Lee, leaving behind tents, 50 badly needed cannons and 10,00 barrels of flour.

The British, based on intelligence they were getting from deserters and Loyalists, believed the Continental Army was: *"broken all to pieces and the spirit of their leaders and their abettors is all broken...I think one may venture to pronounce that it is well-nigh over with them."*[67] British Admiral Lord Howe, and his brother Sir William Howe, issued a proclamation on November 30th offering all men who would pledge *"peaceable obedience"* to the King a *"free and general pardon"*. Fearing imminent defeat of the Colonial Army, almost 5000 citizens took them up on this offer. Considering how the war was going, aligning with the British probably seemed the most reasonable action to take. But Sam and Andrew Fraunces didn't sign and neither did T.C. Campbell.

The Continental Army was now divided between two fronts, and it was imperative that they join forces as soon as possible. Washington wrote to General Lee expressing frustration that Lee had not followed orders to at once join him. The troops of both men were hungry, many without coats, and winter was coming. Washington was at New Brunswick, N.J. when on November 30th, 1776, over 2000 of the militia men from Maryland and New Jersey left without warning at the end of their enlistments, despite, or perhaps because of, the fact that the British were less than two hours away, advancing on their position.

Thomas Paine, famous author of <u>Common Sense</u> who was a soldier with General Greene, was inspired by the courage of those who remained to write <u>The Crisis</u>. Paine's eloquence convinced many

Pacifist Quakers to work in non-combatant roles for the Patriot side. His words still resonate today: *"These are the times that try men's souls; the summer soldier and the sunshine patriot will, in this crisis, shrink from the service of his country; but he that stands it now, deserves the love and thanks of man and woman. Tyranny, like hell, is not easily conquered; yet we have this consolation with us, that the harder the conflict, the more glorious the triumph."*

Washington had no choice but to retreat, this time to Trenton, New Jersey. Fortunately, the British then made a mistake. General Cornwallis could have caught and annihilated the small Continental Army on its retreat, but Howe inexplicably ordered Cornwallis to slow his advance, allowing Washington to reach Trenton on Dec 7th with less than 3000 men. These exhausted, freezing, coatless and shoeless, hungry men were now the only protection between the huge advancing British army and the capital city of Philadelphia, 60 miles away. When Washington sent a rider to warn the Continental Congress to flee, they were shocked as most had no idea how badly the war was going. Sadly, there were plenty of men and arms available to fight but the States refused to send them. When Howe and his large force marched on Trenton, Washington, greatly outnumbered, again retreated across the Delaware River into Pennsylvania on Dec 11th. Washington wisely took all the boats across the river with him, leaving Howe no way to follow.

By December of 1776, Washington had survived one assassination attempt and several important defections, lost four battles and abandoned Fort Lee without a fight. He had started with 20,000 men in

New York City in August, been forced to retreat from Manhattan to Westchester, to New Jersey and now to Pennsylvania. His army was divided between himself and General Lee, and he and his few men were the only thing standing between the British and the capitol of the United States and Congress. Washington had less than 3500 men left under his personal command and almost 2000 of them planned to leave at the end of December when their enlistments were over! That would be the end. The rebellion would fail, and leading Patriots faced certain death. Washington, through his personal eloquence, integrity, and by promising them a bounty for staying, was able to persuade many of the men to re-enlist despite the lack of pay, lack of ammunition, clothes and food and the enormous odds against them.

Washington wrote yet again to Lee urging him to hurry with his 24 pound cannon and was relieved to hear that Lee was finally on his way with 4000 badly needed men. But Lee, moving slowly, stopped to spend the night of Dec 12th at Widow White's Tavern in Basking Ridge, NJ leaving the bulk of his army camped 3 miles away. Local Loyalists informed the British and the following morning, General Charles Lee and 15 of his men surrendered after a brief fight. American General Sullivan collected the rest of Lee's troops and marched them to Washington's camp. He had hoped for 4000 men but less than 2000 of Lee's men were left and they were so battered that their bare feet left blood on the frozen ground as they limped into camp. The British then made another miscalculation.

Wanting to spend Christmas in NY City with his mistress, the wife of Joshua Loring, British Gen. William Howe decided to leave a small

171

detachment of Hessians in Trenton and returned with his main body of men to Manhattan for winter. He thought that Washington, believing the entire British army was camped at Trenton, would not attack there. But, on Christmas Night, December 25th-26th, Washington selected 2400 of the fittest men he had left and crossed the Delaware River. They quietly marched all night in freezing sleet to make a desperate surprise attack on what they believed was the entire British army in the village of Trenton. Instead, they surprised 1500 Hessian mercenaries drunkenly celebrating Christmas. After a chaotic battle, over 900 of the half-dressed, hung over Hessians surrendered along with six badly needed cannons. Washington suffered only 4 wounded men and two deaths, both of men who had frozen to death on the march.

Washington made sure this much needed success was written up in all the newspapers, supplying a badly needed morale boost to the Continental troops, and Patriots throughout the Colonies. Washington and his men were suddenly heroes again. This event was memorialized in paintings called 'Crossing the Delaware'. Washington crossed the Delaware again, through thick ice floes, a few days later and took Princeton, New Jersey from British Lord Cornwallis, capturing 300 more prisoners. He then moved his troops to winter camp in Morristown, New Jersey, setting up his headquarters at Arnold's Tavern. The long first year of war was over and the Patriots hoped for new enlistments and greater success in the spring.

1777 – Spies

Jay's Committee of Secret Correspondence employed secret agents in the Colonies as well as overseas, including Patience Lovell Wright, the wax figure sculptor. General Washington also had spies, civilian and military. Major Benjamin Tallmadge recruited informants like Abraham Woodhull who became 'Samuel Culper', leader of the famous Culper Spy Ring. Many other spies such as the tailor Hercules Mulligan and his slave Cato, Haym Solomon, Elizabeth Burgin, James Rivington, John Cork, Asher FitzRandolph, John VanDruver, Baker Hendricks, Elizabeth Vanderhoven and Samuel Fraunces operated independently. Among these were three brothers from Staten Island, Joshua, Jacob and John Mersereau, owned a tavern in Staten Island and a stage line between New York and Philadelphia. They provided a conduit for transporting covert information for Washington. When the English occupied NY City, the brothers gave Washington their horses. Joshua's sons, Joshua III and John LaGrange Mersereau volunteered to remain on Staten Island behind enemy lines to continue sending information to Washington. Samuel certainly would have known these men as their stages stopped at Fraunces Tavern. Later, Samuel's granddaughter Betsy Fraunces, daughter of Samuel M, married John De Hart. De hart's father was a slave who had been owned by the Mersereau family. And in 1906, architect, William Mersereau of Staten Island was hired to restore the Fraunces Tavern.

General Washington started 1777 in Morristown, New Jersey with only 1000 men, as enlistments expired, and deserters fled the hardships. Washington had great difficulty trying to re-build the Continental Army until Congress finally set up a draft and offered bounty land and higher pay. But Congress had no way to supply reliable arms, clothing or pay for the Continental Army whose recruiters were competing against individual States and towns raising their own local militias and funds to pay them. Militias were filled with middle class men and farmers who joined local militias with 3 month enlistments where they could protect their own property and receive regular pay. They soon learned the rudiments of guerilla warfare.

The average drafted Continental soldier now was a young, poor recent immigrant without property, usually single and uneducated. Washington's army grew that winter to 8298 drafted soldiers, over 2600 of them sick or injured. States taxed citizens for the local militias and again for funding the Continental Army. Resentful Americans began regarding the Continental soldiers as hired mercenaries, like the hated Hessians, believing 'true' Patriots were local militia men. In reality, the militias especially in NJ, saw far more fighting than Washington's Continental Army did.

On June 17[th,] the British, under General John 'Gentleman Johnny' Burgoyne, invaded New York from Canada, capturing Fort Ticonderoga without a fight. He then marched to Saratoga to wait for Gen. Howe and his reinforcements. They planned to cut off New England from the rest of the colonies thus disrupting supply lines. But

Howe and his troops never showed up. He was too busy trying to capture Philadelphia.

On Sept 9-11 Washington and his men were driven back towards Philadelphia by Howe's troops. The 3rd Continental Congress fled to Baltimore. The 'Battle of Brandywine Creek' became the longest one day battle of the war with 11 hours of brutal fighting. Washington retreated again after heavy losses, and the British occupied Philadelphia. But the delay caused by this long battle kept Howe from sending troops to Burgoyne. A month later, on Oct 7th, at the Battle of Saratoga, Burgoyne, greatly outnumbered without Howe's reinforcements, surrendered his entire Army of 5900 men to American Gen. Gates. Following this surrender, Howe retreated to New York City, evacuating all the forts the English had previously captured. Taking Philadelphia had come at high cost.

Currency continued to be a huge problem for the new United States. America could not run a war without money, but the Continental Congress had no power to tax anyone. Each State had voluntarily agreed to supply men, money and supplies to the war but all were delinquent in sending them. Many waited to see which way the war was going. Continental soldiers were not being paid. They were poorly clothed and were living on starvation rations and the Army was horribly short of ammunition. States began printing their own currencies, not backed by anything of value, to send to Congress for their shares. Soon many currencies were in circulation with fluctuating values. Congress also printed $242,000,000 Colonial dollars. Unfortunately, at the start

175

of the Revolution, there was only about $12 million in precious specie in all of America and none was in the hands of Congress, so this paper money was essentially worthless, and everyone soon knew it. Financial hardship had just begun.

Washington and his men made their 2nd winter camp at Valley Forge, about 20 miles from Philadelphia, in December of 1777. First came deep snow, then warms spells and hard rains melted the snow, turning the surrounding roads to deep mud and bogging down the few supply wagons. Cold weather then froze the mud into impassable ruts. When wagons could get through, the local vendors sold their supplies to the nearby British army for hard currency instead of the worthless Continental scrip. American soldiers were so hungry that, after several days with no rations, those that had them, ate their shoes. Over 2,500 of the original 10,000 men died from exposure and disease.

Washington's 2nd housekeeper, 72 year old Elizabeth Thompson, was a very resourceful woman. When local vendors wouldn't accept her continental scrip, she asked Washington to: *"give me an order for six bushels of salt"* which she purchased from a patriotic merchant. The following day, when his dinner table was full, Washington asked how she had gotten food, concerned that she had used her own funds. She explained she had bartered the salt for other provisions.

Washington was desperately trying to provide his men with food and ammunition with little support from Congress. None of his soldiers had been paid, food was so scarce everyone was on ½ rations, and they had no warm coats, blankets or shoes. Many just walked away and went

176

home. He also faced political backstabbing in Congress where a faction agitated to have Washington replaced by General Gates. This got so bad that Congress sent a delegation to Valley Forge. After seeing the truly horrendous conditions and speaking with the troops and Washington, the delegation placed the problems completely on Congress for not supplying sufficient funds. They replaced Quartermaster Miflin with Gen. Greene noting the troops were: *"in little less than a famine"*.

It was during this winter camp at Valley Forge that Baron von Steuben, a decorated Prussian General, arrived and, because he could not get a commission in the American Army, he volunteered his time. He created organizational plans for all Army camps and wrote an operations and training manual that was used by the Army for the next 100 years. Von Steuben soon reformed this rag-tag collection of farmers into a true fighting Army, personally training smaller groups of soldiers to teach others about tactics, fighting and how to use bayonets for combat instead of just roasting meat, when they could get it.

1778 – Prisoners

The Battles of Brandywine Creek and Saratoga convinced France that America actually could win the war, so France agreed to declare war against Britain. In February 1778, US representatives signed 2 treaties in Paris, a *'Treaty of Amity and Commerce'*, and a *'Treaty of Alliance'* which stipulated that neither country would accept a truce unless both parties consented. France officially recognized the new United States of America, becoming the major provider of money, supplies and soldiers to the Continental Army. The American Revolution had now become a World War. Spain allied with France, and both threatened to invade England. Britain declared war on the Dutch for trading with America and France. Britain had no allies until 1781 when Russia agreed to help them.

In May, England's Parliament sent General Henry Clinton to replace General Howe as commander of all British forces in America. He combined his forces in New York and evacuated Philadelphia in June, marching 10,000 men, women and children back towards Manhattan. As Clinton was marching his soldiers from Philadelphia through New Jersey, Washington followed and ordered Gen. Charles Lee, recently exchanged as a prisoner of war after his ignominious capture, and restored to his command, to harass the end of Clinton's long supply train trying to capture badly needed food and ammunition.

General Charles Lee, a distinguished officer in England before the war, was jealous when Washington was made Commander in Chief of the Continental Army instead of himself. To gain glory and undermine Washington, Lee had constantly been slow to respond to Washington's orders. He continued agitating to replace Washington and wrote many letters of criticism to Congress. Lee was captured in 1776, due to his own carelessness, and held prisoner by the British for several years before being exchanged. Years later, in 1857, a letter in his handwriting was discovered among papers of the Howe family, outlining his plan to defeat the Colonials. Since this betrayal was not discovered until long after his death, Lee had been returned to his command.

When Washington ordered him to pursue the fleeing British army, Lee loudly disagreed in front of the troops. Washington overruled Lee and gave young Gen. Lafayette 5000 men to attack Clinton's rearguard. Jealous of the younger Lafayette, Lee then requested the command back, which Lafayette graciously relinquished. But Lee did not provide his soldiers with a plan of attack, and his disorganized American soldiers were soon in chaotic retreat. Washington, advancing with the rest of the army, was furious to see Lee's men racing towards him. He took personal command of the men and angrily dressed down Lee, relieving him of command in public. Lee was sent to the rear, where he wrote two furious, highly insubordinate letters to Washington, demanding a court martial. He soon got his wish.

On Sunday June 28, 1778, Washington's army engaged the retreating British at the Battle of Monmouth Courthouse (now

Freehold, NJ). The battle involved over 25,000 soldiers between the Colonials, British and Hessians and lasted over 7 hours in blistering 100 degree heat. Both sides claimed victory when it ended in a stand-off. They fought until it was too dark to shoot. This is where the *"Legend of Molly Pitcher"*, Mary (Ludwig) Hayes McCauley, originated. She (and many other women throughout the war) carried water to thirsty soldiers in pitchers and to swab cannons between shots. When her husband fell in battle, Mary took up his position, swabbing his cannon throughout the battle and narrowly missed being shot. Her bravery was memorialized in the diary of Joseph Plumb Martin and Washington himself saw her courage that day. He issued her a warrant as a non-commissioned officer, and she was known as Sgt. Molly for the rest of her life. The Americans expected to continue the fight the following morning, but the British retreated silently during the night. They had lost 249 men killed and left on the battlefield. The Americans had lost 69 dead, 161 wounded, and 140 missing. One of those was Sam Fraunces.

Washington convened General Lee's Court Martial at New Brunswick, NY on July 1st, 1778, immediately after the battle of Monmouth. The Court Martial Board found that Lee was guilty of: *"disobeying orders in the face of the enemy, misbehavior and disrespecting the Commander in Chief."* He was relieved of command for one year. Lee continued writing indignant letters trying to overturn this verdict and publicly vilified Washington. This finally resulted in Congress dismissing him completely from the Army on Jan 10th, 1780.

Charles Lee then retired to his farm, Prato Rio in Berkeley County, VA where he bred horses and dogs. Lee had given up large family estates in Britain and the West Indies to join the Patriot cause. He was now bitter and deeply in debt with no income and no pension, living in an unfinished house, the future rooms marked off with chalk and writing about his reduced circumstances to his few remaining friends. On a trip from visiting friends in Baltimore in 1782, he became ill at an inn in Philadelphia, dying several days later of a *"refluxion of the lungs"*, probably pneumonia.[68] He left bequests to several long-time friends and the rest of his property to his sister in England. He owed a very large debt to Samuel Fraunces for food and lodging. Sam spent many years unsuccessfully trying to collect it after the war.

Samuel Fraunces was captured in late June 1778, probably after the Battle of Monmouth. He had been living in Elizabethtown, per his memorial to Congress on 5 March 1785. The British soldiers plundered his home, taking everything of value and brought him to New York City. Sam was then 56 so not likely to have been among the fighting men. He and his son Andrew's NY militia service had ended, and they had made their way to New Jersey to join Elizabeth and the rest of the family. It is possible that Sam was caught supplying intelligence to Washington although he had successfully done so for years. It is more likely that Sam created an opportunity to be captured so he could better spy for the cause. Sam had great respect for Washington. He had already saved his life once and had been passing information to the Patriots for years. Washington had recently asked that his spy master to *"endeavor to get some intelligent person into the City and others of his own choice to be messengers between you and him for the purpose of conveying such information as he shall be able to obtain and give."*[69] When word reached Sam, he knew he could do that effectively. Clinton's army was returning to New York and was his best way back.

If capture was Sam's plan, it was a very risky one. Colonial prisoners of war were kept in horrifying conditions. Soldiers were supposed to be fed and clothed from payments made by the American Army or their State or local Militias. The Colonies and Army were paying minimal amounts to the British, but the money was stolen and many of the soldiers were starving. Soldiers at least had a chance of being exchanged for British prisoners. Neither country or Colonies made any efforts to feed or clothe civilians – and they could not be exchanged. If they had no family money, they often died of starvation.

Sam's dangerous gamble paid off. He was brought to New York City and presented to Gen. Robertson. Robertson knew Sam well and had patronized his tavern for years before the war. Sam talked himself into a job as Robertson's personal chef. Not only did he not have to stay in prison, but Sam negotiated a perk to have all the left-over food. Robertson undoubtedly thought Sam would sell the left-over food and had no idea it would instead be delivered to the American prisoners. Sam later testified that he: *"submitted to serve for some time in the menial office of cook in the family of General Robertson without any pay or perquisite whatsoever, except the privilege of disposing of the remnants of the tables, which I appropriated towards the comfort of the American prisoners within the City."*[70] Sam took the left-over food to

183

the Sugar House on Crown Street, and later testified, *"sometimes the sentries would overset it on the ground and the poor prisoners would lick it up, sometimes the Britons they would come past with a piece of meat or other provision kind and would hold it up to the soldiers that was almost starved to aggravate them."* Helping American prisoners was a crime punishable by prison or death, but Sam regularly delivered food, and collected clothing for them. He lent prisoners' money to escape. His long suffering wife, Elizabeth, was left to support their 7 children in New Jersey while soldiers of both armies ransacked and pillaged around them.

It has been claimed that Samuel was a slave owner based on an advertisement of August 29th, 1778, where Samuel Fraunces at the corner of Dock Street near the Royal Exchange offered for sale: *"one clock, one desk and bookcase, one chest of drawers, a variety of kitchen furniture, looking glasses, some table China, a few mahogany tables, a few boxes of spermaceti candles, one mahogany desk and a variety of other articles too tedious to mention; likewise a negro boy, about 14 years of age, hearty and strong and is used to household work. NB. He has had the smallpox".*[71] This accusation makes no sense. Sam had been captured 2 months earlier in New Jersey and was a prisoner-of-war living with Gen. Robertson at Kennedy House. He would not have been allowed to bring a slave into captivity with him, so this was clearly not 'his' slave (ironically this boy was the same age as his dark skinned son Samuel M). His tavern building was being used to house English officers. Sam was most likely selling these items, including the boy (possibly an officer's slave) at British request. Three months later, on November 14th, there was an advertisement that John and William Smith, Loyalists, had opened Sam's Queen's Head as a Tavern again.[72]

How valuable was Sam's position to Washington's intelligence gathering? At the time of Sam's capture in 1778, General James Robertson was the British Commander in New York City. Since his own home burned in the great fire, Robertson lived at the Kennedy House as Washington had first done. An arrogant man, he undoubtedly felt it fitting that the best chef in America was to cook for the most powerful Englishman, living in the best house in the city. Robertson was about 61 at this time and enjoyed lavish dining and entertaining. He had lived in NY City for many years before the Revolution and knew Sam, then 56, well. He sided with moderate Loyalists, arguing strongly to Parliament that, if Britain gave the colonies representation and negotiated on taxes, the Americans would give up their crazy war. In reality, fewer than 20% of Colonists were Loyalists (although a larger 40% in Manhattan) but his perceptions were clearly influenced by the preponderance of Loyalists he entertained. This belief, his familiarity with Sam, and the lack of Patriots in the city, lulled any caution about discussing military matters over lunch and dinner with his officers and guests. Robertson's household included his senior officers as Washington's did, and his frequent lavish entertainment of Loyalists supplied Sam great opportunities to hear conversations, and pass intelligence on to General Washington. Since, to the British,

185

money was no object, Sam could regularly prepare a surplus of food to deliver to starving prisoners.

1778 was not a good year to be in New York City. Every house was being used as soldiers' barracks and Loyalist owners were restricted to 1 or 2 rooms of their own homes. Canvas Town, where most of the poor and freed slaves lived, began about 50 feet from the Queen's Head Tavern, across Broad Street. There, crude homes were constructed from the ruined walls or a chimney still standing after the Great Fire, extended with salvaged ships spars and canvas. Food was cooked over communal fires and people wore everything they owned to stay warm and prevent thieves from taking the little they had.

Resentment soon grew among Loyalists who had welcomed the British Army with open arms. They were incredulous that the greatest Army in the world had not already crushed the Rebels and were outraged that Gen. Clinton had retreated from Philadelphia. Winning was not the sure thing they had believed, and they feared retaliation if the British lost the war. Their frustration soon turned to anger as idle English soldiers committed serious crimes including thefts, rapes and murder with no discipline from their Commanders and no legal recourse. Clinton's condescension and unwillingness to discuss anything even with the most trusted Loyalists alienated his supporters.

Military law stipulated civilians were to be tried by civilian courts, while captured combatants were prisoners of war and could potentially be exchanged for English prisoners of similar rank. Since the city was under military occupation, there were no civilian authorities. Prominent

186

Loyalist civilians speaking out against the rapes and looting, clergymen objecting to wanton destruction of churches and doctors protesting poor care for the ill and wounded were being arrested and jailed like prisoners of war, contrary to military law. Civilians were not entitled to Army supplies, so their friends and families who could, supplied food, clothing, and money for their needs. Other simply starved. They could not be exchanged, and their only hope was to be ransomed.

The winter of 1778-79 was the worst winter in memory. A huge blizzard hit on Christmas Eve, paralyzing the city. A French blockade prevented supply ships from entering NY ports. The city was surrounded on land by Washington's army, so food and fuel were very scarce. The prisoners of war had the worst conditions of all.

William Cunningham, the Provost Marshal, in charge of land based prisons, was notorious for the inhumane condition in which he kept American prisoners, far harsher conditions than were acceptable at the time. He would hang 5 or 6 men each night without trial. The prisoners were conducted along the streets and hung nightly on public gallows until the women of the neighborhood petitioned Gen. Howe to stop the practice *"as the sufferers praying for mercy and appealing to heaven for justice was dreadful to their ears."* Their bodies were thrown into mass graves; often the very trenches they had dug to defend the city before they were captured.[73]

Military prisoners were supposed to be fed and clothed from funds provided by the American commissary to the British, who were then to issue food and wood for fires. But Congress did not supply sufficient funds and most of that was stolen by the British. Military prisoners

187

were supposed to receive rations twice a week consisting of ½ pound of biscuit, ½ pound of raw pork, ½ pint of peas, ½ gill of rice and ½ ounce of butter. They were to be allowed one fire every three days to cook their food. They slept in bare rooms with no straw or bedding. Water was brought to them in chamber pots. Lice and other vermin infested them all. British Commissary Manager, Joshua Loring Jr., whose wife was the mistress of General William Howe, later admitted to stealing 60% of the funds allotted for the prisoners' food.[74] If that is what he admitted to, certainly it was much more. If prisoners didn't freeze to death or die of malnutrition, they were infected with dysentery, typhoid, smallpox, yellow fever, or tuberculosis.

The worst prison was the Provost, located in the Old Jail building. According to a contemporary account, John Pintard wrote: *"Cunningham roamed from cell to cell, insulting the noblest of the land. He saw them suffering from cold, and he mocked their cry for bread. For slight offenses he thrust them into underground dungeons. The North-east chamber, turning to the left on the second floor, was appropriated to officers and prisoners of superior rank and distinction, and was called Congress Hall. So closely were they packed that when they lay down at night to rest, when their bones ached on the hard oak planks, and they wished to turn, it was altogether by word of command, "right-left" being so wedged and compact as to form almost a solid mass of human bodies."*[75] Joseph Plumb Martin's autobiography noted *"At the Battle of Germantown, in 1777, a Dutchman, an inhabitant of that town, and his wife, fired upon some of the British during the action. After the battle, someone informed against them, and they were both taken and confined in the provost guardhouse and there kept with scarcely anything to sustain nature and not a spark of fire to warm them. On the morning that the HMS Augusta was blown up at Fort Mifflin, the poor old man exclaimed 'Huzzah for General Washington. Tomorrow he comes.' The villain Provost Marshal upon hearing this put him into the cellar, without allowing him the least article of sustenance, till he died."*

New Bridewell Prison was equally bad. Oliver Woodruff spent the winter there, where he "*never saw any fire except what was in the lamps of the city. There was not a pane of glass in the windows and nothing to keep out the cold but the Iron Gate."* Three sugarhouses on Liberty Street along the waterfront, used to store rum, sugar and molasses, were also turned into prisons. They were filthy, and rat infested, stifling hot in summer, and freezing cold in winter with no sanitary facilities. Conditions worsened as the prison population swelled despite the constant deaths. It was so crowded that prisoners organized themselves into groups of 6, so each could stand for 10 minutes by a window.

Many were also held on decommissioned rotting ships called "*the hulks*", anchored in Wallabout Bay. The Jersey was the most notorious of these. Over 85% of her prisoners died. Other prison ships included the Whitby, the Good Hope, the Scorpion, the Prince of Wales, the Falmouth, the Hunter, and the Stromboli. So many dead bodies were thrown overboard that twenty years after the war, bones were still being found along the Brooklyn shore. They were re-buried in a cemetery on the site of the Battle at Brooklyn Heights. While Cunningham and O'Keefe were directly responsible for the death of 2500 mainland prisoners, Naval Commissioner Sprout, in charge of the prison ships, was directly responsible for the death of over 10,500 prisoners.

Fully 1/3 of these deaths were civilian non-combatants, such as preachers who spoke out about criminal activity or civilian men and women accused of aiding the Patriot cause. None ever had a trial. Sam could easily have been among them. What is most astonishing is that all these prisoners could have saved themselves simply by signing an Oath of Allegiance to England. They all refused to do so despite almost certain death as a result. These prisoners were the real heroes of the war.

1779 – Occupation

On May 11th, 1779, Robertson was made Royal Governor of NY while in England, and Sam was finally paroled. The officers to cease imprisoning civilians noting, *"no citizen shall be put into confinement…unless in case of violent breach of peace."* In name "Queen's Head Tavern" was now being used by a tavern on Brownjohn's Wharf owned by Loyalist James Strachan, so Sam reopened his Pearl Street establishment, calling it "Black Sam's" or "Fraunces' Tavern".

All the churches in Manhattan, except the Church of England, had been conscripted as hospitals or barracks and their interiors maliciously destroyed. That summer, Trinity Church property, burned in the Great Fire, became an entertainment Mall for officers and their ladies to walk and hear concerts. Tombstones were removed to widen their promenade. The graveyard was railed in, benches placed, and lamps fixed in trees. The pretty lights and music in the Mall, guarded by occupation soldiers to keep ordinary people out, outraged prominent Loyalist mourners at the many funerals caused by disease, starvation and cold, who had to request permission to cross the Mall to bury their loved ones in their desecrated churchyard.[76] By September, an epidemic raged, but the tone-deaf British held a splendid ball with fireworks on the Anniversary of King George's Coronation.[77] Despite

British controlled news, articles began appearing that *"scarce a day passes that multitudes are not offended."* The Order of the Day on Nov 20th stated that *"the commandant had received many and frequent complaints of inhabitants being ill-treated by officers and servants quartered upon their houses"* and finally directed December, the whole city ran out of fuel because people were too sick to cut wood. Soldiers seized the wood supplies from sugar and still houses without paying. Not only did this incense these Loyalist businessmen, but they could also no longer produce rum which antagonized everyone.

Washington set up winter quarters in the Ford Mansion in Morristown, New Jersey and described the situation of his army as *"alarming"* in circular letters to the states. His men were *"intirely destitute of money and he feared the army would disband within a fortnight without relief."*[78] None had been paid. They were freezing, without blankets or shoes, had no rations and no money to buy food, had any been available. Gen. Nathanial Greene observed angrily that: *"A country once overflowing with plenty, are now suffering an Army, employed for the defense of everything that is dear and valuable, to perish for want of food."* [79]

1780 – Treason

Washington and his family lived at the Ford home between December 1779 and June 1780. Over 28 separate snowstorms hit NY and NJ that winter, piling snow over 12 feet deep in places.[80] William Smith wrote that it was so cold in Manhattan that the ink froze in his pen while sitting 2 feet from a large coal fire. The rivers froze solid enough to support fully loaded wagons, heavy cannons, and a troop of British cavalry, who galloped across the ice from Staten Island to the Battery. All the fences and sheds in Manhattan had been torn down and used for firewood, but the British ordered that "*no fruit or ornamental trees around Gentlemen's Houses shall be cut down*".

Loyalists had originally accepted Martial Law because it suspended taxes, but they were now agitating for a return to civilian rule. The idle soldiers were so out of control that English Lt. Von Krafft wrote in his journal: "*In the evening I took a walk in New York and, on account of the flagrant excesses occurring there, took with me 2 soldiers ....*"[81] He wrote further "*I could narrate many and very frightful occurrences of theft, fraud, robbery and murder by the English soldiers...as they received but little money, they used these disgusting means.*" Shore leave for sailors was finally prohibited after dark because of the disturbances they caused. In rural, strongly Loyalist areas like Long Island, Staten Island and upper Manhattan, officers seized horses, goats, cows and sheep, hundreds of pounds of oats and hay and cut down forests of timber, without paying, to sell in the city for personal profit. These crimes could not be prosecuted because there were no civilian courts and officers would not court martial their men. These harsh acts of the British against their supporters soon turned indignant Loyalist's supporters against them.

The British had plenty of money and no shame flaunting it. Gov. Tryon hosted a dinner for 70 at Sam Fraunces Tavern providing Sam with lots of left-overs for prisoners. A few weeks later, in mid-January 1780, the New York Gazette made note of another lavish celebration, put on by General Field on the Queen's birthday. It was an event of *"uncommon splendor and magnificence"*. The ball began at 8 pm and lasted until 3 in the morning. A public dinner was given by Governor Tryon, at Mr. Hick's Tavern which *"consisted of 380 dishes beside ornamental appendages"*. The entire extravaganza cost over 2000 guineas (L2100) at a time when the richest 1% in the US had an average annual income of only L527 and over 80% of the population lived on between L22 and L100 per year.[82] The British spent in one night enough to support 100 families for an entire year. Extravagance like this, in the middle of a war, while soldiers ran amok and Loyalists were starving and freezing to death, appalled even guests at the event.

Governor Robertson returned to New York from England on March 21st, 1780, just before his 63rd birthday. He had been appointed Royal Governor of NY State and Civilian Commander of the City by the King, hoping to appease the Loyalists by reinstating civilian law.

He requested Gen. Clinton declare Manhattan at peace so he could reinstate Civil Law but Clinton, the military commander, ignored him, refusing to declare peace. Clinton rightly thought that civilian authorities would order financial reparations for seizures, prosecution for criminal acts, and expose his officers to discipline for lack of control. It would allow Loyalists *"exasperated by their sufferings and losses…to conceive perhaps erroneously, that the Restoration of the Government may be conducive to the Gratification of their Revenge."* Martial Law continued.

In May, the American Army suffered their worst defeat when the British captured the entire Southern Continental Army at Charleston. The British lost 225 men.

There was a severe drought and unnatural cold that spring, with frost on the ground until the middle of June. Food was very scarce, and malaria and smallpox were epidemic. Instead of attacking the Americans, Clinton remained in NY occupying his time by erecting an orchestra stage on the north side of Trinity Church, and widening the Mall Promenade, removing more tombstones, and covering several graves and a vault, decidedly not a way to win the hearts and minds of a religiously conservative, exasperated Loyalist population.

On June 5th, Gov. Robertson celebrated the King's Birthday with a *"very elegant Entertainment"* for about 70 Generals, who had *"a great dinner today at 'Black Sam's'."*[83] With all these British entertainments, Sam could supply more food to the prisoners. His tavern became a safe house for those who could escape, and he helped with food, money, clothing, and safe contacts.

A Massachusetts Constitution endorsed in June stated that "*all men are born free and equal*", including black slaves. This anti-slavery language angered the southern states which used this vow to justify their continuing refusal to send their pledged money or men. But this bold statement provided encouragement to Sam that slavery would eventually end.

At General Washington's urging, Congress promoted General Benedict Arnold on August 3rd, giving him official command of West Point and authority over the vitally important Hudson River valley, from Albany to the British lines. Washington considered Arnold an excellent officer and a friend, and this prestigious promotion made Arnold a valued member of Washington's inner command.

But Arnold was a bitter man. He was severely injured twice in battle but was passed over for promotion, and when finally promoted, did not get the retroactive pay he was due. He was then officially reprimanded (after a trumped up court martial) and, feeling unappreciated, financially strapped, and despondent about the state of the war, had approached British Gen. Clinton offering to defect. When Arnold received his promotion, he at once wrote to Clinton, suggesting a plan to defect, deliver West Point, and capture Washington for a payment of £ 20,000.

When Arnold arrived at West Point, he began putting his defection plan into action. He delayed making needed repairs and sent detachments to outlying posts to reduce troop strength. He diminished supplies so a siege would fail. Subordinates noticed but believed he was selling materials for personal profit. While this reflected on his personal reputation, no one even remotely suspected this highly respected officer would defect. Arnold, paranoid and fearing betrayal, insisted that final negotiations for his plot be done face to face.

Loyalist William Smith wrote in his diary on Nov 19th that *"a dinner was given by Col. Williams for Sir Henry Clinton and his staff as a parting compliment to Major Andre who is about to go north to confer with the American General, Benedict Arnold, in a plot to secure the capitulation of West Point which Arnold commands."*[84] Major Andre left Manhattan on the ship Vulture on Nov. 20th, sailing up the Hudson. That day, Sam overheard an officer who had attended the previous night's farewell dinner, quietly but excitedly telling others about plans to take a fort *"without a fight...making a quick ending"* and saw them make a quiet toast to *"Arnold"*. Arnold's recent promotion was well known, and Sam suddenly realized the fort they were talking about must be West Point and that Arnold planned to defect. Sam also knew that Washington and General Rochambeau, leader of the French forces in America, were to meet with General Arnold at West Point in a few days. Sam realized that would be the perfect opportunity to capture both men, putting a *"quick ending"* to the war. Now, how to get this critical information to Washington in NJ without revealing himself?

Janetje (van Reypen) Tuers, her husband and brother, were among only 14 Patriot families in Bergen, New Jersey, a Loyalist stronghold. She sold their produce in Manhattan, and Sam was a good customer. She also helped Sam deliver food and clothing to the Sugar House prison where her brother, blacksmith Daniel van Reypen, had been imprisoned so Sam knew she could be trusted. When Janetje arrived, Sam quietly explained what he heard and how urgent it was to get word to Gen. Washington. Janetje returned home on the Paulus Hook ferry as usual and stopped at her brother's house to pass on Sam's information. Daniel rode 16 miles to Hackensack that night to meet with General Wayne, who brought him to see General Washington the next morning, September 21st. Washington offered a reward, which Daniel declined, asking only that Washington intercede if he or his sister were captured.[85] Washington had trusted Arnold implicitly, and had supported him as an officer and a friend for many years. He was incredulous at this news.

Meanwhile, Andre's ship arrived near West Point, and he was rowed to shore on the night of September 21st to meet with Arnold at the Joshua Hett Smith house in Haverstraw. Returning to the ship on the morning of the 22nd, they found that it had been fired upon and moved downriver, stranding Andre. Time was short. Andre had to get to Manhattan, brief Clinton and get troops north to capture the Generals and the fort in just a few days. General Arnold wrote Andre a civilian pass as John Anderson to get through American lines and gave him drawings of West Point and the schedule of Washington and Rochambeau's visit to his headquarters and Andre left, dressed in civilian clothing.

Early morning on September 23rd, his escort, Joshua Hett Smith, left Andre near Tarrytown, thinking they were within English lines. About 9 am, Andre was captured by 3 militiamen, one wearing a

Hessian overcoat. Andre mistook them for English and demanded they give way before they revealed they were Americans. They detained him, finding the papers in his boot. He insisted that he was on business for Gen. Arnold, and tried to bribe them to let him go, but they refused and took him to Col. Jameson in Tappan.

Jameson sent 'Anderson' off towards General Arnold at West Point that afternoon of Sept. 23rd. Because he felt the papers were so important, Jameson sent them in an express packet to Gen. Washington noting *"The papers were found under the feet of his stockings....he offered the men that took him one hundred guineas and as many goods as they would please to ask...I have sent the prisoner to General Arnold, he is very desirous of the papers and everything being sent with him but I think they are of a very dangerous tendency (that I thought) it more proper your Excellency should see them."* [86]

Major Tallmadge, one of Washington's spies, *"arrived late in the evening of the 23rd and learned the circumstances of the capture..."*[87] Knowing of the plot, but unable to divulge that, he was not happy that the prisoner had been sent to Arnold instead of Washington and after much discussion *"finally obtained his (Jameson's) reluctant consent to have the prisoner brought back."* Jameson insisted on sending a letter to his superior officer, General Arnold, explaining that Major Tallmadge had countermanded General Arnold's direct orders.

The prisoner 'Anderson' arrived back in Tappan the next morning. Watching him pace and turn, Tallmadge thought that he was a soldier *"bred to arms"*, noting he was in *"great agitation and anxiety"*. About 3 pm, after dinner on the 24th, the prisoner requested pen and paper and wrote a letter to Gen. Washington, confessing his identity as Major John Andre, Adjutant-General to the British Army. Tallmadge, upon receiving the unsealed letter, was shocked to learn who his prisoner really was.[88]

Jameson's note to Gen. Arnold arrived at West Point on the 25th while he was eating breakfast with two of Washington's aides who had arrived in advance of the larger party. Arnold suddenly realized that his plot was exposed. Washington and Rochambeau were due at his headquarters in a few hours. He then knew Andre had never gotten to Manhattan and British troops would not be there to capture Washington or take the fort. Far worse, Washington now knew he was a traitor. Arnold fled less than two hours before Washington arrived, asking his wife Peggy to delay pursuit. He rowed to the Vulture, which had moved back upriver to help in the capture of Washington and Rochambeau and sailed back to British held Manhattan. When the express rider finally caught up and Washington received the papers, he finally accepted that his good friend, Benedict Arnold, had betrayed his friendship and his country. Washington and Rochambeau arrived at the meeting planning to take Arnold into custody, but Arnold had already escaped.

Washington tried to exchange Major Andre for Benedict Arnold, but General Clinton refused. Major Andre was court martialed and sentenced to death. Washington personally liked the young officer and sent dinners from the De Wint House to the Old 76 House where Andre was held. Major Tallmadge also became greatly attached to Andre during his imprisonment and cried with many others at his death. Andre was allowed to die in his Regimental uniform. He was hung on October 2nd, 1780. He was a courageous and charming young man who had acted from his honorable belief in England's cause. He died with great dignity, putting the noose around his own neck. His body was re-buried in Westminster Abbey, England, forty years after his death.

Had Washington and Rochambeau, the two top commanders of the war been captured or killed, it certainly would have ended the war. Maj-General Nathanial Greene, who presided over Andre's Court Martial, wrote in his orderly book, "*Treason of the blackist dye was yesterday discovered. Gen'l Arnold, who comm'd at West Point lost to every centiment of honour of private and publick was about to give up that important Poast into the hands of the Enimy. Such an event must have given the American cause a deadly wound if not a fatal Stab, happily the Treason has been timely Discovered to prevent fatal misfortune...*"

Thwarted Gen. Clinton told William Smith he "*blamed Arnold for Andre's capture and lamented that he (Clinton) had everything ready for seizing the Highlands forts and putting an end to the war for he had boats ready for proceeding to Albany...that Arnold had insisted on being part of the Capture (of Washington) and was to have been paid a great price for the Acquisition. He lamented the Loss of Hope of an instantaneous Termination of the War – said that he should have had both Washington and Rochambeau as prisoners had the plot succeeded.*" [89]

Samuel Fraunces had, for the 2nd time, discovered and warned Washington of a plot against him. Although Arnold escaped, West

Point was saved and the two most important Generals in the war escaped capture and death. This was among the most important intelligence of the entire war.

Washington was very anxious to capture Benedict Arnold alive to make an example of him. Arnold was in NY recruiting Loyalists to fight for the British. Washington shared with Major Henry "Light Horse Harry Lee" his idea to have a soldier ride through the pickets and get to NY City where he would claim to be a deserter and gain Arnold's confidence. Then, with an accomplice, he would kidnap Arnold and take him to a waiting boat. Major Lee proposed the plan to John Champe of Loudon County, VA who accepted the assignment. He was most bothered by *"the ignominy of desertion, to be followed by the hypocrisy of enlisting with the enemy."*[90] On 20 Oct Champe rode off with arms, saddlebags, orderly book and five guineas (supplied by Lee). He was spotted and chased by a patrol but managed to escape. He was eventually introduced to Arnold who made him one of his recruiters. Their plan failed and Champe eventually deserted and rejoined Lee's command. Washington gave him a public commendation and excused him from further service, and he returned home to his wife and 7 children. He became the doorkeeper for the Continental Congress in Philadelphia. He died at 46 in 1798. The accomplice who was to help Champe abduct Arnold? Samuel Fraunces *"a negro man, who kept a tavern there"* and who received Washington's instructions in a cyphered letter.[91] Sam Fraunces had been supplying Washington with intelligence since Clinton and his officers were staying at Sam's Tavern.

Benedict Arnold became a hated man. He had sold his honor for money. He was promised L 20,000 but only received L 6,000 plus an annual pension of L 360 because his plan had failed. Arnold was made a Brigadier General and led British against his former troops but was very unpopular and many refused to serve under him. Arnold died in a delirium at the age of 60 on June 14th, 1801, suffering from gout and dropsy and was buried without military honors. He left a small estate plagued by debts which Peggy tried to pay. She died in London in 1804 at the age of 44. They are buried at St. Mary's Church in Battersea.

1781 – Discontent

On January 1781 there was mutiny in the Continental Pennsylvania Line. The men had not been paid for months, then they received scrip which was worthless. Several men were sharing a single blanket in the bitter cold because supplies were not arriving. Most of the soldiers believed their 3 year enlistments had expired but they were not allowed to go home and told they had to remain until peace was declared. Short timers were reenlisting and getting signing bonuses every 3 months while they starved. So, a group of the soldiers began marching from their camp at Morristown to Philadelphia to appeal to the Continental Congress and Pennsylvania Council.

Gen. Clinton heard about it from Sam's old friend, Andrew Gautier[92] at about the same time on 3 January that Washington did. Andrew Gaultier was living in Paulus Hook and working as a secret spy for British Gen. Clinton. Both Generals wondered if the men would defect to the British. Clinton, hoping to entice defectors and get information, sent messengers to the American line, offering to pay their back wages in British gold without any expectation of further military service, if they would defect. The mutiny leaders immediately turned the messengers over to Washington. They didn't want to defect they just wanted to be paid. Congress's continuing refusal to pay and feed the Army, which led to their long festering, justified fears about promised pensions and bounty lands led to another mutiny in January when the New Jersey line also mutinied. Washington was now faced with the real possibility that his entire army would simply rise-up and walk home.

Back in New York City, a hurricane of rain, hail and snow hit the city at the end of January causing great damage. Governor Robertson was still stymied by Gen. Clinton, unable to establish civilian rule. There were terrible shortages of fuel and food, and more thefts and rapes by idle soldiers with too much time on their hands. Loyalists realized that Robertson was powerless. He was described by Smith, a former supporter,[93] as: *"General Robertson talks in this pitiful Strain. He is a Dotard and abandoned to Frivolity. He has Parties of Girls in the Fort Garden, in the midst of his own Fears and the Anxieties of this Hour…"* He spent much of his time socializing and seems to have given up any further attempt to fight Clinton for civilian control of the city, so the military occupation continued.

On March 19th, 1781, Samuel Fraunces offered his tavern for sale with the description: *"the whole in extraordinary good repair and is at present a remarkable good stand for business of any kind and will, upon a reestablishment of civil government, be the most advantageous situation from its vicinity to the North River and New Jersey."*[94] The building was located in an occupied city, near a harbor full of gunships, in the middle of a war. Not surprisingly, no-one bought it and Sam remained in place.

In March, British General Cornwallis suffered heavy losses at the Battle of Guilford Courthouse in North Carolina. He retreated to Yorktown, Virginia, and sent word to Clinton that he had only 7500 men left and needed urgent evacuation. Clinton promised to send the fleet and ordered him to wait there. Unfortunately, that location was not defensible against attach. Still, Cornwallis followed orders. But Clinton delayed.

Gen. Washington was overjoyed to hear that the long awaited French fleet under Comte de Grasse was heading to Yorktown. Washington and Rochambeau marched their combined troops, with no British opposition, to Virginia. Comte De Grasse arrived off Yorktown, landing his troops who met up with Lafayette and surrounded Cornwallis. Washington and Rochambeau's men soon joined them. The English fleet finally arrived, far too late to evacuate Cornwallis, and at the Battle of Chesapeake, the French fleet decimated them. The badly damaged British ships limped back to New York, leaving Cornwallis stranded and surrounded. He surrendered his entire remaining army of 7000 men on Oct 19th, 1781, at Yorktown, Virginia. This surrender was particularly galling to England because the victors were 4000 French soldiers under General Rochambeau, 2500 Americans led by French General Lafayette and Comte de Grasse's French fleet. News of Cornwallis' surrender hit New York like a cannonball and Clinton was widely vilified for his delays in sending the fleet. Even worse, when news of Cornwallis's surrender at Yorktown reached England, the anti-war Whig party won the next election.

America now seemed likely to win the war, but the 13 States continued bickering. Congress had tried accepting contributions of food and clothes toward each State's pledged payments, but that was a dismal failure and didn't provide the funds needed to conduct the Nation's business. Financial matters were in crisis with over 7 years of back pay owed to soldiers. Civilian merchants who had supplied bullets, food and clothing to the Army were unpaid or had received worthless scrip. All the justifications for the earlier mutinies were still unresolved and the entire Continental army was seething with anger. Washington knew an armed military coup by his angry men was entirely possible and again warned Congress things were coming to a head.

Congress finally appointed a Superintendent of Finance. Wealthy financier Robert Morris had loaned his personal funds to the Continental Congress for years. He now established the Bank of North America with another loan from France and approached wealthy financiers like Haym Salomon to subscribe to the bank, lending their own money to the Government in exchange for Debt Certificates. He at once suspended all pay for the Continental Army, decreeing they be paid only in Debt Certificates or Land Grants until a peace treaty was signed, an obviously unpopular move. He combined the debt owed to other countries, by then so huge that Congress could make only interest payments. He reduced the Civilian Service List, firing many, and required competitive bidding for all contracts, trying to reduce rampant graft and profiteering. In October he issued a circular letter outlining the state of country's finances, including the loans from Europe, and

208

insisted that the delinquent states begin taxing to raise their promised funds. The states were angered by all this and moved slowly with much bickering. Morris retired from public service in 1789 and died in 1806 in relative poverty at the age of 73. Haym Solomon also died young, leaving his family in poverty despite all the funds both had raised at critical times for the Continental Army.

Portrait of Samuel Fraunces owned by the Mason family

After the War

1782 – Peace

There are 2 portraits claiming to be of Samuel Fraunces. One, hanging in the New York Fraunces Tavern Museum, depicts an aristocratic looking white man wearing a fancy blue coat and powdered wig. That portrait was donated to the Sons of the Revolution of the State of New York. This portrait has been proven to be of a Prussian aristocrat and is NOT Samuel Fraunces.

The other known portrait is an etching or engraving published in a book Stage Coach and Tavern Days, by Alice Morse in 1900. It was made from a painting attributed to John Trumbull and owned by a direct descendant of Samuel Fraunces, Mrs. A. Livingstone Mason of Newport, RI. (The etching has been enhanced by this author). It appears to be from the period of 1780-1790 when men's jackets began to have collars that folded over. There was less embroidery on the jackets and waistcoats, but the cravat was more ornate. Men often wore their hair natural, without a wig. It is impossible to determine the sitter's age from this etching, but in 1780 Samuel would have been 56 years old.

Artist John Trumbull was an aide-de-camp to Washington during part of the war and often made portraits, pencil sketches and small oils to be used for larger paintings. From 1789 to 1794 he lived in New York, producing some of his best work, including over 250 miniatures painted on mahogany. Several of Trumbull's paintings were made into engravings to print numbered copies for sale and this may be one of those. This engraving was owned by Edith (Hartshorn) Mason.

Edith Bucklin (Hartshorn) Mason (1855-1906) was the founder of the Society of Colonial Dames in Rhode Island and documented her family history well. She was the daughter of Isaac Hartshorn (1804-1877) and Elizabeth D. Gardiner (1825-1916). Edith's mother, Elizabeth D Gardiner, was the daughter of Nathanial Gardiner (1792-1881) and Eliza Stensin Fraunces (1797-1842). Eliza Stinson Fraunces, Edith's grandmother, was the child of Andrew Gautier Fraunces (1759-1805) and his wife Sarah Pye (1766-1825). Sarah died at the home of Eliza and Nathanial Gardiner in 1825. Andrew Gautier Fraunces, Edith's great-grandfather, was the oldest son of Samuel Fraunces (1722-1795) and his wife Elizabeth Dally (1734-about 1799). Provenance is well documented adding credibility that this is a true representation of Samuel Fraunces.

Peace was finally in sight. After Cornwallis's surrender at Yorktown, the anti-war Whigs gained control of Parliament, which voted to end all support for the war in America and requested the King to negotiate for peace. In April 1782, Sir Henry Clinton was removed as Commander in Chief and Sir Guy Carleton, in Canada, was appointed to replace him. Carleton arrived in New York on May 6th, 1782. In early June, he issued General Orders of Peace as the first step to restore civil government and met daily to hear citizen complaints. He arranged to have the prisoners better supported until they were

216

released. On Oct 6th, the first convoy of 460 Loyalists sailed from New York for Nova Scotia. As the British pulled out of other cities, more Loyalist arrived in the NY.

Preliminary articles of Peace were signed by John Adams, Ben Franklin, John Jay, and Henry Laurens in November 1782 in Paris. The French had expected that, per the original treaties, the Americans would coordinate with them before signing. But the American delegation found that, while France supported independence, they did not support America gaining added territory, preferring to confine America to the area east of the Appalachian Mountains. The delegation, not fully trusting the French, began secret direct negotiations with England. They were able to obtain all the land east of the Mississippi River, south of Canada and north of Florida. They also gained fishing rights off Canada. England agreed to all this, hoping to set up a profitable trade partnership, and of course, to aggravate arch enemy France. France, who had supplied huge loans, soldiers, weapons, and fleets to support America in its war against Britain, was left on the verge of bankruptcy. Ben Franklin was able to diplomatically defuse the volatile situation.

The war had cost the United States about $66,000,000 (in specie). Congress had issued $242,000,000 Continental dollars but, without the specie to back them, they had depreciated in value to only 1 cent per dollar. This loss of value hit the soldiers hardest as their wages, years past due, declined in value every month they waited to be paid.

The New York Congress, like all the States, was struggling to raise money they owed to the Continental Congress. They were inundated with 'memorials' requesting payment from vendors who had supplied the Continental Army with clothing, ammunition and food. NY Militia men were also requesting their promised pensions. They put almost all these requests on hold. But they did pay Sam Fraunces.

Samuel Fraunces received *L* 200 from the New York State Congress at the end of 1782 *"as a gratuity for his kindness in feeding our Prisoners in New York and for Secret Services. This was done indiscriminately to the Continental Troops and Militia."*[95] This payment, made when so many others were being postponed, shows the importance the New York Congress attached to his services.

1783 – Powder Keg

Loyalist Mayor Mathews read the King's Proclamation from City Hall in New York on Feb 14th, declaring the formal end of the war. It was met with anger and despair by Loyalists, terrified of reprisal. Sir Guy Carleton, now Commander in Chief of all British Forces in North America, was negotiating the withdrawal of all British troops from the United States. He moved into the Kennedy House in Manhattan and Robertson sailed back to England where he died in London on 4 March 1788. General Washington, headquartered in Newburgh, received the *"ratifications of the Articles of Peace"* from Carleton and responded with *"satisfaction"* at receiving the *"Joyful Annunciation"*, replying that he would issue orders to *"suspend all acts of hostilities"*.

In April 1783 all the remaining Prisoners of War were released from New York ships and prisons. All were ill and none had funds to get home. Meanwhile the frustrated and unpaid Continental Army troops were getting more agitated. The war was over, and they were about to be sent home. Many had been fighting for almost 7 years with only intermittent pay in worthless scrip, and they believed that Congress had no intention of paying them their past due pay, their promised bounty lands or their promised pensions of half pay for life. Sadly, they were right.

Congress was, at this point, an Association with representatives from each state. Congress had no power to compel the States to pay what they owed, and all were in arrears on their pledges. States also were also faced with the need to pay for their own state militias. While Congress debated what to do, several states passed legislation forbidding their representatives to support the lifetime half-pay pension that had been promised to Army enlistees. Congress voted twice on proposals for shorter pension terms but both proposals were defeated. A few frustrated members of Congress spread a rumor that the Continental Army would refuse to disband until it was paid, hoping to force the states to vote to pay them. This rumor soon became truth.

On March 11th, 1783, Washington learned that a delegation of officers from each state's Continental Army troops had sent a memorial to Congress asking for their back pay and for confirmation of their promised pensions. Congress rejected their petition! The furious officers arranged a meeting to discuss what their response should be. Washington heard about the meeting and, believing they would decide on an armed revolt, cancelled it and scheduled another for March 15th to be presided over by Gen. Gates. Gates had been maneuvering with the dissatisfied officers and members of Congress to remove Washington as head of the Army, take over the government and declare martial law. This became known as the Newburgh Conspiracy. Washington unexpectedly showed up, surprising his angry officers and the shocked Gates stepped aside. Washington made a dramatic speech in which he pledged to stand with his men to address their concerns with Congress. Pulling out his glasses, which few had seen, and noting that he had gone almost blind in service of his country, he pledged his full cooperation and urged them to not take actions contrary to all they had been fighting for. As Major Samuel Shaw wrote in his journal, *"There was something so natural, so unaffected in this appeal as rendered it superior to the most studied oratory. It forced its way to the heart, and you might see sensibility moisten every eye. This caused most of the men to realize that Washington, too, had sacrificed a great deal, maybe even more than most of them during the years for this glorious cause. These men, of course, were his fellow officers, most having worked closely with him for several years. The conspiracy collapsed."* Washington was so well respected by his men that they agreed with his plea and pledged their continued loyalty to the United States. Thomas Jefferson later noted that *"The moderation and virtue of a single character probably prevented this Revolution from being closed, as most others have been, by a subversion of that liberty it was intended to establish."* Washington wrote yet another strongly worded letter to Congress, again urging them to address the men's justified grievances in which he said, *"For if, besides the simple payment of their wages, a farther compensation is not due to the sufferings and sacrifices of the officers, then have I been mistaken indeed. If the whole army have not merited whatever a grateful people can bestow, then have I been beguiled by prejudice, and built opinion on the basis of error. If this country should not, in the event, perform everything which has been requested in the late memorial to Congress, then will my belief become vain, and the hope that has been excited, void of foundation.*

221

And "if," (as has been suggested for the purpose of inflaming their passions) "the officers of the army are to be the only sufferers by this revolution; if retiring from the field they are to grow old in poverty, wretchedness and contempt; if they are to wade through the vile mire of dependency, and owe the miserable remnant of that life to charity, which has hitherto been spent in honor," then shall I have learned what ingratitude is, then shall I have realized a tale which will embitter every moment of my future life. But I am under no such apprehensions; a country rescued by their arms from impending ruin, will never leave unpaid the debt of gratitude." Sadly, not only was the debt left unpaid, but these men were vilified.

The country now had over 200,000 armed angry young men, many of whom had been unwillingly drafted or who had re-enlisted for the promised bounty. Over 30% of the original draftees had been captured or killed. The rest had fought for years with insufficient ammunition, frozen from lack of clothing, shoes, blankets or tents, barely surviving on partial rations because Congress could not properly provide for them and had done it all without pay. In 1776 pay for Privates had been set at $6.66/month or $79.92 (*L*18) per year, Corporals and drummers got $7.33 or $87.96 (*L*20) per year. Sergeants got $8 or $96 (*L*21.60) per year, Ensigns got $20 or $240 (*L*54) per year, Lieutenants $27 or $324 (*L*73) per year, Captains received $40 or $480 (*L*108) per year, Majors got $50 or $600 (*L*135) per year, Lt. Cols $60 or $720 (*L*162) per year and Colonels got $75 or $900 (*L*202) per year, plus various bonuses for re-enlisting, often in land grants. Their infrequent pay had been made with 'Bills of Credit' that were now almost worthless. The lack of pay left their families destitute. Congress finally approved a pension of 5 years full pay instead of half-pay for life (30 years or more). This was not only a huge reduction of the promised amounts but a meaningless vote since they still had no money to pay it. The new country was sitting on a powder keg.

On April 18th, Washington made a formal announcement to his troops about the Cessation of Hostilities. He congratulated his army telling them that: *"having participated in a great drama on the stage of human affairs, nothing now remains but for the actors of this mighty scene to preserve a perfect unvarying consistence of character through the very last act; to close the Drama with applause; and to retire from the Military Theatre with the same approbation of Angels and men which have crowned all their former virtuous actions."* In other words, please go home quietly.

The 7th article of the preliminary Peace Treaty circulated in the spring of 1783 required Britain to withdraw from the United States: *"without causing any destruction or carrying away any Negroes or other property of the American inhabitants."* By the time a copy of this agreement reached North America and was published, the British had already evacuated as many as 6000 freed black slaves from South Carolina and Georgia. But New York City, filled with thousands of escaped slaves, reacted with *"anguish and terror"*.[96] The city was filled with owners and agents, trying to recapture former slaves. This terror continued until General Carleton stated his position on this issue at the peace negotiations.

223

On May 4th, 1783, Gen. Washington, Governor Clinton, General Scott and other officers visited West Point before arriving in Tappan for the Peace Conference, where they were met by Sam Fraunces who provided them with a fine dinner there.[97] On May 6th, George Washington, met with Sir Guy Carleton at the De Wint House in Tappan, New York on the western side of the Hudson River near the New Jersey border.[98] A reception was held with prominent local citizens including NY Governor Clinton for an hour of conversation before commencing negotiations. Sam's son, Andrew Gautier Fraunces, probably met his future wife, Sarah Pye, there. Her father was a prominent local politician who attended the meeting.

Sam Fraunces catered the first international conference for the United States. Because of the large number of attendees, they took their "*plentiful repast*" under a tent. It was "*a most sumptuous dinner served to about 30 who ate and drank in Peace and good fellowship without drinking any toasts.*" Great pomp and ceremony were maintained throughout this conference. While together there, Sam and George Washington found time to have private conversations. One of these involved Washington's painful dental issues. Sam knew a French dentist who had applied to Washington for help to leave the country. Washington had sent the man to the French minister in Philadelphia. However, during their conversation at the conference, Sam reminded Washington, "*that this man was a well-known dentist of whose skill much has been said*", suggesting he could help. Washington at once contacted an assistant, noting that Sam had reminded him about the dentist, and asked the assistant to request he join Washington in

Newburgh. Samuel's bill for the catering amounted to $L500$, presented on May 6th, 1783. There was no charge for his advice.

Washington opened the Peace Negotiations with discussion of the resolution in the Versailles treaty *"regarding the delivery of all Negroes and other property"*. Carleton responded that he had already sent off over 6000 refugees in his efforts to *"speedily facilitate the evacuation"*. When Washington insisted this was against the specific language in the treaty, Carleton said that his interpretation of the treaty meant *"property that was owned by Americans at the time of the treaty signing but would not include those who had responded to British pleas for help years before."* Carleton insisted that the British would never have agreed *"to reduce themselves to the necessity of violating their faith to the Negroes"* and that *"delivering up Negroes to their former masters…would be a dishonorable violation of the public faith."*

That night, after the first meeting, Washington sent a letter to Carleton, stating again his opposition to the removal of slaves and warning of further discussions at dinner the next day. Carleton pled illness and did not attend the 2nd dinner. He instead had a brief private meeting with Washington and followed up with a written response to his earlier letter. Carleton wrote *"the Negroes in question, I have already said, I found free when I arrived in New York. I had therefore no right, as I thought, to prevent their going to any part of the world they thought proper."* He then added *"I must confess the mere supposition that the King's minister could deliberately stipulate in a treaty, an engagement to be guilty of the notorious breach of public*

225

faith towards people of any complexion, seems to denote a less friendly disposition than I would wish, and I think, less friendly than we might expect." Carleton had acted on his own in this matter, but his actions soon received the blessing of Parliament who considered his policies "*an act of Justice*" and "*perfectly justifiable.*"[99] Carleton assured that, if removing the slaves was later proven to be an infraction of the treaty, the British government would make compensation to the owners. To ensure this, he proposed a registry so that "*the owners might eventually be paid for the slaves who were entitled to their freedom by British Proclamation and Promises.*"

This registry, the <u>Inspection Roll of Negroes</u>, was compiled by Gen. Birch, Carleton's Aide, between April and November 1783. Birch held meetings for over 2 hours each Wednesday at Samuel Fraunces' Tavern. Canvas Town, where most of the former slaves lived, was just across the street. This <u>Inspection Roll of Negroes</u> still exists. It is a set of 2 ledgers each about 200 pages long, listing the name, age, distinguishing marks, occupation and the name and location of their former master, for 1336 men, 914 women and 750 children.[100] They received Certificates of Freedom from General Birch. After the Evacuation, about 7000 blacks remained in New York City. British ships transported about 3,000 freed slaves to Nova Scotia for resettlement. Among the first were Henry and Deborah Squash, former slaves of General Washington. Other Washington slaves left on later ships. Several of General Washington's slaves left after he became

President. They included Oney Judge and Hercules, the chef. They remained in the United States.

In June 1783, the main part of the Continental Army was officially furloughed, a leave of absence from duty, rather than discharged. This was planned so the men could be marched home under control of their officers to prevent mutiny. Also, the British had not yet completely evacuated, and Congress wanted to be able to call them up again if needed. Most importantly, men on furlough were still technically in the army so could not demand their pensions and bounty lands. The Continental troops included about 9000 blacks who had joined the American side. Slaves had been promised freedom and free blacks had enlisted for the Cause, the pay and bounty land. The Continental Army was about 25% black.

The Army was still not paid so Robert Morris, Superintendent of Finance, pledged his entire personal fortune in an emergency loan to Congress and issued $800,000 in notes to the soldiers. Each soldier received one month's pay in cash and the rest in Morris Notes, redeemable for cash plus 6% interest at a later date.

A group of 300-500 Continental Army soldiers near Philadelphia, furious over the mistaken belief that they were to be discharged before they could receive Morris's promissory notes, surrounded the Congress Building demanding a hearing. Congress sent word to the Governor, requesting protection of the Pennsylvania Militia. The Governor refused to call out the militia, partly in sympathy with the soldiers and partly because he feared the militia would support the soldiers and escalate the situation. The men were promised that they would get the Morris Notes and returned to camp without violence. Congress, stating they were *"grossly insulted"* by this demonstration, moved to Princeton, NJ.[101] This altercation later led Congress to establish Washington, DC as a federal district under their control.

The men were grudgingly allowed to keep their uniforms and muskets. Without any other clothing or food, most spent their cash and sold their possessions to support themselves and their families. Many sold their certificates at deep discount to speculators for cash. The promised pensions were not paid until 35 years after the war ended. In 1818, the Federal Pension Act was finally passed. It supplied pensions only for poverty stricken or disabled Continental troops, and they had to supply a schedule of assets and income. Those who qualified were to receive $20 a month for officers and $8 for non-officers. This act excluded militia men, assuming their states would care for them, and excluded most Black veterans, saying that because they had served in exchange for freedom from slavery, they did not deserve additional rewards. Only 18,880 veterans, out of hundreds of thousands who served, received any Federal pension. It was only in 1828, after most had died, that poverty or disability requirement was eliminated.[102]

Most land bounties were never paid either. States had issued land bounties as did Congress. Most were problematic. In NY State, the bounty lands included Indian land, recognized by prior treaties, and not legally available. Poor surveying resulted in overlapping competing claims in other areas. Many soldiers, believing they would never get the land, sold their ownership to speculators. The Continental Congress acts of the 1780s limited bounty lands to settlement on military land, on properties larger than 4,000 contiguous acres. That was larger than even a major general's allotment. Theoretically men could combine their claims and settle together but, in reality, land speculators bought the shares at deep discounts from soldiers unable to find other men with contiguous claims. Some officers put together large holdings and resold plots to soldiers who should have owned them outright.

The Continental soldiers were sent home *"without the means to support or comfort their families"*, and *"liable to arrest for debts they had contracted while in the service."* Once they were safely disbursed, they were officially discharged. Washington was truly distraught that his men, who had fought so hard, suffered through such terrible hardship and won the war against all odds, were: *"to be ushered off without pay, with paper pensions and grudging recognition of their service"*. Washington could only lament: *"To be disbanded like a set of beggars, needy, distressed and without prospect.... will drive every man of Honor and Sensibility to the extreme horrors of Despair."*[103] What happened was even worse.

The Continental soldiers soon became targets of a smear campaign led by Congressmen and newspapers from delinquent states. States faced with raising the money to pay for Continental soldiers as well as their own Militia men refused, calling the Continentals greedy aristocratic pretenders wanting to live off their pensions. This animosity stunned the now bitter soldiers who were marched off without even a *'Thank You'* from the Congress they had made possible. After eight years of fighting against overwhelming odds, they were still

229

unpaid, in debt, most without land or jobs and now were being attacked by those they had fought for. In May a group of officers started the Society of the Cincinnati. Concerned about the financial desperation of so many officers, they set up a fund for indigent officers and their survivors. Their goal was to remind citizens of the need to defend liberties and to keep alive the memory of the sacrifices they had made. They created 13 state associations, and one in France for French officers, and Washington was their first President. Membership was hereditary, passing to the oldest male relative. Critics claimed they were trying to create an aristocracy.

In June, Washington wrote a letter from Newburgh to Lt. Col. William Stephens Smith in New York City, asking to be remembered to Samuel Fraunces and to old Mrs. Thompson, his housekeeper.[104] Sam's family had joined him in still occupied NY City and that year, Samuel and his oldest son, Andrew G. Fraunces, were listed in the Parish Register at Trinity Church in New York.[105]

In July 1783, the Supreme Court of Massachusetts abolished slavery and all slaves were immediately freed. That same year New Hampshire began gradual abolition of slavery. These abolition efforts caused outrage in the Southern states, which used it to justify their continuing refusal to pay their debts to Congress.

The British were still in control of Manhattan when on August 18th, 1783, Sam wrote to General Washington:

Sir

It is with the profoundest respect I presume to approach your Excellency on this most happy occasion, the return of Peace to my bleeding Country. This Event, so grateful in itself, is still heightened in the preservation through so many toils and dangers of a life so valuable, so dear to every individual.

May I beg your Excellency to believe I shall ever esteem this the happiest moment of my life that affords me the opportunity of presenting and craving your Excellency's acceptance of my most grateful acknowledgements for the many favors you have so generously conferred upon me; and if (as I presume to hope) your Excellency views with a favorable Eye my small endeavors to aid the general Cause, allow me to say my peculiar situation would not permit the greater exertions my inclinations prompted—Wherein my good Fortune may have made me in the least serviceable I think my Services greatly overpaid by your Excellency's condescendingly approving smile which gives a Sanction to the pleasing Sensation that ever accompany good intentions.

Yet Sir while I confess my utmost Ambitions already overpaid, I cannot help applying to your unbounded goodness for some small token of your good opinion that may serve to close the mouth of calumny and detraction and introduce me to that public on whom rests my dependency for a livelihood as one deserving of their future favor.

I hope your Excellency will not think my request unreasonable when you advert to my past situation that exposes me to the insidious representations of Rivals which my base professions can never obviate

231

and through which however undeservedly must be involved the Fate of a Wife and numerous offspring to whom I owe the tenderest Care— Influenced by the warmest Gratitude I beg leave to subscribe myself Your Excellency's Most Obedient and very Humble Servant....Samuel Fraunces

Since Sam had been, and still was, in occupied New York, a rumor by competitors suggested he was Loyalist and should not be patronized. His efforts during the Revolution to save Washington's life, to feed and clothe the prisoners and to foil Benedict Arnold's treason were not known to those outside Washington's immediate circle. Neither were the names, nor exploits of other Patriot spies who had worked in New York during the Revolution. Sam was asking for a positive sign from General Washington to allay suspicions of his loyalty. Indicating the regard in which Washington held Sam, despite everything else he was dealing with, including the potential mutiny of his Army, Washington responded to Sam the same day!

Sir:

I have received with satisfaction your favor—congratulating me on the happy return of Peace, & the prospects of Returning to our former Walks of Life.

I take pleasure in complying with your Request of a Recommendation to the Citizens of America—as I am happy to find, by the Concurrent Testimony of many of our suffering Brethren, & others, that you have invariably through the most trying Times, maintained a constant friendship & Attention to the Cause of our Country & its

Independence & Freedom—& this Testimony is also strengthened by my own Observations, so far as I have had Opportunity of knowing your Character personally.

I do therefore hereby recommend you to the several Executives & to all the good People of these States, as a warm Friend—& one who has not only suffered in our Cause, who has deserved well of many Individuals, who have experienced the rigors of Captivity in N. York, and therefore One who is deserving the favor & attention of these U. States.

I wish you Health & prosperity—with a gratefull Reception with your fellow Citizens, And am Sir Your Most humb Srt. – George Washington."

It is noted in an annotation to the Washington papers that this letter was unusually long and wordy for Washington, and that he appeared to be extremely circumspect, since the 'service' Sam was referring to was intelligence passed on during his tenure in the still English occupied city.[106]

On September 12th, 1783, George Washington wrote to Daniel Parker who was acting as his agent in New York:

Sir

.....If there are Wine & Beer Glasses (the latter of the same shape but larger) exactly like those which Mr. Frauncis brought to Orange Town; of which he will have a perfect recollection, I should be glad, if an opportunity offers to Alexandria, to get six dozn or more of the first, and three dozn of the latter with as many water or finger glasses

233

together with a dozn & half of Neat quart Decanters and as many Water Bottles for Table use, carefully packed (which I am sure Mr. Fraunces will see to the doing of for me) and sent to that place....

If a neat, & compleat sett of Bleu & White Table China could be had upon pretty easy terms, be pleased to inform me of it, and the Price—not less than six or eight dozn Shallow & a proportionable number of Deep & other Plates, Butter Boats, Dishes & Tureens, will suffice. These things sometimes come in compleat setts ready packed— shou'd this be the case, altho' there may be a greater number of Pieces than I have mentioned I should have no objection to a case on that acct.

Be so good as to let me have your answer as soon as convenient, as it will prevent an application elsewhere, or may render one necessary—I wish also to know if you have received a line from Colo. Cob respecting Tea &ca. I am Sir Yr Most Obt Hble Servt, Go. Washington

P.S. Will you be so good as to inform me what goods—for family use—are very low in New York, and if they are to be had cheaper, than Goods of the same kind & quality at Philadelphia.

Go. W."

Clearly, Washington knew Sam would obtain the correct items for him. On September 18th, 1783, Daniel Parker replied to George Washington from New York:

Sir

I had the honor to receive your Excellency's favor of the 12th instant since which I have caused the Glasses to be procured by Mr. Fraunces as per inclosed Bill—.... I requested Mr. Fraunces to obtain the lowest price that a neat and compleat set of Table China could be obtained for, he has made particular enquiry and can find none on better terms than the inclosed which I think is higher than they can be bought for in Philadelphia—We can find no compleat setts that are ready packd in this City.

I have the Honor to be with the greatest Respect Your Excellency's Most Obedt servt, Danl Parker"

Sam did buy from Edward Nicoll, Jr. on Sept. 10th a large assortment of glassware at a cost of L47.10, and a set of 205 pieces of Blue and White China on Sept. 18th, 1783. The receipts are in Washington's papers.

On November 2nd, Washington published his Farewell Order to his furloughed men. He told them that "the singular interpositions of Providence in our feeble condition were such, as could scarcely escape the attention of the most unobserving; while the unparalleled perseverance of the Armies of the U[nited] States, through almost every possible suffering and discouragement for the space of eight long years, was little short of a standing miracle." He believed that the blending of people from every colony into "one patriotic band of brothers" was a major accomplishment and urged the veterans to continue this in civilian life. He thanked them for their assistance, acknowledged that Congress had failed to pay them and encouraged their patience saying *"Nor is it possible to conceive, that any one of the U States will prefer a national bankruptcy and a dissolution of the union, to a compliance*

235

with the requisitions of Congress and the payment of its just debts; so that the Officers and Soldiers may expect considerable assistance in recommencing their civil occupations from the sums due to them from the public, which must and will most inevitably be paid." He also encouraged them to settle on the western bounty lands to help expand their new country.

General Washington wrote his final Circular Letter to the States, expressing his opinion that America was entering a period *of "political probation"* in which events would determine if the nation would become *"respectable and prosperous or contemptible and miserable."* He listed four developments he believed essential for the nation to succeed: *"Formation of an indissoluble union, under one federal head; demonstration of a sacred regard to public justice; adoption of a proper peace establishment; and cultivation of a public character able to see past local interests to a general good."* Each state was acting in its own interest, and not in the interest of the whole country, and Washington saw the need for a strong Federal Government.

The British evacuation was finally completed on November 25th, 1783. The Pennsylvania Packet wrote of Washington's arrival in New York City on Nov 25th: "Their Excellencies the Governor and Commander in Chief were escorted by a body of West Chester Light Horse under the command of Captain Delavan. The procession proceeded down Queen (now Pearl) Street and through the Broadway to Cape's Tavern. The Governor gave a public dinner at Fraunces

236

Tavern at which the Commander in Chief and other general officers were present." Samuel Fraunces received L97.12.00 "for an Entertainment for the Military and other Public Officers on entering the City".[107] The Governor also hosted Washington and his general officers as well as many others at Samuel Fraunces Tavern. The bill for that dinner, presented on Nov 26th, 1783, amounted to L85.10.6.[108]

Washington stayed at Fraunces Tavern for 10 days after the British evacuation.[109] Washington's papers showed that he remained at Fraunces Tavern until Dec 4 at an expense of L113.1s.3d and had a dinner party there on Nov 30th at a cost of L35.[110] All this patronage undoubtedly repaired Sam's reputation. Following the evacuation and several more days of celebrations, Washington invited his officers to a personal farewell dinner, also at Fraunces Tavern at 12 o'clock on Dec 4th, 1783. It was here that he announced he was retiring his commission and returning to civilian life.

General Tallmadge's memoir of this luncheon noted that Samuel Fraunces: *"was always in the room, very resplendently dressed in wig and small-clothes, watching over the service provided by his assistants."* Samuel, ever conscious of proper decorum, had the staff polish the windows and wax the floors until they gleamed. *"In the main room of the tavern waiters were preparing a large buffet lunch on linen draped tables that held hot and cold joints and slices, platters of bread, golden mounds of butter and heaps of green garden sauce. Along each of the long tables, decanters of wine sparkled beside stacks of polished glasses."* As the Long Room filled at 12 o'clock on that cold December day, Washington entered the room slowly and began to speak to his audience, each one holding a glass of wine: *"I cannot come to each of you but shall feel obliged if each of you will come and take me by the hand."* After dining with the men, Washington delivered his emotional Farewell Speech to his officers. *"With a heart full of love and gratitude I now take leave of you. I most devoutly wish that your latter days may be as prosperous and happy as your former ones have been glorious and honorable."* Tallmadge noted that Washington was "suffused in tears" as he embraced his officers one by one and "such a scene of sorrow and weeping I had never before witnessed and fondly hope I may never be called to witness again." Having shared so much, it certainly was a sad farewell. But it may also be assumed that some of these tears were prompted by disillusionment and embarrassment that he had failed to get these men the pay they deserved or the appreciation of an ungrateful country. It is estimated that there were 18 officers among the 44 guests. When Washington asked for the bill, Sam declared there was nothing to pay. Washington insisted but was finally forced to compromise with Sam by giving him a piece of paper inscribed: *"To my friend Samuel Fraunces, from his obliged guest, G. Washington."*

Sam then handed a personal letter to Washington:

Sir:

I cannot but with heartfelt anxiety think of your leaving so soon your sincere friends, together with your humblest of servants. However reluctant, we must acquiesce, since it is the resolution of one of the [first] and best of men. Your extreme goodness and generosity will pardon any impropriety in this small Address since the motive rises from the overflowings of a gratefull heart.

Let me intreat your Excellency to accept the sincere wishes of one who is proud to say he has been but too much Honored—for which you have the constant prayers of a numerous [illegible which a] sensibility and a thorough knowledge of your kindnesses inspires.

And that all happiness in this life may attend you & your good family; and everything the Blessed expect from [] and the sincere and daily prayers of Your Excellency's intirely devoted Servant, Samuel Fraunces

N.B. I most earnestly beg your Excellency will order about the Carriage of a small piece of Shell Work which I have lately compleated for Mrs. Washington purposely—whose acceptance of it will confer the greatest Honor on me—the [field] is Hector and Andromache adorned with Shell Flowers the collection of a number of years—I have but one more wish, that is at any time your Excellency's commands are laid on me, to think they will be undertaken with the greatest pleasure & that I always shall be as I am at present—I dare hope your Excellency sooner or later will not deprive my family & self the satisfaction of hearing of yr health.   S. Fraunces".

This letter references a shell-work of Hector and Andromache that Sam was giving to Mrs. Washington. He offered this gift as Washington was retiring from public service to return to private life in Mt. Vernon.

It was soon widely known that Washington planned to resign his commission. Washington traveled for 4 cold days from New York to

Philadelphia, mostly on horseback, feted throughout the trip, arriving in Philadelphia on Dec 8 again to great celebration and many letters of appreciation in the papers. Washington then traveled through a brutal winter blizzard to Baltimore where there were more celebrations and on to Annapolis for what he tiredly hoped would be his final official reception. There was a grand ball with 500 people at the State house there for George and Martha on the 22nd and Washington danced every set.

On Dec 23rd he addressed the Continental Congress, with Martha in the audience, recognizing those who had helped achieve the victory and said, "Having now finished the work assigned me, I retire from the great theatre of Action; and bidding an affectionate farewell to this august body under whose orders I have so long acted, I here offer my commission, and take my leave of all the employments of public life." He handed his original parchment commission from 1775 as Commander in Chief to Mifflin, President of Congress, and formally resigned. Washington's willingness to relinquish his powers and return to civilian life was so astonishing that it made him an international celebrity. The King of England said in wonder, "he is truly the greatest of men".

1784 –Civilians

George and Martha Washington finally arrived home in Mount Vernon in time for Christmas. The Treaty of Paris was officially ratified by the United States Congress on Jan 14th, 1784. The war had caused financial problems for him, as it had for everyone. He had served without pay for over 8 years. He had many receipts and notebooks to be tallied for reimbursement and had to calculate the fluctuating value of all the currencies. His Mount Vernon estate was 8000 acres divided into five plantations along the Potomac River, each with a small village of African and Virginia-born slaves: Mansion House (90 slaves), Dogue Run (45 slaves), Union (76 slaves), Muddy Hole (41 slaves), and River (57 slaves). They raised wheat, corn, hemp, and flax, had a small fishing fleet, and bred sheep His businesses included gristmills and sawmills, weaving facilities, blacksmith shops and a whiskey distillery which by 1799 was the largest in America.

Sam was struggling in New York. In January of 1784 an ad invited "*Merchants who were importers of goods from Great Britain, previous to, and who have been in exile during the war, are requested to attend a General Meeting at the house of Samuel Fraunces on Wed the 28th at 5 o'clock.*"[111] On March 1st Samuel wrote a letter to

241

Washington from New York with another small gift and his good wishes:

Sir:

I have the honor of conveying by an unexpected opportunity, my most sincere and dutiful respects to your Excellency of a grateful heart that is fully sensible of the immeasurable obligation your unwarranted favors have laid me under, therefore your Excellency's native goodness will pardon any presumption that may seem on this.

My prayers shall at all times be most devoutly for the health and happiness of your Excellency and family.

My wife and daughters beg to be remembered likewise with every sentiment of esteem. They send Mrs. Washington a couple of utensils for cutting paste "the best that could be procured" and hopes will meet with approbation. They present their most respectful compliment to her in the meantime and I remain with unfeigned sincerity…your Excellency's most obedient and most devoted humble servant.. Samuel Fraunces"[112]

Sam and Elizabeth closed Fraunces Tavern that spring. On September 3, 1784, there was another ad for the sale of Fraunces Tavern: *"To be Sold at Publick Auction on Friday 10 of September at 12 o'clock at the coffee-house: That spacious well-built Freehold Estate situate in Great Dock Street well known as Frauncis's Tavern. The premises are extensive and admirably well contrived for a Hotel or Tavern, the cellars are capacious and good, the upper rooms large, convenient for company and the attick story well adapted to the uses of a numerous family; its vicinity to the New Market and the probability that new and elegant houses will soon be built in that part of the city, must considerably add to the value of the Estate. Though so famed and well contrived as a tavern, it has the peculiar advantage that it may be readily converted into two separate houses at very moderate expense. Further particulars may be known prior to the day of sale, on the premises or of Viner Van Zandt, 202 Water Street."*[113] Sam had unsuccessfully tried to sell the Queen's Head before. It did not sell this time either.

Sam and Elizabeth's last child, Hannah Louisa Fraunces was baptized on Oct 27, 1784, at Trinity Church in New York City. Baptism records noted her birth on August 24th to Samuel and Elizabeth Francis (sic) with daughter Elizabeth Francis (later Thompson) and Gifford and 'Hannah' Petit Dally (sic) as witnesses.[114] Sam was 62 and Elizabeth was 44 years old. Given Elizabeth's age, Hannah was possibly not their child. She could have been a grandchild that Sam and Elizabeth agreed to raise as their own. Their oldest children, Andrew (25), Margaret (23) and Elizabeth (18) were not yet married.

On November 11th, 1784, Samuel and Elizabeth Fraunces placed another ad for a Public Sale at 49 Dock Street in New York, this time for the contents of the Queen's Head Tavern. The ad mentioned a: *"large and more valuable collection of household and kitchen furniture than has been exposed for sale for many years, consisting of some: Elegant mahogany bedsteads and common same; a variety of dining, card and other tables; a few sets of neat Mahogany chairs and some common ones; a few elegant looking glasses and some carpeting; some pieces of elegant wax and shell work in neat mahogany cases; Mahogany book cases and chests with drawers; a few pairs of elegant branched lights for a table; also a complete set of elegant table linen etc.; A quantity of beautiful chased plate; a Quantity of table china of all sorts; a grand variety of jelly and blancmange forms; also copper pans, stew kettles of all sorts and sizes, and good variety of other articles too tedious to mention. The vendue to begin at 10 o'clock and will be continued every day until sold."* And so, the Queen's Head Tavern in the De Lancey Mansion ceased to operate. It is interesting to note that the sale items included *"some pieces of elegant wax and shell work in neat mahogany cases"*. Still not able to sell the building, Sam leased it out to various tenants and moved his family to Monmouth County, NJ.

Despite being a famous restauranteur, the Frauncis family was in dire financial straits due to the country's economic depression. He had served for years without pay in occupied New York under the threat of death if caught as a spy. Sam was hoping to be repaid some of the large sums of money he had loaned to prisoners and for credit he'd given to officers of the Army and Loyalists during the war. Repayment of these debts would have allowed him to live comfortably. He was now 63 years old and had worked long days and nights 7 days a week for many years. Elizabeth was 44 and now had 8 children including an infant, and she too must have felt the burden of continuing the Tavern was too great. Surely both were tired and looked forward to some peace of their own.

1785 – Depression

George Washington was now a private citizen living at Mount Vernon. Continental Congress met in New York City Hall for the next several years, Jan 11, 1785 to Nov 13, 1788, and the Department of Foreign Affairs, the War Office, and the Treasury rented space at the Fraunces Tavern Building from January 11th, 1785 to April 30th, 1788.[115] Despite the critical matters that Congress was dealing with, they considered a petition submitted by Sam on March 5th, 1785: "*That your memorialist most respectfully submits, being from the principle attached to the cause of America, removed from the city of New York previous to its being taken possession of by the British Forces into Elizabethtown, in the State of New Jersey. That he was here made prisoner by the Enemy which, after plundering his family of almost every necessity, brought him to the City of New York*

That he was the person that first discovered the conspiracy which was formed in the year 1776 against the life of his Excellency General Washington and that the suspicion which was entertained of his agency in that important discovery occasioned a public enquiry after he was made a prisoner on which the want of positive proof alone preserved his life.

That your memorialist for many years before the war a responsible Inn-holder in this city, submitted to serve for some time in the menial

245

office of cook in the family of General Robertson without any pay or perquisite whatsoever except the privilege of removing the remnants of the table which he appropriated towards the comfort of the American prisoners within the city, to whom the exercise of the commonest acts of humanity was at that time considered a crime of the deepest dye.

That in this station and others precious to the war, he served with zeal and at the hazard of his life, the cause of America, not only by supplying prisoners with money, food and raiment, and facilitating their escape but by performing services of a confidential nature and of the utmost importance to the operations of the American Army.

That your memorialist in consequence of the heavy advances he had made to American prisoners the far greatest part of which is not yet reimbursed and the solid proof of his zeal for the cause of Freedom as to see himself, his wife and numerous family on the precipice of beggary unless the generous and humane hand of your Honorable House should be extended to his relief.

These facts your memorialist can support by indisputable evidence in this city sanctioned by the most ample certificates from the late Commander in Chief, General Lee and several officers of rank in the French Marines who were witnesses of his exertions in the common cause. He therefore flatters himself that the United States in Congress will graciously condescend to order an enquiry to be made into the Premise and to extend their relief in such a manner as the nature of your memorialist pretension shall in their wisdom require. And your memorialist as in Duty bound shall ever pray……Samuel Fraunces.[116]

246

Submitted with his memorial was a letter of support from Maj. General Arthur St Clair (Aide-de-Camp to Washington, later President of Congress) dated 29 March 1788; affidavits, dated 18 March 1785, from R. Graham and M. Martin; a letter from Col. Samuel Smith (Commander of Ft. Mifflin and Congressman, many of his men had been prisoners) dated April 22nd, 1783; a certificate from General Charles Scott (Chief of Intelligence for Washington before Tallmadge) dated June 11th, 1784; 3 letters from George Washington dated Sept 7th, 1785, June 30th, 1783, and July 17th, 1785; Certificates from Martha (Stewart) Wilson (young widow of Robert, who lived in Hackettstown, NJ where she passed information to Washington's HQ nearby) and AW Fraunces dated June 9th, 1784; Certificate from Sarah McDonald dated June 7th, 1784; and letters from E. Robins (prisoner); Wm. Everett; H. Mulligan (Hercules Mulligan was another spy); James Tyler (a prisoner of war); McGuire; John Gautier (French speaking private, prisoner from Gen. Hazen's Canadian Brigade); Capt. Duguam; Mr. Wilmier; General Lee (Washington's 2nd in Command); Colonel William Duer (a spy and Commissary of the Army); Col. George Smith (Lt. Col. of First Battalion of Philadelphia County Militia); Governor Clinton (Gov. of NY); and French Admiral Comte De Grasse (who defeated the British Navy at Yorktown). With all these supporting documents, Sam's petition was quickly reviewed by a committee, read to Congress on March 15th, who passed a resolution on March 28th stating *"That it appears to them from authentic papers that the memorialist has been uniformly and steadily attached to the interests of America. That they have reason to believe that he was instrumental in discovering and*

247

defeating a design upon the life of Gen'l Washington. That he frequently communicated the most important intelligence to the Commander in Chief. That his house was an asylum to our countrymen when prisoners as well as to the subjects of our ally (the French) as appears by a variety of certificates. That he expended considerable sums, acquired by his daily labor in the support of the captive Americans. That in order to render their situation more easy he advanced them specie upon certificates without any expectation of profit thereon. That from these circumstances the memorialist is greatly reduced, that his house now occupied by the Secretary for the Department of Foreign affairs and the Secretary in the War office is under mortgage for the sum of L650 New York currency, that unless we afford him the means of discharging the mortgage it must be disposed of at much less than its value. Your committee are therefore of opinion that Congress come to the following resolutions:

1ˢᵗ Resolved, That the Secretary of Congress take a lease from Mr. Samuel Fraunces for his house now occupied by the public for the term of two years at the rate of L325 per year.

2ⁿᵈ That an order pass in favor of the said Samuel Fraunces for the sum of L650 upon the treasury of the United States in order to enable him to discharge the mortgage and that the same be charged to the rent on house.

That in consideration of the singular services of the said Samuel Fraunces and of his advances to the American Prisoners, that the sum of $2000 dollars be paid to the said Samuel Fraunces on account of the

Loan offices Certificates in his hands and that they be delivered up and cancelled." This was done on April 4th. [117]

On April 4th Congress also *"Resolved by nine states: That the secretary of Congress take a lease from Samuel Frauncis for his house, now occupied by the public, for the term of two years, at the rate of $812.50 per year. (*a large increase from the originally intended rent of $325) *That a warrant be drawn in favor of the said Samuel Frauncis for the sum of $1625 on account of the said rent and to discharge a mortgage on the said house:*

By nine States: That in consideration of the singular services of the said Samuel Fraunces, and of his advances to the American prisoners, the sum of two thousand dollars be paid to the said Samuel Fraunces on account of the Loan office certificates in his hands and that they be delivered up and cancelled."

So, Sam was awarded $1625 plus $2000 for his certificates. The $1625 paid off the $650 mortgage so he could sell the Pearl Street building and provided the new owner with $325/yr. in the agreed upon rent for 2 years, leaving him with $325 plus the certificates. However, when the certificates were presented, due to rampant inflation, they were worth only $1293 which is what Samuel was reimbursed. Sam was finally able to sell the Fraunces Tavern building to George Powers, a Brooklyn butcher. On April 25th, 1785, *"Samuel Fraunces, late of the City of New York, Innkeeper, but at present of the County of Monmouth, New Jersey, farmer, and Elizabeth his wife,"* sold Fraunces Tavern to *"George Powers, butcher, of Brooklyn for L1950."*[118] Samuel took a small loss on the sale as he had paid L2000 for it in 1763. Elizabeth signed her name on the documents, proving her equal partnership in the business, very unusual for the time. They had no income but would have now about $3568 in cash from the sale of the building and the redeemed certificates. Sam was owed substantial sums for credit he had offered to members of the New York State Congress as well as to individual Army officers who had run tabs at his establishment. He was also trying to collect on past due bills from Loyalists who had left New York without paying him. Among Sam's large debts was that of the disgraced and now deceased Gen. Charles Lee. Sam contacted George Washington, retired in Virginia, asking for his help in collecting this debt and Washington agreed to help. On June 26, 1785, Samuel wrote a letter from New York to Washington referencing earlier correspondence they had shared.

"Sir,

I received your letter from Governor Clinton and can but say I received the greatest honor in your kind acceptance of the grotesque work. (this is the shell work miniature he sent to Mrs. Washington which had finally been delivered and for which Washington had sent Sam a thank you letter.)

I know not in what manner to apologize to your Excellency for my boldness in enclosing Mr. White's letter in this but my reliance on your goodness so often experienced. My circumstance has obliged me to quit the city and dispose of my House. I have put some dependence in the State's aid but find it vain. I cannot either collect my debts so as to clear me from the world under this situation. I have made bold to beg Your Excellency's favor in recommending the enclosed Mr. White

250

perhaps you may be acquainted with and it will be of the greatest weight as there is upwards of five hundred and fifty pounds due me from the Estate of Gen. Lee. Mr. White has the account from Col. Hamilton the enclosed is open with a request to direct favor to me under cover to the Governor who will kindly forward any. I must again beg pardon for my assurance but your Excellency may believe me I am forced through necessity and therefore reaffirm the hope of being once more relieved through your Excellency's goodness.

I have the honor to remain with the utter respect to your lady and self, your Excellency's most obedient and humble Servant.... Samuel Fraunces.

Mrs. Fraunces and family desire their respects to you and your lady."[119]

Samuel noted that he '*had been obliged to quit the* city' and noted a debt of *L*550 pounds due from General Lee's estate. This amount would have easily supported his family for several years. Alexander White, a Virginia lawyer retained by Lee's sister in England, was executor of Gen. Lee's estate and refused to pay the debt for General Lee's food and lodging during the war. He was stonewalling because Lee's estate was bankrupt. Washington contacted Alexander White from Mount Vernon on 14 July 1785 on Sam's behalf.

"Dear Sir,

Mr. Fraunces's letters to you and to me the last of which I also enclose for your perusal are so expressive of his wants as to render it unnecessary for me to add aught on the occasion of them. He had been considered (tho confined within the British lines) as a friend to our cause. It is said he was remarkably attentive to our prisoners in the city of New York, supporting them as far as his means would allow in the hour of their greatest distress. This it is which has both Governor Clinton and myself to continue to support him. It is the cause I presume of his applying thro me to you and must be my apology for giving you the trouble of this letter.

With respect to his demand against the Estate of Gen Lee, I know nothing. His letter to the best of my recollection is the first intimation I ever had of his being a creditor. The propriety of justice therefore of the claims must speak for themselves and will no doubt have their own weight. The time of payments seems interesting to him.

The subject of this letter reminds me of an account of my own against Gen. Lee's estate which I put into your hands at the spring last year. With great esteem, I am ....G. Washington." Apparently, Washington was also a creditor. White responded to Washington's letter of the 16th saying that the estate was bankrupt because Lee owed great sums to Congress who refused to grant Lee's estate any bounty lands that could have been sold to settle his estate, due to his dismissal from service. Lee's sister had to send $L4500$ to White to settle the estate. Sam's debt was not among them.

George Washington often referred to Samuel Fraunces as '*Black Sam*' as we see from a letter he wrote to Clement Biddle on Sept 7, 1785: "*Inclosed is a letter to Mr. Fraunces [sic] als 'Black Sam'*", in which Washington asked for Sam's help in finding a housekeeper for Mount Vernon.

"*Sir:*

As no person can judge better of the qualifications necessary to constitute a good housekeeper or household steward than yourself, for a family which has a good deal of company and wishes to entertain them in a plain but genteel style, I take the liberty of asking you if there is any such as one within your reach whom you think could be induced to come to me for reasonable wages. I would rather have a man than a woman but either will do if they can be recommended for their honesty, sobriety and knowledge of their profession, which in one word is to relieve Mrs. Washington from the drudgery of ordering and seeing the table properly covered and things economically used. Nothing more therefore need be said to inform you of a character that would suit me than what is already mentioned.

The wages I now give to a man who is about to leave me in order to get married (under which circumstances he would not suit me) is about $100 per annum but for me who understands the needs perfectly and stands fair in other respects I would go as far as $125.

Sometime ago I wrote to Col. Biddle and to Mr. Moyston who keeps the City Tavern in Philadelphia to try if they could procure such a person as I want. I therefore beg if you know one that would suit me, and is to be had upon the terms above, and who can attend properly to a large family (for mine is such with a good many workmen) that you would immediately inform Col Biddle first before any engagement is entered into on my behalf, lest one should be provided at Philadelphia and embarrassments arise from the different engagements.

I am sorry to give you so much trouble but I hope you will excuse it ....

G Washington"

Clearly, Washington continued to correspond with Sam as a trusted friend. Sam's response to this letter has been lost. On Sept 28th Sam wrote responding to Washington's letter about the Lee debt.

"Sir

With the utmost respect I have the honor to address your Excellency and return my sincerest thanks for your kind interposition in my business with Mr. White. I shall never be able to recompense with my poor services the many obligations your goodness lays me under for still I am afraid necessity forces me to be troublesome, I beg your Excellency's patience to hear my numberless misfortunes.

I am not at present in this city but have been obligated to sell my property for very little to pay off a mortgage and have bought a small retreat in New Jersey, notwithstanding I am still unfortunately in debt and cannot receive one penny of or from those that owe me to discharge the same. All the dependence I have is that your influence being kindly interposed will encourage Mr. White to be speedy in assisting me. As my account is no more than a Book debt, I have no further vouchers (which Mr. White requires) than my Books, which have for the past 30 years been always proved just and a certificate from Gen. Lee which your Excellency is acquainted with. My son kept my books and anything that he can do to satisfy Mr. White shall be done but I know not whether there be occasion.

Your Excellency's goodness emboldens me to tell you I have through necessity been obliged to accept a small subscription from a few gentlemen to relieve my family from wants. I can ask such a favor of you and I would but I have been too much an imposition on such extreme generosity already.

I have only left to offer up my prayers for your health and happiness and that the latter may exist here and hereafter. I am Sir you Excellency's most obedient and devoted Humble Servant... Samuel Fraunces."

Executor White would not accept the Tavern's accounting books, using this as a stalling tactic. Sam was hoping that another follow-up from Washington would induce White to pay him. Sam had not yet learned that Lee's estate was insolvent.

In this letter Sam says that he had bought a *"small farm in New Jersey"* and he mentions a *"small subscription from gentlemen"*, knowing that he could ask Washington, but feeling *"already too much in his debt"* to do so. Sam was probably selling shares in a future business venture.

1786 – Troubles

Sadly, Sam was not the only person suffering as the depression continued through most of 1786, with a shortage of currency, high taxes, and a great number of foreclosures. Congress was continually petitioned by creditors but was bankrupt because States would not pay their war debts. The fact that Congress had addressed Sam's 1785 petition so quickly underscores their recognition of his contributions.

On March 14, 1786, Governor Clinton submitted to the New York State Legislature another petition from Samuel Fraunces and recommended *"his peculiar case"* to their attention being *"Convinced of the truth of so many of the most material facts therein stated."* On May 5, 1786, NY State Congress appropriated *L*200 to Samuel Fraunces in thanks for the *"support of New York prisoners of war and for sundry services"*. Sam was again reimbursed at a time when NY State had no money to pay anyone.

Sam and Elizabeth's oldest son, Andrew Gautier Fraunces married Sarah Pye about 1785. Sarah (1766-1825) was a daughter of David Pye (1740-1796) from England, a family with a long white heritage. Her father disowned Sarah in his will in 1796. He bequeathed only 20 shillings (less than *L*1) to his daughter Sarah, *"to be paid from the funds*

257

her husband, Andrew G. Fraunces, owes to my estate." He left the rest of his substantial lands and estate to his sons John, David and Isaac Pye requiring them to support their mother and sister Ann and left Ann *L*100 pounds to be invested.[120]

Shay's Rebellion, a series of armed protests in 1786-1787 soon arose over Congress's inability to pay the veterans. The weary, wounded, unpaid soldiers had returned home to rebuild their lives. Their neighbors reviled them for wanting their pay and pensions, whipped up by newspaper articles from states who objected to northern abolition of slavery and to being taxed to pay for the war. Men who had spent years fighting without pay had no money to buy land and no income. With no job skills and few jobs due to the depression, many were destitute. Men hoping for agricultural jobs found that those with land had lost all their livestock to foraging armies and their fallow fields would take several years to become income producing again. Most of the New England population lived on subsistence farms, buying goods on credit until crops were harvested.

In coastal areas, however, there was a wealthier merchant shipping class. When trade resumed, Europe's merchants demanded payment in British pounds because the US still had no monetary system. The barter system broke down when American merchants demanded English currency from customers who simply had no way to get it. Massachusetts state government, dominated by politically connected merchants, then raised property taxes to generate funds to pay war debts, leading to widespread foreclosures. As more families lost their land, a great groundswell of anger developed. Widows and orphans, unable to collect the promised pay or pensions from States or Congress, were thrown into the streets. Men had fought and bled for a country that would not pay them. That same government was now confiscating their homes for non-payment of taxes, one of the reasons they had gone to war. Their land which they had cleared and defended through the French and Indian War and the American Revolution was being confiscated by banks and sold to wealthy speculators for a pittance. Armed uprisings soon blew up in Massachusetts, New Hampshire and other states. After a year of these large armed riots, everyone realized there would be another revolution if a solution wasn't found fast.

1787 – Constitution

The 13 colonies originally formed a Confederation in which they volunteered to act in agreement with each other for the war and each had pledged funds and men to the Confederation. Now, several years after the end of the war, most states still owed millions in unpaid pledges. Congress had no funds of its own and no power to tax or to force the states to obey their decisions. Congress could sign international treaties, but states violated them with impunity. Some states began imposing tariffs on good from other states, there was no national monetary system, and the economy was in free fall. Congress, unable pay the army, had no way to repay huge foreign debts accumulated during the war either. Most representatives in Congress realized the system was flawed. It was imperative to create a national currency. A Constitutional Convention was held in Independence Hall in Philadelphia in 1787, while Congress continued meeting in New York.

George Washington was elected President of the Constitutional Convention which determined to set up a functional national government and to create a national monetary system. Washington and a group of supporters felt the state sovereignty system was simply not workable as Congress was constantly deadlocked over state disagreements. These Federalists became convinced that only a strong central government could work. There were 73 delegates chosen by states (excluding Rhode Island), but only 55 delegates attended the Constitutional Convention, the greatest men of the day, including 21 war veterans and 8 signers of the Declaration of Independence. They were regular men, farmers, merchants, lawyers and bankers and their average age was 42, including the brilliant 36 year old James Madison and 81 year old Ben Franklin. What they created was an entirely new form of government.

The new Constitution established 3 branches of Government: Executive, Legislative and Judicial, to disperse power within a system of checks and balances, to prevent control by a majority. It closely mirrored the English system, causing some opposition. A single executive was especially unpopular as it resembled monarchy. Only Washington's personal integrity convinced many that this was a workable solution because most believed he would be the first President.

Sam, in New Jersey and still struggling financially, sent another letter to Washington, while he was President of the Constitutional Convention in Philadelphia. During this critical work, Washington sent Sam's letter to the Continental Congress on May 11th, 1787, who appointed a committee to review it.

"Report:

It appears to your Committee that Congress on the 4th April 1784, resolved "that in consideration of the singular services of the said

Samuel Fraunces and of his advances to the American Prisoners the sum of $2000 to be paid to the said Samuel Fraunces on account of the Loan office Certificates in his hands and that they be delivered up and cancelled.

That in consequence of this Resolution the Loan Office Certificates of the said Samuel Fraunces amounting to Two Thousand Dollars were presented to the proper Officers of the Treasury to be cancelled, that upon being liquidated their specie value appears to be $1293 63/90 Dollars for which sum a warrant issued in his favor on the Treasurer of the US.

That on a subsequent application of the said S. Fraunces, Congress of the 15ᵗʰ ᵒᶠ Sept 1785 ordered that the full sum of Two Thousand Dollars should be paid to the said Samuel Fraunces in consequence whereof he was paid the farther sum of $706 27/90 Dolls.

Your Committee farther reports that the said Samuel Fraunces alledges that he did advance during the War to the American Prisoners two thousand dollars in specie, for the Loan Office Certificates aforesaid influenced by no other motives than an attachment to the cause of America, and from some testimonials produced by him, your Committee are induced to believe this was the fact.

Your Committee have examined a number of Letters and Papers submitted to them by the said S. Fraunces by which, as well as from his general character, it appears that the said Fraunces was firmly attached to the Interest of his Country, rendered very essential services to the Prisoners and furnished useful and important intelligence, by means of which he expended very considerable part of his property.

Your committee therefore in consideration of the services rendered and the losses sustained by the said Samuel Fraunces and in consideration of the report, that the Board of Treasury take order for paying to Samuel Fraunces the sum of $500."

So, Sam was paid the additional $706 to the face value of his certificates and was also paid another $500 in consideration. Once again, Congress prioritized his petition at a time when they had no money to pay anyone.

Continental Congress in July approved the Northwest Ordinance, creating new states north of the Ohio River. It included a Bill of Rights guaranteeing freedom of religion, the right to trial by jury, public education, and a ban on slavery in the new states. Jefferson had proposed a complete ban on slavery, but it was defeated by 1 vote.

On Aug 14, 1787, Samuel's 19 year old daughter, Catherine, married Cornelius J. Smock, 25, in Middletown, Monmouth, New Jersey. Cornelius Smock (1761-1836) was a son of Johannes 'John' Barnes Luyster Smock (1727-1811) and his wife, Femmetje Teunison (1718-1778). John Smock was a New Jersey Patriot, who had served as a Lt. Col. in the New Jersey Militia. The Smock family had been in New Amsterdam since the early 1600's and were a well-known, prominent white, former slave owning family. They lived in Monmouth, New Jersey where Cornelius served in the Militia with his father, brother, and uncle. In 1792 they moved to New York City but remained on the tax rolls in New Jersey.

264

During August, the Constitutional Convention debated details like the length of the terms for President and legislators and the power of Congress to regulate commerce. They also decided only the national government could coin money and regulate its value. States could no longer print money or issue bills of credit. The national government was given the power of taxation to be used to pay off national debts. Only the national government could regulate foreign and interstate commerce. At the insistence of the Southern states, a 20 year ban was placed on any further Congressional action concerning slavery. On September 17, 1787, 39 of the 55 delegates signed the final draft of the new Constitution and made it public.

It at once created huge controversy. People who were not involved in politics had expected the Convention to revise the original Articles of Confederation, not create an entirely new form of government, with a strong national government like the English system they had just gotten rid of, including taxation. The new Constitution needed the approval of 9 states to be ratified. The Federalists, who supported a strong central government, began to publish essays in favor of ratification. Eighty-five articles, written by Alexander Hamilton, James Madison and John Jay in support of the new Constitution, were widely circulated and later published as the <u>Federalist Papers</u>.

The Anti-Federalists wanted a weaker central government, giving greater power to the States, but were far less effective in their communications.

Delaware (Dec. 7) was the first of the states to ratify the Constitution. It was soon followed by: Pennsylvania (Dec. 12), New

Jersey (Dec. 18) and Georgia (Dec. 31). By the end of the year, four states had signed. Five more were needed and newspapers inflamed both sides.

1788 – Ratification

This was a good year for Sam and his family. On Jan 27, Samuel was a godparent for his grandchild Andrew Fraunces Smock, son of Cornelius and Catherine (Fraunces) Smock, born 5 months after the marriage of his parents.

On May 8th, 1878, Sam opened a new tavern in a house at 16 Nassau Street, corner of John St. in New York, formerly occupied by William Marrener.[121] Sam's tavern soon became a meeting place for Federalists and Sam heard many debates over the new Constitution. In May, he submitted a claim to the New York Court as a creditor of Frederick Philipse. A letter from Richard Morris, Chief Justice of the State of New York, shows he approved the payment of $L27.06$ from the confiscated estate. Philipse had spent much of the war entertaining Loyalists lavishly with Sam's catering services. Tories were declared traitors and all Tory lands were confiscated by Congress in 1784. Sam petitioned for payment from his confiscated estate.

Connecticut approved the new Constitution on (Jan. 9). Five signatures down, four needed. Then Massachusetts became the sixth signatory (Feb. 7). In March, Rhode Island rejected the Constitution in a popular referendum. Maryland then signed (April 26), and South

Carolina signed (May 23). They were the 7th and 8th states to sign. Now only one more state was needed to ratify the Constitution. Patrick Henry, George Mason, and other states' rights champions fiercely opposed Virginia's ratification of the Constitution. Richard Henry Lee called for a national Bill of Rights (like the Northwest Ordinance). Roger Sherman suggested a compromise for membership in the House of Representatives to be based on population while the Senate would have equal members for all states. At the insistence of the Southern states, black slaves were to be counted at 3/5th of their number to determine the number of House members although slaves could not vote. At the time free black men could vote in 5 of the 13 states, including North Carolina. The Federalists, led by James Madison, finally prevailed and Virginia ratified. On July 2, 1788 a formal announcement was made that the United States of America had a new Constitution.

A few weeks later, on July 28, 1788, Sam's daughter Margaret Amelia married John Battin in Trinity Church in New York City.[122] Battin was a well-educated British soldier who liked America, so he hid on Long Island to evade the Evacuation. He became a successful Tavern owner in Jamaica, LI. In 1786 he opened the Porter House Tavern in NY City at the sign of the Blue Bell in Slote Lane. He then moved to 37 Nassau St, just down the street from Sam and Elizabeth's new Tavern at 15 Nassau, where he met and soon married Margaret. John Battin later became a hosiery merchant on Broadway between Dye and Cortlandt Streets where their son, also named John, kept the business after his father's death. Margaret died young but John Sr. lived to be 101, walking the Battery every day, a well-known character until his death.

On Dec 30, 1788, the General society of Mechanics and Tradesmen had their annual meeting at Sam's tavern at the corner of John and Nassau Streets where they partook of elegant entertainment for the day. The left-over food was taken to the debtors in the New Jail who sent a thank you note. Samuel was still helping to feed prisoners and the poor whenever he was able.[123]

1789 – Steward

On Jan 6th, 1789, the Society of Mechanics and Tradesmen held an anniversary meeting at Samuel Fraunces' new tavern in Cortlandt Street where he had recently moved. Samuel's daughter, Elizabeth married Acheson Thompson on Jan 14, 1789, at Trinity Church in New York City. Elizabeth was 23 and he was 34.[124] Acheson was a tailor but in April, probably with the assistance of Sam, he opened a tavern at the house formerly occupied by Daniel Hadley at 9 Mile Stone, about 155th St. Mile Stones were laid out from New York City Hall, one per mile, in 1769 by Postmaster Ben Franklin along the Post Roads to Albany and Boston as well as to Philadelphia. Acheson Thompson kept taverns and inns in New York and Philadelphia for the rest of his life. He catered to mariners, and several made him executor of their wills and left him their property.

In February, Sam and Elizabeth Fraunces and son Andrew stood as godparents at the baptism of John Fraunces Batten, first child of Margaret and John Battin in Trinity Church.[125] This child was also born about 7 months after his parent's wedding.

On April 14th, 1789, Charles Thomson, secretary of Congress, arrived at Mount Vernon to inform George Washington that he had been unanimously elected as the first President of the United States.

Despite Martha's reluctance, Washington accepted and, feeling an urgency to get the country organized, at once left for New York. He instructed Tobias Lear, his secretary, to find a Steward for the Presidential household in NY, recommending Sam for the post. Martha stayed behind to organize things for the move to New York. With over 8000 acres on 5 separate plantations, over 200 slaves and several ongoing businesses to make arrangements for, it would take her several weeks to arrange managers for their affairs, so she was still in Virginia when Washington made his triumphant arrival in New York on the 23rd of April 1789. The streets were thronged, and all the houses were illuminated. People cheered and wept, exclaiming that they could now die content, knowing Washington would be the father of their new country. He truly was universally admired and loved. On April 30th, 1789, George Washington and John Adams were inaugurated as President and Vice President on the balcony of the Federal Hall in New York City. The bible used for their oath was from St. John's Mason Lodge and the oath was administered by the Chancellor of New York State, Patriot leader, Robert Livingston. After the oath was completed, Livingston shouted *"Long Live George Washington, President of the United States!"* Livingston and Washington were Masons, John Adams was not. The crowd cheered and a 13 gun salute, one for each state, was fired. Washington was then 57 years old.

Congress had arranged for the use of Mr. Samuel Osgood's home at 3 Cherry Street as a temporary home for the President and Washington moved into the house before his inauguration. He lived in the small but fully furnished home for 10 months, from his inauguration on April 30th, 1789, to Feb 3rd, 1890. Congress rented the house for $845 per year. It was a 4 story brick residence with 5 windows on each side facing Franklin Square. It contained the living quarters for the First Family, a private office for the President and public business offices.

Tobias Lear convinced Sam to leave his new Cortlandt Street Inn in Elizabeth's capable hands to become Steward to the President. Lear supplied a glowing recommendation of Sam's food.

"We have engaged Black Sam Frances (sic) as Steward and Superintendent of the Kitchen, and a very excellent fellow he is in the latter department – he tosses up such a number of fine dishes that we are distracted in our choice when we set down to table and obliged to hold a long consultation upon the subject before we can determine what to attack. Oysters and Lobsters make a very conspicuous figure upon the table and never go off untouched."

Samuel started as the First Presidential Steward on May 1st, 1789 placing ads in the New York papers noting that *"no account would be opened by any servant or others employed by the Household of the President"* signed Samuel Fraunces, Steward of the Household.[126] Another ad on May 9th assured clients that: *"Mrs. Fraunces would be managing the tavern and inn at 49 Cortlandt St, where the General Stage office is kept as usual and patrons could expect the same service and items"* and he *"hoped for their continued support."*[127] There were 169 taverns in New York that year and Elizabeth kept up with the best of them, a formidable force in her own right. The Societies of St.

273

George, St. Patrick, St. Andrews, and the Holland Mason's Lodge all met regularly at her establishment.

On May 7th, the first inaugural ball was held but winter weather had delayed Marth's arrival. After waiting several weeks, it was decided to go ahead with the ball. Washington danced the minuet gracefully with several New York matrons. Martha arrived 2 weeks later.

Washington's first presidential term started on March 4th, 1789. He was so inundated with visitors, leaving him little time for his official duties, that he decided to *'receive visits of compliment'* on only 2 designated days, for one hour only, and announced he would do no entertaining at dinner.[128] His household was large with George and Martha, and her two grandchildren Nelly and Wash Cutis then 8 and 10. The President's private secretary, Tobias Lear and his wife lived in as did Col. David Humphreys, secretaries Lewis and Nelson, Maj. William Jackson an aide de camp, Sam as Steward, a chef and multiple servants to care for the people and horses.

Washington received a salary of $25,000 which was not sufficient to the expenses of his household and at times he paid additional expenses from his own pocket. As Steward and General Manager of the President's House and grounds, Samuel managed a staff of 20 people, black and white, slave and free. It was his job to greet guests and escort them to the President as well as to manage all household employees. He was the purchasing agent for the family and staff and kept all household financial records. President Washington employed 5 white servants at $84/year each (plus liveries at $29 per person), 2 free black maids at $46/year each, a housekeeper at $96/year and 3 other women at $36/year, a valet at $162/year and the Steward, Samuel Fraunces, for $300/year. At this time, a typical clerk in the Treasury Dept. was making $500/year. Washington also had 7 black slaves who received no pay but did get housing and clothing. They were William Lee, Christopher Shekels, Giles, Paris, Austin, Moll and Oney Judge. Slavery was still legal in New York and Sam, a free man of mixed-race with several dark children himself, surely felt empathy with these slaves he managed.

Washington's first State Dinner as President was held on May 29th, 1789, the day after Martha finally arrived in New York. "*Although The President makes no formal invitation, yet the day after the arrival of Mrs. Washington, the following distinguished personages dined at his house, 'en famille', their Excellencies the Vice-President–the Governor of this State–the Ministers of France and Spain–and the Governor of the Western Territory–the Hon. Secretary of the United States for Foreign Affairs–the Most. Hon. Mr. Langdon, Mr. Wingate, Mr. Izard, Mr. Few, and Mr. Muhlenberg, Speaker of the House of Representatives of the United States.*"–Gazette of the United States. Pain Wingate, a Senator from New Hampshire, left the following description of this dinner: "*It was the least showy dinner that I ever saw at the President's. As there was no clergyman present, Washington himself said grace on taking his seat. He dined on a boiled leg of mutton, as it was his custom to eat of only one dish. After the dessert, a single glass of wine was offered to each of the guests, when the President rose, the guests followed his example, and repaired to the drawing-room, each departing at his option, without ceremony."* [129] Dinner and decorum soon improved.

As the Steward, Samuel was responsible for establishing proper decorum for the new household, now equivalent in hierarchy to the Kings of Europe, with centuries of ceremony and rigid rules of conduct without creating any appearance of royalty. It was his duty to supply a bountiful, elegant table, showing the best of America's foods. Sam was always present *"resplendently dressed in wig and small clothes."* His ideas of proper elegance soon clashed with the legendary frugality of George Washington. Washington was very conscious of the need to behave as a common man to avoid any impression of royalty to the sensitive American public. Although Washington was willing to spend his own funds to live graciously in Virginia, he was very concerned about his household costs being reviewed and paid for by Congress and allocated a surprisingly small amount to Sam for the household budget. Sam, who was expected to entertain Royalty and Ambassadors from all over the world, as well as Senators, Governors, and other American officials, struggled to provide the level of service and elegance he believed proper. After one disagreement, Sam reputedly said:

"Well, he may discharge me, he may kill me if he will, but while he is President of the United States and I have the honor to be his Steward, his establishment shall be supplied with the very best of everything that the whole Country can afford."

Samuel set up the protocols for the President's House for his successors. Accounts of the stewardship at the White House note *"Almost every question governing the State dinners is within the control of the steward of the White House, who is in a position to be very arbitrary if he chooses. Even the President's wife has very little to say about the culinary department or household affairs. Moreover, this supervision of all the details of the household is no sinecure, for an account must be rendered of every dish or utensil, broken or worn out, and no piece of broken glass or china can be destroyed except upon the order of the Superintendent of Public Buildings and Grounds. The present steward is the embodiment of discretion in matters pertaining to his official duties."*

The President held formal visiting hours for men on Tuesdays from 3-4 pm. Martha would hold levees on Fridays, less formal affairs with men and women. Dinners for members of Congress and government officials were held on Thursdays. Meals were always *"bountiful and elegant"* to Sam's high standards. The menu was decided each day by Sam, who visited the market, selecting the best to be had within his strict budget. The actual meals were cooked under his direction and served by staff that he had trained.

"Formal dinners began at 4 P.M., and there was no waiting for unpunctual guests. If no clergyman was present, Washington himself said grace. In mixed company, the President and Martha sat across from each other, halfway down the long table, with a secretary at the head and the foot, to aid the serving and the conversation. Samuel

Fraunces, in a dazzling white apron, white silk shirt and stockings, velvet breeches, with powder in his hair, presided in the dining room and placed the dishes on the table, while the carving and helping were mostly done by the secretaries. When the ladies retired to the drawing room, it was Washington's habit to follow after fifteen minutes to join them for coffee, leaving one of the secretaries to entertain the gentlemen who wished to linger over the wine. If there were no other ladies present, Martha sat at the head of the table, with a secretary at the foot, and the President half way between. For the family meals they reverted to the side-by-side chairs at the head of the table, with a carver at the foot. "[130]* Meals were served *"to from ten to twenty-two guests. At the central table, laid exquisitely in fine linen, was a long mirror, made in sections and framed in silver, on which stood china statuettes. The silverware which had been melted down and reproduced in more elegant style with each piece displaying abounded, with jelly, fruit, nuts and raisins, were on the table before the guests made their entrance. After the meal, the President would raise his wine glass. All would drink a toast, and the ladies would retire to the drawing-room, leaving the men to their after dinner indulgences. The Washington's served good wine, but ordinarily a silver mug of beer stood beside the President's plate, except at state dinners. An invitation to dinner was not regarded as a command, and there were instances of regrets being sent for one reason or another. Half a dozen or more servants were in attendance at these dinners, in the white and scarlet livery of the Washington household."* [131]

Sam supplied breakfast for the household including family of 12 plus staff of 20, cakes and refreshments for the afternoon receptions, the 4 o'clock dinners for 20 or more guests, plus a separate dinner table for the staff of 20, and later light evening suppers for the household of 32.

Samuel and Elizabeth's daughter Sarah also soon married, early in 1789, to Thomas Charles Campbell, Sam's old partner in the purchase of Hampden Hall before the war. Sarah was 16 and the much older Campbell was a widower with children older than she was. Campbell had gone back to his linen business by 1787, located at 67 Maiden Lane where he sold broadcloths, blankets, Irish linens, Shetland wool hose, and chintzes and calico.[132]

Samuel became a Mason in 1789. He and son Andrew G. Fraunces were listed in the Holland Lodge #8 in New York City.[133] This was considered the premier lodge in the city with many prestigious members including honorary members George Washington and Baron von Steuben.

On June 6, 1789, John Battin (who had married Margaret Fraunces the prior year) placed an ad that he had moved into the house lately occupied by Samuel Fraunces at the corner of John and Nassau Streets where he hoped for a continuance of their favors.

Sam's wife Elizabeth was successfully managing the Fraunces Tavern and Inn, On the 4th of July, General Malcolm's brigade under command of Col. Chrystie paraded by the house of President Washington who, although ill, appeared at the door in full regimentals.

279

The officers then dined at 4 o'clock at Elizabeth's Fraunces Tavern in Cortlandt Street.[134]

On the 18th of August, newly married daughter Elizabeth (Fraunces) Thompson wrote to President George Washington, at her husband Acheson's urging, asking President Washington to intercede with Congress to aid their request for payment. Acheson Thompson, also an innkeeper, had been caring for George Morgan White Eyes, a 19 year old Indian ward of Congress and had bought clothing for him with the approval of Washington's secretary, Mr. Lear. Congress had not reimbursed him, putting the Thompsons in financial distress.

George Morgan White Eyes had a tragic and short life. His father was an Indian chief who married a white woman who had been kidnapped as a child and raised by Indians. George Morgan their bi racial son, was made a ward of Congress following the murder of his father by his supposed allies, the American Militia. At the age of 7 he was sent to live with George Morgan, a friend of his father for whom he had been named. Unfortunately, Morgan was often away from home and his wife and son resented young George and treated him like a charity case, even though Congress was sending them funds for the boy's support. George M. was brilliant. He excelled at school and was attending Princeton College when he was suddenly removed before completing his senior year and dumped in NY City at the Thompson's Boarding House, with no money and without even a change of clothes. His foster father, George Morgan, wrote to Congress asking that they send him to another College to complete his studies, but Congress did nothing, leaving the boy with no money, no means of support and no college degree.

When George M's request for a job to earn money to support himself went unanswered, he despondently returned to his tribal lands, walking the whole way. This intelligent man, raised as a white man, who could read and write several languages, was unable to assimilate back into his native culture. He was tragically killed at the age of 27 in a drunken brawl.

Elizabeth (Fraunces) Thompson's letter of Aug 18th, 1789, to George Washington, said:

"I once more take the liberty of addressing myself to your Excellency requesting that you will be so good as to give your approbation to the payment of Mr. Thompson's acct for the articles provided by him for George M. White Eyes, which articles he would not have supplied him with had he not thought he was acting upon a surety of its being by your desire."

She said that her husband was facing debtor's prison, leaving his family in distress, and that the people from whom the clothes were bought would no longer wait for payment. In another letter written shortly after this she requested:

"a few moments hearing from your Excellency relative to the Account of George M. White Eyes which I am sorry to hear is disapproved of – and which would not have been done had not Mr. White Eyes said it was by the particular order of Mr. Lear, that he should be supplied with everything he wanted that was necessary."

Elizabeth had been taught to read and write well by her mother, something few women in those days could do.

Andrew G. Fraunces, oldest child of Sam and Elizabeth, was a clerk at the Treasury Department. That year, Andrew G. was listed as a member of the Dutch Reformed Church in New York City. [135]

George Clinton's election as Governor of New York was celebrated by a grand Jubilee at Fraunces Tavern in Cortlandt St. But the stage stop moved to a different tavern which may have hurt Elizabeth's business. On Oct 9, 1789, a notice appeared in the newspapers noting that Passengers for the Boston and Albany stages are asked to enter their names at the "Stage House" which has been "removed from Mr. Fraunces to Mr. Isaac Norton's at #160 Queen Street opposite Mr. Walton's."[136]

1790 – Philadelphia

Samuel started the year of 1790 as the Presidential Steward at the Osgood House at 3 Cherry Street, New York. That year, well known painter John Trumbull advertised his plan to do a series of paintings including one of the Farewell of General Washington to his Officers. It is at this time that Trumbull sketched the faces of those who attended that Farewell Dinner at Fraunces Tavern. A set of numbered engravings were made from the larger paintings, selling for 3 guineas per print. This is probably the source of the etching later found at the Edith Hartshorne Mason house. Washington sat for Trumbull on many occasions from February to July, and Sam was, of course, present.

Feb 2nd, 1790, the First Supreme Court of the US was convened in Manhattan and, that evening, the Grand Jury of the US for the district of NY gave a *very elegant entertainment*" in honor of the Supreme Court at Fraunces Tavern. The list of attendees included the names of the leading lawmakers of the US at the time.[137] On February 8th the Grand Jury for the United States gave another *very elegant entertainment*" to the Chief, Associate and District Judges, Attorney General and the officers of the Supreme and District Courts again at Fraunces Tavern in Cortlandt Street.[138] Elizabeth was keeping Fraunces' Tavern with great success.

283

President Washington had been complaining that Samuel and the cook, Mrs. Read, were too extravagant. Samuel, unwilling to further compromise the quality of his food to Washington's frugality, resigned his position in early February 1790. This was at the time when President Washington was to move to a different house. When Sam left, Washington gave him a bonus and there were apparently no hard feelings. Sam, no longer working for President Washington, returned to help Elizabeth run their tavern. I wonder how that went? She apparently had been successful enough that the family income didn't depend on the *L*25 per month Sam's position as Steward provided.

President Washington and his family then moved to the much larger Alexander Macomb House at 39-41 Broadway where they all lived from February 23rd to August 30, 1790. The prior tenant, the French Minister, had left this house furnished and Washington bought all the furniture, including all the mirrors and draperies, with his own funds, when they moved in. The Washington family returned to Mount Vernon on August 30th, 1790, when Congress recessed for the summer. Samuel had been replaced as Steward by John Hyde and his wife who, to the great consternation of George Washington, between February and August, spent considerably more running the household than Sam had. John Vicar from Baltimore was also hired as a cook at an additional $15 per month because the Hyde's *"didn't cook"*.

Philadelphia was widely expected to become the capital of the new nation, but after the incident when the Governor refused to call out the militia, members of Congress became convinced that they needed an independent location, where Congress would be in charge. Slaveholders, fearing influence from Philadelphia Abolitionists, insisted it be in a non-abolitionist area. Virginia and Maryland each agreed to cede 10 square miles of land for a new Capitol City. Congress then agreed to meet in Philadelphia for 10 years, while a new city was built in the District of Columbia.

Meanwhile, the first census was held in 1790. The statistics from this census enlarged the House of Representatives from 69 to 105 seats, based on population. About 25% of the buildings in New York City at the time were taverns. The largest city was New York (33,131), followed by Philadelphia (28,522), Boston (18,320), Charleston, SC (16,359), and Baltimore (13,503).

This first Census noted that Samuel's household consisted of 6 people: 1 White Male 16+ (Samuel), 4 free White Females (wife Elizabeth, daughters Elizabeth Thompson, Sophia, and Hannah), and 1 Slave (believed to be dark skinned son Samuel M. Fraunces). Since Elizabeth (Dally) Fraunces, a white woman, probably gave the census taker the information, she and the rest of the household were identified as 'white' and the census taker likely assumed the only black person he saw was a slave, even though it was almost certainly, Samuel's 16 year old son, Samuel M., who was not accounted for elsewhere in the census.

On October 27th, 1790, Samuel Fraunces placed a newspaper notice that he had relocated his tavern which *"moved from 49 Cortlandt*

Street to Broad Street in the house formerly occupied by Widow Blaaw near the Exchange. He has some rooms for genteel boarders and will provide entertainment for clubs and companies. He particularly noted to ship captains and gentlemen in the mercantile line that he offered for exportation, pickled and fried oysters, lobsters and beef almode which he will warrant will keep to go to any part of the world. He particularly invites his brothers of Tammany Society and respective Lodges of the city. " This location was very near his original Queens Head Tavern by the Exchange.

After the summer recess, President Washington moved into the first Pennsylvania Executive Mansion – the Masters-Penn House at 524-530 Market Street in Philadelphia with his family, 9 black slaves and 16 white servants. His slaves included Oney Judge, Moll, Austin, Hercules, Richmond, Giles, Paris, Christopher Sheels and Joe Richardson who had been with him in New York City. The house belonged to his friend, financier and Congressman Robert Morris who had expanded and furnished it and gave it to the President for use as the Executive Mansion. The house was still too small for them all, so Washington designed some additions, including a large 2 story bow on the south side and a one story servants hall on the east side of the kitchen. He also built a private office and expanded the stables. During a public archaeology project in 2007, the foundations of the back buildings and the bow front that he added were found. This site, next to the Liberty Bell Center and Independence Hall National Historical Park, has now expanded its interpretive center to include information about slavery during the Revolution, especially Washington's slaves, who lived and worked on this site.

President Washington was becoming frustrated with household problems. Before their move to Philadelphia, Steward John Hyde, who had replaced Sam, had expressed his dissatisfaction to Washington about his position. Washington wrote his secretary, Tobias Lear, and noted that he didn't want to pay for the Hyde's move to Philadelphia, only to have them leave after arrival, and asked Lear to confirm Hyde's intentions. He also asked Lear to compare Hyde's accounts to those of Samuel Fraunces. Washington complained that the dinners were "*lacking*", and he felt that "*several of his cooks could provide better dinners and desserts, but the pride of the Hyde's would not allow them to do so.*" Hyde also had trouble managing the servants and, to Washington's dismay, Lear found that Hyde's expenses exceeded Samuel Fraunces' by L4 to L5 per week although Lear did say more people were being accommodated and he did not suspect dishonesty. Washington was unhappy with Hyde and even wrote to Lear that he strongly suspected that "*nothing was brought to his (Washington's) table of liquors, fruits or other items that was not used just as profusely at the Hyde's table.*" Mrs. Hyde claimed she couldn't keep up with all her duties which included superintending the washerwomen, cleaning the house, preparing desserts and making cake, tea and coffee for the large establishment. Washington hated change and he was concerned that, if Mrs. Hyde resigned, there would be no one to make the deserts, and felt strongly that her husband on his own would not be any better than William, one of the existing servants. Washington wrote to Lear:

*"Francis (*sic – Sam Fraunces*), besides being an excellent cook, knowing how to provide genteel Dinners and giving aid in dressing them, prepared the Dessert, made the Cake and did everything that Hyde and wife conjointly do; consequently the services of Hyde alone is not to be compared with those of Frauncis's."*

The Hydes both agreed to stay with the household and moved to Philadelphia. Chef John Vicar, who had joined the household in New York, also moved to Philadelphia with his wife. His meals were lacking and uninspired and he didn't bake cakes, but Decatur called him "*the best cook that could be obtained*".

1791 – Slaves

The First Family arrived in Philadelphia at the end of November 1790. In February, three months after they arrived, John Hyde, despite his prior assurances, suddenly gave one month's notice and left at the end of March. Four months after that, in July 1790 the Hyde's opened a tavern in Philadelphia on 10th Street!

As soon as Hyde gave notice, Washington asked Lear to contact Sam in New York and invite him back saying he would *"be most welcome to rejoin"* the President's house. Lear was to ensure that, whoever the Steward hired, be told *"that it be understood that wine is not admissible at their Table; if it is so under any pretense whatsoever, it will terminate, as the permission given Hyde has done."* It appears that in addition to being poor managers, the Hyde's had abused his permission to have the best food and wine at the servant's table, and frugal Washington was not about to allow it to occur again.

Sam graciously agreed to come back. This must have taken some persuasion as he now had to close his profitable tavern and move his family to Philadelphia. He started as Steward again on May 12th, 1791, helped by a new housekeeper, Ann Emerson, a widow with 3 children who earned $133.33 per year. She was frugal and much appreciated by the Washington family. She and Samuel worked well together, and she supervised the house cleaners and washerwomen. Chef John Vicar, the uninspired cook, was still with the President's household when Sam came back. Washington noted in his letter to Lear to tell Sam that "*if upon trial he finds, as I am sure is the case, that we can do without Vicar, he may be discharged.*" Sam soon discharged Vicar and promoted Washington's slave Hercules to replace him.

Hercules had learned how to cook from Washington's long time slave cook Old Doll and became chief cook at the Mansion House Plantation by 1786. He was about 36 when Washington brought him to Philadelphia. He was described as "*a dark-brown man . . . possessed of great muscular power. The Steward and the whole household treated the chief cook with great respect....*"[139]

Detailed records, recently made available by Mount Vernon, supply a rare view into the sheer magnitude of his work. During the week of May 19th, for instance, the Mt. Vernon kitchen "*prepared 293 pounds of beef, 111 pounds of veal, 54 pounds of mutton, 129 pounds of lamb, 16 pounds of pork, calves' feet (for sweet colonial Jell-O), 44 chickens, 22 pigeons, 2 ducks, 10 lobsters, 98 pounds of butter, 32 dozen eggs, myriad fruits and vegetables, 3 half-barrels of beer, 20 bottles of porter, 9 bottles of "cyder," 2 bottles of Sauternes, 22 bottles of Madeira, 4 bottles of claret, 10 bottles of Champagne, and 1 twenty-eight-pound cheese.* Working in an 18th century kitchen was backbreaking, with heavy iron pots swinging on cranes, whole animals turning on spits, and tin reflector ovens beside the roasting-hot fires. Even the basic tasks, such as purifying sugar from large loaves, were a lengthy chore. But the meat – regularly more than a quarter-ton each week, give or take a pig – was an astounding amount for a staff of seven to butcher, boil, roast, or fry *into "fricaseys," "ragoos," pastry-wrapped "coffin crust" pies, and scallopini-like "collops" rolled "olive-style" around forcemeat."*

Hercules soon established a reputation in Philadelphia as a highly accomplished chef. He was treated as a favored servant by the Washington family and allowed unusual freedom for a slave. He would enter and leave the Executive Mansion through the front door, unlike tradesmen, who had to approach the kitchen. The Washington family gave him the rights to '*kitchen leavings*', the perk Samuel had used to assist the prisoners of war during the revolution. This supplied a nice income and was usually only bestowed on top chefs like James Hemmings. This perk is estimated to have earned Hercules about $200 per year, about the salary previously paid to Vicar, plus he was fed, clothed and housed for free. Hercules was soon quite well to do. He loved fine clothing and was known as quite a dandy. He was often rewarded with gifts from the Washington family, receiving tickets to plays and to the Circus, according to the Washington Account Books. He was given 3 bottles of rum after the death of his wife, Lame Alice, and he was allowed to bring his son, Richmond, to Philadelphia as a kitchen scullion and chimney sweep, despite the boy being considered a troublemaker. George Washington Parke Custis, Martha's grandson, who lived with the Washington family, remembers Hercules, known as 'Uncle Harkless' to him and his sister Nelly, ran his kitchen with great discipline.

Imagine the excitement and joy of this talented man, born a slave, reared in the deep country, suddenly living in the largest Abolitionist city in the country, walking the streets of Philadelphia with thousands of free blacks, seeing, smelling, and tasting wonderful food from all over the world. Hercules and the other Washington slaves certainly met and became friends with the many free blacks in Philadelphia. The Gradual Abolition Law passed in 1780 in Pennsylvania prohibited keeping slaves in the state for longer than 6 months and gave slaves the legal power to free themselves after 6 months residence there. The Quakers formed the Society for the Abolition of Slavery and there was a Free African Society active in the city to help them. By 1790, there were over 1800 free blacks in the city and only 273 black slaves, including Washington's.

When Congress agreed to move to Philadelphia, slavery became an issue. President Washington took the legal position that he was a resident of Virginia, in Philadelphia only temporarily, and that the Gradual Abolition law should not apply to him. However, to avoid any legal challenges, he simply rotated his slaves in and out of the state in 6 month cycles so they could not prove their 6 month residency. He recognized that his plan was a violation of the Pennsylvania law.

"I wish to have it accomplished under the pretext that may deceive both them (the slaves) and the public" Washington wrote to Lear. *"This advice may be known to none but yourself and Mrs. Washington."*

Of course, it didn't take long for the slaves to learn about the law and figure out why they were being moved back and forth every 6 months. They may have been illiterate, but they were not stupid.

James Hemmings, the well-known chef of Thomas Jefferson, had accompanied Jefferson to Paris where Jefferson paid for his apprenticeship to a French chef. His sister Sally Hemmings came over later with Jefferson's youngest daughter. James and Sally learned to speak and read French and could have stayed in Paris and been free, but Jefferson promised James his freedom if he would return and train others at Monticello to cook. Sally was promised that her children (with Jefferson) would be freed. So, both returned to Monticello with Jefferson in 1789 and Jefferson did eventually keep both promises.

James Hemmings, a gifted Paris trained chef, lived just blocks from the Executive Mansion in Philadelphia. Certainly, Hercules, James and Samuel exchanged ideas on cooking. Perhaps they taught Hercules to read and speak French since Sam and James were both fluent in it, and French was the language of fine cuisine. As these 3 men sat around a table getting to know one another and sharing their histories, surely the subject of freedom came up. James Hemmings was being paid for his work as a chef while waiting for the date of his emancipation. Jefferson's housekeeper, James' sister Sally, had been promised freedom for her children with Jefferson. Sam, his family, and most blacks in Philadelphia were all free. Massachusetts had abolished slavery. Slaves who fought for the English had been freed. Freedom was in the air everywhere but in the President's house.

293

1793 – Fevers

In March of 1793, Sam's son Andrew G. advertised in newspapers looking for a loan. Andrew had bought, on speculation discounted Treasury notes from the time when Morris encouraged wealthy financiers to supply funds for the war, hoping to redeem them for their full amount. When the Treasury refused to redeem his notes, it placed Andrew in a precarious financial position. He was, shortly afterward, terminated from his Treasury position during a Congressional cost cutting measure but, believing he was being singled out, began a personal feud with his former boss, Alexander Hamilton, Secretary of the Treasury. Hamilton's political opponents tried to use Andrew G. to prove corruption in the Treasury Department, drawing him deeper into their intrigue and encouraging him to continue his feud in the newspapers for their political gain, which soon ruined his reputation. Andrew G. Fraunces was described as "*a man of no principals, a drunkard and avaricious*" and this was by an ally. On April 3rd, 1793, Andrew, having lost a lawsuit against Hamilton, enlisted in the Artillery and Engineers and placed a notice in the newspapers that he had been "*driven from his family and lost everything and had no recourse*" but to do so. He apparently changed his mind or was kicked out, because on April 20th he announced he had opened a Notary Public office at his home at 60 Crown Street in New York City, where he offered to assist in suits against the Government, and on April 27th noted that he had moved to 44 Hanover Square.

In May he was again denied payment by the Treasury Department and on July 30th, he appealed directly to President Washington, leaving an angry letter with Samuel at the President's house in Philadelphia. We can only imagine Sam's embarrassment at having to present this letter from his son to the President. In August, Washington's secretary, Tobias Lear, replied to Andrew G. Fraunces from Philadelphia:

Sir:

The President of the United States has received your letter of the 30 July. The matter of it being of a serious nature, he has directed the Secretary of the Treasury to report to him in writing how far the representation is founded in facts and the reasons on his part for declining the payment of the warrants. But it is not expected that he can consistently with objects of more general concern, make his report till sometime in the ensuing week, in the course of which you will be informed of the result of your application.

I am yours – Tobias Lear, SPUS.[140]

During the summer of 1793, a yellow fever epidemic was raging up and down the east coast. Mrs. Washington, with grandchildren Wash and Nellie, went with Washington to the Deshler-Morris House in Germantown. Many cities would not allow refugees from Philadelphia and the city was effectively quarantined. It was believed that people of African descent were immune to yellow fever, based on their partial immunity to malaria, so overwhelmed doctors asked the Free African

Society in Philadelphia to help with nursing and removal of bodies. Hospitals would not admit anyone infectious, so the sick were moved to a square on 12th Street. It is estimated that well over 1000 people were buried in '*Congo Square*' (now Washington Square) including many of the blacks who had so generously responded when asked to help and who, it turned out, were just as susceptible as whites. That hot summer over 5000 people died, 10% of Philadelphia's population. The epidemic did not end until frost killed the mosquitos.

Sam and Mrs. Emerson were left in Philadelphia in charge of the Executive Mansion. Washington wrote to Sam to let him know that he had asked his officers to look in on them. A letter from Sam replied on Oct 23, 1793:

"Sir:

I received your letter last evening and it gives me the greatest satisfaction that my conduct meets your approbation. Was any accident to happen in the family it would not be for want of my care and attention. I strictly adhere to your directions in every event – the house is clean and ready for your return and everything in perfect order.

I long to see you home where I think you will be as safe as anywhere as our neighborhood is entirely clear of any infection. The fever still continues to abate in the city but rages in Southwark and other outposts.

You mention if any of the family should be taken ill to take advice, which cannot be done as there are no persons of any consequence left, but I hope we shall want none, as your direction is quite sufficient.

Several families however begin to return as it is thought they may with safety. I know that the President lent Mr. Osborn money and in consequence made an enquiry before I received your letter.

I found none but fifteen dollars with his effects and wife which she took to the hospital with her. His trunk and some of his clothes are here which I detained until I heard from you. The trunk is locked, what is in it I do not know.

Mrs. Emerson is well and gives her duty to Madam. She is much afflicted in spirits. Yr dutiful Serv…. Samuel Fraunces."[141]

William Osborne, the President's valet referred to here, had recently married and given notice that he planned to leave Washington's service to open a tavern in Philadelphia in October. He had asked for a loan of $200 from Washington and Washington had lent him $100. Unfortunately, William Osborn died of the fever in September before he could repay the debt. Ann Emerson was worried about her children. This is what Sam referred to in the above letter.

In October Sam's son Andrew G., continuing his public feud with Alexander Hamilton, published a pamphlet entitled *"An Appeal to the Legislature of the US on the Conduct of the Secretary of the Treasury"* demanding payment of the disputed Treasury Warrants and continued to send petitions to Congress about his case.

1794 – Retirement

In June 1794 Samuel Fraunces retired again as the Presidential Steward. There is no indication why, although it was apparently on good terms. After leaving the First Family, Samuel opened a tavern called the "Tavern Keeper" in Philadelphia. An ad in Philadelphia on July 17th, 1794, informed his friends and the public that he "*intends to open an Ordinary in his house in Second Street next door to the British Ministers #165 on Thursday the 17th of July where they may rely on every attention.*" He planned to offer "*Beefstakes and soup every day from 12 to 2, breakfasts in the morning and lodging for a few gentlemen by the year*". He also wanted "*a young man or woman of good character who understands kitchen work.*" Rooms were available for club meetings and catering was offered.

Sam bought a property with his son Andrew G. Fraunces who now lived in Philadelphia. It may be assumed that Samuel and Elizabeth paid for this house and perhaps gave it to Andrew. The large property on Filbert St near 3rd for which they paid $2000 in gold and silver coins, was sold to pay Andrew's debts in 1795.[142]

Samuel M. Fraunces, Samuel's youngest son, was still living in New York City, where he married Elizabeth Stevens on 5 Oct 1794 at

Trinity Church. Samuel M. opened an 'Intelligence Office' (a placement office) to supply clerks, barkeeps, wait-staff, servants, housemaids, wet nurses etc. His office was found at 7 Cortlandt Street near Broadway in New York. This was the same block where Sam and Elizabeth had run the Fraunces Tavern before moving to Philadelphia.

Sadly, Sam and Elizabeth's daughter Margaret Amelia (Fraunces) Battin died that year in New York at only 33 years of age, after the birth of her 4th child, Joseph Battin.

1795 – Death

On June 17th, 1795, Samuel placed an ad in the Philadelphia Gazette announcing a "move to 59 South Water Street of Fraunces Tavern from #166 South 2nd Street to a large and commodious house between Chestnut and Walnut streets lately occupied by Mr. Isaac Hazelhurst, on which he has spared no pains or expense to make it convenient and agreeable for the reception of gentlemen. This was the same site on which the noted 'Beef Steak and Punch House' formerly stood, has the advantage of the best water in the city, known long since by the name of Green Tree Water. There are several elegant rooms, sufficiently large to accommodate any society of company of gentlemen and from his well-known abilities to please in the line of his business, he flatters himself with a continuance of that patronage which he has experienced since he first opened a public house in this city and for which he begs leave to make a publick acknowledgement. For the accommodation of small parties, the large coffee room on the ground floor is conveniently fitted up with a number of boxes, constructed in such a manner as to admit gentlemen to be as private as they please – where may be had at any hour soups, beef-steaks, relishes &tc. He has on hand and will keep a constant supply of spirituous and malt liquors of the best qualities. Breakfasts provided, also dinners and suppers cooked in the most approved manner at short notice and pastry of all sorts, made to order in the house or to send out at any hour. He has several well-furnished bedchambers for Borders and Lodgers by the week, month or year. PS The large convenient stores and vaults underneath the house with the office above to be rented either separate or together"[143]

Samuel spared no expense on his new venue.[144] This was to be the pinnacle of his long career. The property was two buildings wide, at 59-61 Water St. plus a connected counting house and a large dry goods store. There was a fine kitchen, water pump and cistern connected to the Delaware River. He offered boxes (private booths) for small parties in the coffee room. Food was served at any hour, and he offered the finest liquors, and catering services. President Washington, foreign diplomats, and the wealthy of Philadelphia all dined there. His inn provided bedrooms with extremely handsome, mahogany furnishings and sparkling chandeliers. In his cellar were over 100 gallons of wine, and a stock of fine brandy and whisky. Sadly, Sam's new establishment had only been open only a few months when he died on Oct 10th, 1795. Sam's brief obituary simply said:

"DIED – On Saturday evening last, Mr. Samuel Fraunces, aged 73 years. – By his death society have sustained the loss of an honest man and the poor a valuable friend."

What a simple statement for a man who had accomplished so much.

Samuel Fraunces was interred on Oct 12th, 1795, in St Peter's Episcopal Church Cemetery at 3rd and Pine Street. His grave was unmarked until recently. There probably was a grave marker that was lost over time. His wife Elizabeth and their daughter Elizabeth and Atchison Thomson were all in Philadelphia. Samuel M., a successful business owner in NY, was named executor of his estate. Andrew was in Debtor's Prison, but Sam's other daughters were married to well off, socially prominent men. It is hard to imagine them not providing a headstone... After Sam's death his hotel property was listed for rent. Another of their properties on Filbert between 8th and 9th street was also sold.

Over the years there has been much speculation over Samuel Fraunces' race. The following genealogical research proves conclusively that Sam was of mixed race. When he was identified as a West Indian, the term was understood to mean a person of mixed race. He was noted as black by contemporary writers, specifically at the time of the Stamp Act riot when Vauxhall was damaged, and a contemporary letter referred to it as "the house where a black family had formerly resided". (Letter by E. Carther, 2 Nov 1765). He was widely referred to as "Black Sam". A Tory spy noted the Battery on Black Sam's Hill in 1776.[145] Washington's 1776 receipt for dinner at "Saml Frances, Alias Black Sam, for dinner, L3.14.0." The British occupiers called him 'Black Sam', noting his Majesty's Council had "a great dinner today at Black Sam's."[146] Tobias Lear called him 'Black Sam' in 1789, "We have engaged 'Black Sam' Frances as Steward and

Superintendent of the Kitchen." George Washington Parke Custis, grandson of Martha Washington, noted in his memoirs that Sam was "commonly known as 'Black Sam' because of his dark complexion". A news article in 1832 noted that he was called 'Black Sam' from the "swarthy embrowned hue of his complexion" and commented that he was a witty and good humored host. It is clear from these early references that Sam was recognized as black in his lifetime.

Elizabeth Dally was a white woman. Their older children married white spouses from prominent families and records noted them as white. But the most important evidence is Sam's youngest children.

The youngest children, Samuel M., Sophia (Fraunces) Gomez and possibly Hannah Louise Fraunces were always identified as Black. Samuel M's descendants all identified as Black. Sophia married a Black man and was identified as Black as were her children. Hannah appeared late in life with a great nephew and identified as Black. The only possibility for Black descendants is that Samuel was of mixed race.

Sam risked his fortune, family, and his life to support the Patriot cause, serving for years as a spy. He saved many prisoners from starvation, supplying a safe house and money for those who could escape.

He saved Washington's life twice, literally changing the course of the Revolution.

He overcame racial prejudice when slavery was still the law of the land, and the President he served owned slaves.

He is remembered at the reconstruction of his Fraunces Tavern in Manhattan. Philadelphia too has finally honored him. In 2010 his name, birth and death dates were engraved on a large pillar at St Peter's Cemetery where he is buried. Sam's story, and those of the slaves who served Washington at the Presidents House, will finally be told at the Liberty Bell National Park.

Samuel Fraunces was a proud and successful hero, and he deserves to be remembered and honored for his contributions to America.

307

Fraunces Genealogy

Elizabeth Dally

Elizabeth Gifford Dally married Samuel Fraunces on November 30th, 1757, at Trinity Church in New York. Born about 1740, and baptized in New York City, she came from a long line of wealthy Dutch settlers in Manhattan. Her parents were Hendrick Dally (1716-1756) and Sarah Gifford (1718-1784).

Paternal grandparents Nicholas Dally (1680-1722) and Elizabeth Creiger (1678-1718) married in 1702 in New Amsterdam colony where both were born.[147] In 1703 they lived in the East Ward of Manhattan.

Paternal great-grandparents Jan Madou Dally (1650-1708) and Elizabeth Obee (1652-1700) married in 1668 in the Dutch Reformed Church in New Amsterdam. Elizabeth was a daughter of Hendrick Hendrickszen Obee and Aeltje Claes. The Obees lived in Block G, #8 house in NYC on Costello Map of 1660 on the East Side of Broadway. They were among the earliest settlers in New Amsterdam where Hendrick Obee became the Excise Collector. In 1685 John and Elizabeth (Obee) Dally sold his father's Staten Island property to Paulus Richards for 82 L 4 Shillings and took a 7 year lease at 4L 2 shillings and 6 pence per year. His son John remained on Staten Island until his death there in 1708.

Paternal great-great-grandfather Jean D'Ally (1615-1691) from Tournai, Belgium, a Huguenot, married Marguerite Madou (1688-1691) at the French Church of London. Moved to Staten Island,

Richmond County NY in 1677. In 1677 the Dally tract was mentioned in a land patent for John Dally. In 1691 he was elected to first NY Assembly representing Staten Island, with a large Huguenot settlement. The tract fronted on the bay. He built a house, barn, and stables on the property. At his death in 1691, his wife's name was erased from his will (because she was near death), and Nicholas Bayard was named Executor. Bayard was his chief creditor. Most of his wealth had been lost in the wars in Maine before his move to Staten Island. Margaret Madou Dally died the same year as her husband.

Paternal great-great-great grandfather was Simon Dally (D'Ailli) from Tourai, Hainault, Belgium. This family was originally from the Somme Valley in Picardy, France and can be traced back to Robert d'Ailli in 1090.

Maternal grandparents of Elizabeth Gifford Dally Fraunces (1740-1811) were John Parker Gifford (1698-1742) and Catherine Borrows (1691-1741).

Maternal great-grandparents were William Gifford (1675-1723) and Sarah 'Sary' Parker. William was born in Long Branch, New Jersey and died in Manasquan, Monmouth, NJ.

Maternal great-great grandparents were Hananiah Gifford (1646-1709) and Elizabeth Wardell (1645-1729).

After Samuel died in Philadelphia, Elizabeth (Dally) Fraunces moved back to Manhattan and in 1798 opened a restaurant in the Columbia Hotel with her son-in-law, Cornelius Smock at 12 Water

Street.[148] She was about 58 and had been successfully running restaurants on her own for years.

Elizabeth was a full partner with Samuel in life and in business. In addition to raising their children and schooling them, she managed the Queen's Head, Vauxhall and Hampden Hall and their other taverns for extensive periods, maintaining a superb reputation for fine food and excellent service.

As we can see from her family lineage, Elizabeth was 100% white.

Children

Sam and Elizabeth's children were named in his will, probated in Philadelphia. Their older children appear to have been light enough to pass for white. They married white spouses and they, and their children, primarily identified as white although several were occasionally noted as '*mulatto*' or '*dark complexion*'. But records show that the 3 youngest of Sam and Elizabeth's children and their descendants were always identified as '*Black*' or '*Mulatto*' during their lifetimes. Samuel and Elizabeth (Dally) Fraunces had the following children:

1. **Andrew Dally Gautier Fraunces** (1759-1806) married Sarah Pye (1766-1825)

2. **Margaret Amelia Dally Fraunces** (1761-1793) married John Battin (1751-1852)

3. **Elizabeth Dally Fraunces** (1765-1820) married Acheson Thompson II (1760-1830)

4. **Catherine Dally Fraunces** (1768-1825) married Cornelius Smock (1761-1836)

5. **Sarah Dally Fraunces** (1773-1861) married Thomas Charles Campbell (1755-1822)

6. **Samuel M. Dally Fraunces** (1774-?) married Elizabeth Stevens (1777-?) *both identified as black*

7. **Sophia Dally Fraunces** (1776-?) married John Gomez (1770-?) *both identified as black*

8. **Hannah Louisa Dally Fraunces** (1784-after 1795) *named in Samuel's will.*

1 – Andrew Gautier Dally Fraunces (1759-1806)

Andrew Gautier Fraunces, Sam and Elizabeth's first child, married Sarah Pye (1766-1825) from a prominent white family. He served in the NY Militia and went to work at the Treasury Dept. after the war. He bought discounted Treasury Bonds, gambling that he would make a profit, but went bankrupt when payment was denied. He engaged in a very public feud with Alexander Hamilton, encouraged by Hamilton's adversaries, accusing Hamilton of illegal acts in newspapers, and demanding a congressional hearing. When Congress determined he had no case, he published accusations that Congress was rigged and was sued for defamation.

Well-educated, Andrew G worked as a Notary Public and Attorney, filing suits and handling real estate contracts, moving offices every few months, probably as he became arrears in rent. He and Sarah moved in Sept 1794 to a house in Elizabethtown, New Jersey where he ran a grocery store and Conveyance Office and let out part of the house for dancing classes. This house was a property his parents had deeded to AG and Sarah in 1792. He was sentenced to a year in debtor's prison in New Jersey in May 1795, being still incarcerated for over a year during which his father died. He advertised asking friends for 'any relief' they could offer. All his property was sold to pay off his debts. He took the family and returned to Manhattan and opened a Notary Office at 6 Lombard Street behind New City Tavern in 1796.

In 1797 he published an apology and retraction of his charges against Hamilton. That spring, Andrew and Sarah's infant son was killed when a nurse dropped baby William from the 2nd story window of 73 Liberty Street. Oddly, there was no further mention of this tragedy or prosecution of the nurse. Andrew issued a public advertisement of thanks for support during the *'tragic time'*, also requesting business. Later that year, despite his earlier apology, he published another letter accusing Hamilton of defaming him.

In 1798 congress refused his last appeal for payment.

Andrew G. died in 1806 at the age of 47 in New York City, still obsessed with resentment against Hamilton. His first burial was at the Cemetery of the Dutch Reformed Church. His remains were moved to Green-Wood Cemetery in Brooklyn, NY with his baby son William Martin Fraunces (1796-1796) and his sister Catherine Fraunces Smock (1768-1825).

Sarah Pye (1764-1825) was born in 1764 to David Pye, Esq. (1724-1805), a lawyer and surveyor from an important family in England and his wife Mary Martine (1740-1783). David was an early founder of the town of Clarkstown, Rockland County, NY on the west side of the Hudson River and a staunch Patriot. He owned cloth mills, weaving, and dying businesses and lots of land, so Sarah grew up in a wealthy, elegant household. Sarah Pye and Andrew Fraunces likely met at the peace negotiations at the DeWint house in Tappan in May 1783. David Pye and his family were among the 30 guests invited to the

DeWint House to meet Gen. Washington. Sam Fraunces was catering this peace meeting.

Andrew and Sarah married about 1784. Sarah's father did not approve. When David wrote his will in 1794 (8 years after their marriage and 10 years before he died) he disowned Sarah, leaving her only 24 shillings *'to be paid from the sum then owed to him by her husband Andrew G. Fraunces'*. Andrew was in Debtor's Prison when David Pye wrote his will, and 30 year old Sarah had 5 children to support on her own, so this was a very harsh repudiation. Sarah's brothers received large tracts of land and prosperous businesses and her sister Ann received over *L*100 in addition to a life estate in the family home.

Following AGs release from Debtor's Prison, their young son, William Martin Pye Fraunces, was tragically killed when dropped by a nurse from a 2nd story window in 1797. Her last child was born just months later.

These hard years for Sarah continued with the death of her husband Andrew in 1806 and the death of another son George Washington Fraunces in 1809 of yellow fever, on a trip to the West Indies. Her son David Pye Fraunces moved first to Cooperstown, NY and then to Philadelphia where he was a bookbinder. Son Andrew Gifford Pye Fraunces married and moved to Pennsylvania. Sarah moved in with her youngest child, Eliza and her wealthy husband, Nathanial Gardiner in Manhattan. She died in 1825 after a short illness at the age of 63 and her funeral was held from the Gardiner home at 54 Dey St. in NY City.

She was originally buried in the Dutch Reformed Churchyard and later re-interred in Greenwood Cemetery. Andrew and Sarah Pye Fraunces had the following children – all identified as white:

1.1. David Pye Fraunces, Sr. (1780-after 1852) son of Andrew and Sarah (Pye) Fraunces, opened a bookstore and bindery in Cooperstown, NY in 1808. He was in the Delaware Militia in 1812. He was last noted when he placed an ad, trying to find his sister, Mary Marguerite (Fraunces) McBride in Philadelphia in 1852. He and his family always identified as white. His children included:

1.1.1 David Pye Fraunces Jr. (1825-1865), the only positively identified child of David P. Fraunces Sr., was described as an indentured servant, '*dark complexion*', in an ad when he ran away from a Straw Hat maker in 1838 in Philadelphia. He married Harriet Harvey and had 2 children – all identified as white:

1.1.2 Sarah Ann Eliza Fraunces (1826-?) possible daughter of David P Fraunces Sr. married Edward Bates, a band box maker (1820-?) in Philadelphia in 1845. They were last found in 1860 census, identified as white.

1.2 Andrew Gifford Pye Fraunces II (1787-1831) married an unknown wife. His children were born in Pennsylvania and Delaware. No census records were found so racial identification is unknown. His 3 children identified as white:

1.2.1 George Washington 2 (1815-1898) married Mary J and had 6 children. He moved to Washington DC where he was a bookbinder. They lived at 648 A St NE.

1.2.2 Andrew Gifford Pye Fraunces III (1818-1881) was born in Delaware. He enlisted in St. Louis, MO on 18 Dec 1843, and was described as 25, with '*dark complexion*', dark eyes and dark hair, 5'8" tall. He never married. He moved to Tuolumne, CA in 1852 and was committed to the State Insane Asylum in 1880 where he presumably died. Official records noted him as white.

1.2.3 Joseph Pye Fraunces (1825-1881) married Eliza Post in NY City on 31 May 1841. He worked as a house painter and lived in the Fordham area. They had 6 children, and all identified as white in census records.

1.3 Unnamed Child of Andrew Gautier and Sarah Pye died at 8 months old.

1.4 George Washington Pye Fraunces 1 (1789-1809), son of Andrew Gautier and Sarah (Pye) Fraunces, died at the age of 20 in 1809 in St. Bartholomew, West Indies of yellow fever. He never married. No racial identity noted.

1.5 Mary Margaretta Pye (Fraunces) McBride (1793-?) was baptized in New York in 1793. She was the daughter of Andrew G and Sarah (Pye) Fraunces. She apparently became estranged from her family after her marriage to a man named McBride. Her brother David

Pye, Sr. tried to locate her in 1852 when he placed an ad *"seeking Mary M. McBride (formerly Fraunces) will hear something much to her advantage by calling on her brother, David P. Fraunces at Altemus Bookbinder in Philadelphia. Reward for information to locate Mary"*.[149] Nothing further was found for her. No racial information found.

1.6. William Martin Pye Fraunces (1796-1797) son of Andrew G and Sarah (Pye) Fraunces, died at 7 months old when he was dropped from a 2nd story window in New York by his nurse. He is buried in Green-Wood Cemetery in Brooklyn with his father.

1.7. Elizabeth 'Eliza' Stensin Pye (Fraunces) Gardiner (1797-1842) daughter of Samuel G and Sarah (Pye) Fraunces married Nathanial Gardiner (1792-1856) of a prominent white family descended from Lion Gardiner who arrived in America in 1635. It is she who passed down the etching of her grandfather, Samuel Fraunces, mentioned earlier in the book, to her descendants. Her mother Sarah (Pye) Fraunces lived with Eliza and Nathanial Gardiner at 54 Dey Street in NY City at the time of her death at 63. They all identified as white. Eliza and Nathanial Gardiner had 4 children – all identified as white:

1.7.1 John Bray Fraunces Gardiner (1821-1881) attorney, never married

1.7.2 William Henry Fraunces Gardiner (1822-1879) physician, unmarried

1.7.3 Mary Fraunces Gardiner (1825-1836) died at 11

1.7.4 Elizabeth Dayton Fraunces Gardiner (1831-1916) married Isaac Hartshorn had 3 children – all identified as white:

1.7.4.1 Nella W Hartshorn (1853-1926) never married

1.7.4.2 Edith Bucklin Hartshorn (1855-1906) married Arthur L. Mason (1852-?) and inherited the etching

1.7.4.3 Gardiner Hartshorn (1857-1858) died at 1

2 – Margaret Amelia Dally (Fraunces) Battin (1761-1794)

Margaret was the 2nd child of Sam and Elizabeth (Dally) Fraunces. Her wedding announcement noted her as the 27 year old daughter of Samuel Fraunces of John Street, when she married John Battin (1751-1852) in Trinity Church. John was a British soldier who stayed behind after the Revolution. He owned a succession of taverns becoming quite well to do. In 1813 he offered 3 properties for lease, a boarding house at 41 Nassau, a house as 39 Hudson with a river view and 29 Warren St. Margaret died at the age of 33 following the birth of her last child, Joseph Fraunces Battin. John Battin married again after Margaret died and had 4 more children. He died, a well-known and beloved character, at the age of 101 at his home on Greenwich St in New York City. Margaret and John Battin had the following 3 children – all identified as white:

2.1. - **John Fraunces Battin** (1789-1826) oldest son of Margaret and John Battin fought in the War of 1812 and married Catherine Beekman in 1813. He partnered with Peckwell in the Broadway House Tavern in New York City, corner of Broadway and Grand. He died in 1826 at the age of 37 after a lingering illness (probably consumption). Catherine also died of consumption in 1836. He and Catherine Beekman had the following children – all identified as white:

2.1.1 – Sarah A Battin (1796-1876) never married

2.1.2 – Margaret B Battin (1815-1836) consumption at 21

2.1.3 – Amelia Battin (1816-1835) of consumption at 19

2.1.4 –William B Battin (1820-1868) Civil War vet, moved to Burns, Allegany, NY where he is buried

2.1.5 – Elizabeth Battin, died young

2.1.6 – John E Battin, died young

2.2 - Amelia Sarah Fraunces (Battin) Edgar (1792-between 1870-1880) 2nd child of John and Margaret (Fraunces) Battin, married Thomas Edgar (1790-1849) in 1825 in NY City and moved to Woodbridge, NJ. Thomas died in 1849 and in 1850 Amelia (60) and her 3 children, Thomas E (21), Anna A (20) and Henrietta L (18), lived on their farm. In 1860, Amelia, Anna and Henrietta Edgar were living with the Thomas M. (32) and Martha Marshall (40) family in Woodbridge, NJ. Amelia died between 1870 and 1880. Her 3 children were:

2.2.1 Thomas E Battin Edgar (1829-1906) Amelia's son Thomas moved to Massachusetts where he died in 1906. He identified as white.

2.2.2 Anna Battin (Edgar) Wood (1830-1880) In the 1870 census Amelia and Henrietta Edgar lived with her oldest daughter, Theodore and Anna (Edgar) Wood, all white. Anna Edgar Wood died in 1880 and left the property which she and her sister Henrietta had inherited from their parents to her children. Amelia Battin Edgar and all her descendants identified as white.

2.2.3 Henrietta L Battin Edgar In 1855, Amelia (63) and Henrietta (23) Edgar were living with the John H. and Mary M. (Battin) Hedley family in Southfield, Richmond, NY. Mary was Amelia's stepsister (daughter of her father John's 2nd wife).

2.3 – Henrietta Louisa Fraunces (Battin) Tuthill married Theodore M Tuthill (1823-1905) and had 3 children:

2.3.1 Catherine Eliza Battin Tuthill (1847-1905) did not marry.

2.3.2 Alice Courtney Battin (Tuthill) Mott (1850-1900) married George Henry Mott and had 3 children. All identified as white.

2.3.3 Daniel Edgar Battin Tuthill (1853-1899) married Anna S Hedley and had 1 son. All identified as White.

2.4 - Joseph Fraunces Battin (1793-abt 1894) opened a drygoods store with his father. His store at 200 6th Avenue specialized in men's hosiery. He lived at 28 Bank Street. He never married. He was identified as white.

3 – Elizabeth Dally (Fraunces) Thompson(1765-bef 1820)

Elizabeth was the 3rd child of Sam and Elizabeth (Dally) Fraunces, born on 26 Dec 1765 in Philadelphia and baptized at Christ Church there. Several records noted that she was *'dark complexioned',* but she was identified as white in official records.

She married Acheson Dick Thompson (1760-1830) in 1789 in Trinity Church in NYC and they owned restaurants and inns. They took care of George Morgan White Eyes for several years supporting him when the US Congress refused to allocate the money promised to him after the murders of his parents. He was educated at Yale and forced to leave before his graduation due to the lack of funds.

Elizabeth and Acheson moved to Philadelphia in 1793 and were there when her father, Samuel Fraunces, died. Acheson was a Mason in Lodge 59 in Philadelphia in 1797 and in 1810 both were registered in the Universalist Church which was vigorously anti-slavery. Acheson was a popular man, owning taverns/inns that catered to seamen. Several made him their executor and heir. He was a character witness for Simon Sparks at his naturalization in 1805. Sparks later married Acheson's mother and left him a small estate when he died. Acheson's tavern in 1809 was at the corner of Front and South St. in Philadelphia in the Southwark Ward. Elizabeth died after the 1810 census and before 1820 when Acheson was noted as a widower. They had 6 children:

3.1 - Sarah Fraunces Thompson (1790-1798) was born 2 May 1790 and baptized 14 July 1790 in New York City at Trinity Church.

Witnesses were Samuel M. Fraunces and Sarah (Fraunces) Campbell, her maternal aunt and uncle. She died of yellow fever.

3.2 - Maria Fraunces Thompson (1793-?) was born 26 Oct 1793 in Philadelphia and baptized at Christ Church in April 1797. A Maria D Anners signed seaman certification papers for 16 year old George Harrison Thompson in 1821. By this date, their parents were both deceased. However, Maria Fraunces Thompson was NOT married to Thomas S. Anners. Thomas married Mary Frances Reed, confirmed by marriage docs and will. His son Henry F. Anners married Jeannette Ferguson. The info on FindAGrave is NOT CORRECT. Maria may have married an Anners but it was NOT this Anners family of Philadelphia.

3.3 Samuel Acheson Fraunces Thompson (1796-1851) did not marry.

3.3 - Anna Moore Fraunces Thompson (1798-?) was not conclusively found after baptism at Christ Church, June 1799 in Philadelphia.

3.4 - Allen Acheson Cunningham Fraunces Thompson (1801-1851) married Adeline Morgan (1806-1857) and lived in Washington, DC where he was a printer. He died of consumption at the age of 51 in 1801 and is buried in Congressional Cemetery with his wife and Josephine Whiting Thompson, his grandchild, the youngest child of his son David and America Thompson. He lived on F Street between 13th and 14th Streets. He and Adeline had 7 children, and all identified as white.

3.4.1 unknown Morgan Thompson (1830-1830)

3.4.2 Annie Elizabeth Morgan (Thompson) Griffith (1832-aft 1920) married George Washington Griffith (1853-1901). They had 1 child, Charles, and all identified as white.

3.4.3 Allen Morgan Thompson (1833-1876) born in DC was also a bookbinder. He named his brother George W Thompson as his next of kin. He was in a home for disabled soldiers when he was just 40 because of rheumatism. He never married. married. He died in Millcreek, VA 2 March 1876 and his body was sent to Baltimore for burial. Identified as white.

3.4.4 Ellen Adelia Morgan (Thompson) Couch (1840-1892) married Alfred F. Couch and moved to Great Barrington, Berkshire, Mass. They had no children. They identified as white.

3.4.5 George Washington Morgan Thompson (1844-aft 1928) married Catherine (born in Germany) and had 2 children. They lived in DC where he worked at the Treasury. Then moved to Baltimore where he opened a restaurant before 1880. He remained in Baltimore and died aft 1928. They identified as white.

3.4.6 David A Morgan Thompson (1845-1904) married Laura America Maddox and had 9 children. They remained in DC where he worked as a bookbinder and worked at the Government Printing Office. He died of a stroke. Identified as white.

3.4.7 Alice Adeline Morgan Thompson (1849-aft 1919) never married. Worked as a clerk and lived at 218 Maryland Ave NE.

3.5 - James Calvin Fraunces Thompson (1803-?) was born in Philadelphia.

3.6 - George Harrison Fraunces Thompson (1805-) was a mariner and noted in a seaman's application as short (5'2") with dark hair, black eyes and a '*swarthy complexion*'. His Seaman's Certificate was signed by a Maria D. Anners. His sister Maria Thompson is NOT married to Thomas S Anners of Philadelphia. He married Mary Frances Reed. Thomas's son, Henry Francis Anners, married Jeannette Ferguson. Marriage records and wills prove those connections. Maria Thompson may have married an Anners, but it was not of this Philadelphia family.

4 – Catherine Dally (Fraunces) Smock (1768-1825)

Catherine was the 4th child of Sam and Elizabeth (Dally) Fraunces, born on 26 Jan 1768 in Philadelphia and in 1787 married Cornelius J. Smock (1761-1836), son of Johannes John Barnes Luyster Smock (1727-1811) and Femmetje 'Phebe' Cornelius Folkerts Teunison (1735-1778) a prominent Monmouth, New Jersey Patriot family. Cornelius, his father, brother, and uncle all fought in Revolution for the NJ militia. The family homestead was in New Jersey, but they also had a home in Brooklyn, NY. Samuel's widow, Elizabeth (Dally) Fraunces, lived with her daughter, Catherine Fraunces (1768-1825) and Cornelius J. Smock after Samuel died. They ran the Columbia Hotel in New York City in 1798, noting that Elizabeth Fraunces was experienced in tavern keeping. Catherine Fraunces Smock died at the age of 53 in Brooklyn and was buried from the home of her son Andrew, 9 Elizabeth St. She and Cornelius, who died in 1836, are buried in Green-Wood Cemetery in Brooklyn, NY. Catherine and Cornelius had 6 children – all identified as white:

4.1.- Andrew Fraunces Smock (1788-1827) was born in NY City, married Hannah Simons at Trinity Church in NYC. His mother Catherine was living with him a 9 Elizabeth St. when she died in 1825. He died of consumption in 1827 at the age of 39 at the same home at 9 Elizabeth St. in New York City. He had been a butcher. Andrew F and Hannah had 2 sons – all identified as white:

331

4.1.1 – Andrew F. Smock Jr. (1824-1844) died of a long severe illness (consumption?) at the age of 20. His funeral was also from the 9 Elizabeth St. house in NY.

4.1.2 – Paul H Smock (1827-1870) married Anna Jane Goble (1832) in New Jersey in 1852 and had 6 children. he died at 41 and is buried at Riverside Cemetery in Tom's River, Ocean County, NJ.

4.2 - Elizabeth Fraunces (Smock) Schenck (1789-1855) Elizabeth the 2nd child of Cornelius and Catherine (Fraunces) Smock, was baptized at Trinity Church in NYC in Oct 1789. She was 19 in 1808 when she married Peter Coert Voorhees Schenck, 33, (son of Courtenius (Coert) Schenck and Sarah Voorhees) and became stepmother to the 5 children of his first wife Sarah Shepherd: Sarah (1791-1805), Elisha (1794-1871), Peter (1797-?), Gitty (1802-1876), and Henry (1805-1891). Peter V. was a Revolutionary War hero. The Schenck and Smock families were early NJ settlers and frequently intermarried.

In the 1830 census Peter V Schenck was noted with 1 white male under 5 (son of Elizabeth born 1825?), 1 Male 20-29 (Henry), 1 white male 50-59 (Peter), 1 white female 20-29 (Gitty), 1 Female 40-49 (2nd wife Elizabeth) and a *'free colored male'* under 10 and a *'free colored female'* 10-23. Peter and Elizabeth identified as white. The *free colored male* remained with them through the 1840 census where Peter, Elizabeth, a female 15-19 (Elizabeth's daughter born 1821?) and a free colored male 10-23 were listed. In the 1850 Census Peter and Elizabeth are still in Freehold and Henry lived adjacent. Elizabeth died in 1855 and Peter in 1857. They are buried in Maplewood Cemetery, Freehold, NJ. There do not appear to be any children of Elizabeth's buried there and no birth records were found, although it is believed that she had a girl in 1821 and a boy in 1825.

Note: There were many *Black* Schencks/Schancks in the Monmouth, NJ area, possibly descendants of freed slaves who had taken the Schenck/Schanck name. Several *Black* Schencks appear adjacent to or living with members of the extended Fraunces family in several census records.

4.3 – Phoebe Fraunces (Smock) Rogers (1792-1848) was the 3rd child of Cornelius J and Catherine (Fraunces) Smock. Born in 1792 she was baptized in Freehold/Monmouth. She married Elihu Mount Rogers (1787-1852) a waterman in 1811 in Monmouth, NJ. She died in Nov 1848 and is buried with Elihu in Holy Trinity Lutheran Memorial Church, Manasquan, Monmouth County, NJ. Elihu died in 1852. Both identified as white. They had the following 5 children – all identified as white:

4.3.1. Cornelius Elihu Smock Rogers (1816-1866) was a wood merchant. He married Susan A Smock Eldridge and they had 2 daughters Catherine Cornelius Eldridge Rogers Osborne and Cornelia Cornelius Eldridge Rogers Palmer. They all identified as white.

4.3.2. John Elihu Smock Rogers (1817-1890) worked as a farmer before he went to sea. He became a Captain and amassed a

333

fortune. He married Sarah Moore Jackson in 1846 and had 9 children. They all identified as white.

4.3.3. Elihu Smock Rogers Jr. (1819-?) identified as white fisherman was (31) and living with Hannah Brooks (60) *Black* in the 1850 census. They shared a property with the Lewis Cay family, also *Black*.

4.3.4. Andrew F. Elihu Smock Rogers (1821-1908) married Mary C. Eldrige (1827-1893). Eldridge family members also married Cornelius Rogers, and his brother Andrew Rogers. Aunt, Catherine Amelia Smock, married George W Eldridge. Andrew was a grocer. They and their 6 children identified as white.

4.3.5 Susan Ann Rogers (1826-1827)

4.4 – Catherine Amelia Fraunces (Smock) Eldridge (1793-?), 4th child of Cornelius and Catherine (Fraunces) Smock, married George W. Eldrige (1790-1867) in 1809 in Trinity Church. Catherine, widow of George, was in Manhattan from 1867-1880 in directories but no census records were located denoting race. George W is buried in Green-Wood Cemetery in Brooklyn. Catherine is not noted as buried with him.

4.4.1 Susan A Smock (Eldridge) Rogers (1820-bef 1866) married Cornelius Rogers (1816-1866) a first cousin, the son of Elihu Rogers and her mother's sister, Phebe Fraunces Smock in New York in 1842. In 1850 census in Brooklyn, they were identified as white, and Cornelius was a wood merchant. They lived in Monmouth, NJ where both died. His brothers John S and Andrew F were executors of his will.

4.5 - Margaret Fraunces (Smock) Dibble (1794-1820) married David John Slason Dibble (1790-1826) in 1812. David was a shoemaker. His father John Dibble fought in the American Revolution. They had 4 children. All identified as white.

4.6 – George Washington Fraunces Smock (1806-1852) 6th child of Cornelius and Catherine (Fraunces) Smock, married Mary Ann Floor and had 5 children. He was a butcher in Manhattan. He and Mary Ann are buried in Green-Wood Cemetery in Brooklyn. They and their descendants all identified as white.

4.7 – Cornelius A. Fraunces Smock (1812-1842) 7th child of Cornelius and Catherine (Fraunces) Smock had a difficult life. His mother died when he was 14. His brother Andrew died when he was 16 and his father died when he was 25. He had been suffering from consumption (TB) for several years and committed suicide with laudanum. Family confiscated the first bottle he brought home, so he went out and bought another and drank it at once. He immediately fell ill and was brought home where he soon died. He was 30. News accounts mention a wife, but she was not named. His funeral was held from the 9 Elizabeth St. house in NY City.

5 – Sarah Dally (Fraunces) Campbell (1773-1861)

Sarah was the 5th child of Sam and Elizabeth (Dally) Fraunces, born and baptized in New York. She married Thomas Charles Campbell (1755-1826), the older widowed business partner of her father when she was 16. TC and Elizabeth had helped run the taverns with Samuel until the English occupied Manhattan. TC Campbell owned a linens store at 87 Maiden Lane. After his death, Sarah moved in with her only child, daughter Marie Campbell Dow. Sarah died in 1861 and is buried in the Trinity Churchyard in Manhattan. Sarah and Thomas Campbell had only one child:

5.1. Marie Fraunces (Campbell) Dow (1804-1887) married John Hall Dow in 1826 at the age of 22. Her husband was 42. They 8 children before her husband died, leaving Marie a widow. Her mother Sarah moved in to help care for the children. A relative of John Dow from Scotland, William and his son William (7) were also living with her in 1850. They lived at 125 E 12th Street. By 1860 Maria had moved to 231 E 35th St and opened a boarding house with 10 guests, 2 servants, her mother, a married daughter, Sarah Campbell Berdan, and her unmarried children. Maria then moved to 159 West 23rd St by 1880 and was still running a boarding house. She then moved in with daughter Sarah Berdan. She is buried at Green-Wood Cemetery. All identified as white.

6 - Samuel M. Dally Fraunces (1774 - ?)

Samuel M. was the 6th child and 2nd son of Sam and Elizabeth (Dally) Fraunces. Samuel M. and his descendants were always identified as *Mulatto* or *Black*. In the first census in New York in 1790, he was almost certainly the *'black slave'* noted in the home of his father, Samuel. Since his white mother probably gave the information, the dark child was probably assumed to be a slave by the census taker. All the children except Samuel M. were noted in this census.

In August of 1794, Samuel M. opened an 'Intelligence Office', a placement service for wait staff, barkeepers, maids and servants at 7 Cortlandt St. near Broadway in NYC.[150] Most of these clients would have been white.

Samuel M. married Elizabeth Stevens (1777-?) on 5 October 1794 at Trinity Church in New York. Her parents are not known, and Stevens is such a common name that it is almost impossible to verify without further information.

When Samuel Fraunces Sr. died in Philadelphia in 1975, Samuel M. was named executor of his father's estate and guardian (with Thomas Armstrong Esq.) for his minor sisters Sophia and Hannah. At this time, he and Elizabeth moved to Philadelphia to settle Sam's affairs and apparently continued to run the tavern at 59 South Water Street in Philadelphia. On December 21, 1795, he offered a property of Sam's at public auction in Philadelphia. It was a 3 story brick house on the south side of Filbert Street between 8th and 9th St., adjoining the land office. The house built *'in modern fashion with as many conveniences*

339

as any house of similar dimensions in the city', included a handsome garden with trees vines, shrubs, a brick coach house and stables for 2 horses with a 9 foot alley and court leading to them. It had a mortgage of *L*500 on it and was leased until the 10th of October 1796, after which the purchaser could have possession. It did not sell and was offered again on 5 April 1796.

Sam M. also owned a livery stable in Philadelphia in July 1796, located on Lombard between 2nd and 3rd Streets, and advertised a Real Estate Brokerage office on 63 South 3rd Street in Philadelphia with a partner, John Van Reed.[151]

In June 1797 Samuel M. had a real estate office at 147 Chestnut Street in Philadelphia, handling judgement bonds, mortgages and notes and advertised that he could draw conveyances and deeds, articles of agreement and partnerships, bills of sale, and leases.

In 1830, Samuel M and his wife Elizabeth were living with their oldest daughter Elizabeth 'Betsy' (Fraunces) de Hart and her husband John DeHart, their 2 sons and several other free colored persons on Staten Island in Castleton, Richmond, NY. It appears that Hannah Louisa Dally Fraunces may have been there as well.as there is a free colored female of appropriate age in the census with them.

Samuel's wife, Betsey, was in the 1840 NY Ward 5 census, as the head of a household with 3 *Free Colored Males* 24-36 (sons John, Joseph and William), 1 *Free Colored Female* 24-36 (Hannah Louisa Dally Fraunces?) and 1 *Free Colored Female* 36-55 (Betsey). Her oldest son, Samuel III, lived next door with his wife Caroline (Sands)

Fraunces. They were also next door to Sophia Dally Fraunces Gomez. All were identified as *free colored persons*.

In 1850 Betsey (Stevens) Fraunces (70) was again living with her daughter Betsy and her husband John DeHart, a fireman, and their children in Ward 8, District 1, of New York. All were identified as *Black*.

In 1857 she was listed in the NY directory as Elizabeth (*Colored*) widow of Samuel, residence at 17 Marion St. She was at that same location in 1870 when she was 90. Samuel M. and Elizabeth 'Betsey' (Stevens) Fraunces had the following children:

6.1. – Elizabeth 'Betsy' Stevens (Fraunces) De Hart (1805-?) married John DeHart I about 1825. John Dehart was the son of Sam DeHart a slave born in the Daniel De Hart family and later given to his wife's family member, John Mersereau. Sam's wife, John's mother, was Betty Cruzer born a slave in the home of Cornelius Cruzer (Croeser). Cornelius willed Betty and all her children (including John) to John Mersereau who owned her husband Sam De Hart in 1807. Ironically a descendant of the Mersereau family, an architect named William H. Mersereau from Staten Island, was hired to lead the restauration of Fraunces Tavern in 1905. A Gradual Emancipation Act was passed in NY that said that all children born after July 4, 1799, would be free but indentured until 28 (women until 25). Slaves born before that date however remained enslaved. In 1827 a new law passed that freed those born before 1799 on July of that year. John was indentured until 1827. His older brother Nicholas 'Claus' born before

341

the proclamation, was not freed until 1827. He was the last slave freed on Staten Island. Elizabeth and John were always identified as *Black*.[152] Elizabeth and John DeHart I had the following children – also identified as *Black*:

6.1.1- Samuel Fraunces Dehart (1827-1893), 1st child of John and Elizabeth (Fraunces) DeHart, was a *black* waiter in 1850, living with his parents and grandmother.[153]

6.1.2. - John Fraunces DeHart Jr. (1833-?), 2nd child of John and Elizabeth (Fraunces) DeHart, was a barber in the 1850 census, living with his parents and grandmother Betsy. John worked as a porter on Wall Street until 1868. He married a woman named Jenett. They moved to Union, NJ where John worked as a laborer. In the 1870 census the family is in Elizabeth, NJ (about 5 miles from Staten Island) in the same house as James Schenck (40) and wife Catherine (35). All of them are identified as *Black*.[154] There was almost certainly a familial connection with this Shenck family as there are black DeHart and Schenck families found living close together in other census records. John and Jenett had the following children – identified as *Black*:

6.1.2.1. Ada W. DeHart (1863-1954)

6.1.2.2. John DeHart III (1866-?)

6.1.3 – Jane de Hart (1850-aft 1870)

6.1.4 – Sarah E De hart (1855-1884) Sarah E married George B Madden. She died at 22 years old in Feb 1884 of septicemia (blood poisoning). Her baby Carrie died at 6 months old in October 1884. George B died at 34 in 1892.

6.2. - Samuel Stevens Fraunces III (1809-1882) 2nd child of Samuel M. and Betsey (Stevens) Fraunces worked as a whitewasher. He always spelled his name Francis. He married Caroline A. Sands (1821-?) in New York about 1840. They lived in NY City and Queens. The 1840 Census in NYC lists Samuel III as a free *Black*, age 24-36, with wife 24-36. The 1850 Census lists him as a Laborer, living with wife Caroline, and children Caroline (3) and Edward (1) in a home on the property of a white druggist named Simeon Seger.[155] The 1855 NY census shows Samuel working as a porter.[156] Elizabeth Sands (70) (mother-in-law) is living with them. In 1870 Samuel was a white-washer in New York City Ward 17. In 1880 he was noted as a white-washer. Caroline was a laundry worker, and they were living with David Walton Sands his brother-in-law. Samuel died in 1882. Samuel III and Caroline Sands Francis had the following 6 children – all identified as *Black*:

6.2.1 - Mary L Sands Francis (1841-aft 1880) was listed in the 1870 Census in Hunterdon, NJ as a 19 year old *mulatto* domestic servant. In the 1880 census she was listed as a 39 year old *black* laundress, caring for her cousins Dora (11), Walter (9) and Essy (4) Francis, all *black*. It is not clear who the parents of these children were.

6.2.2 - Elizabeth Sands Francis (1843-1929) was living with her parents in 1860 all noted as *black*. They were still together in 1870. She was living with a cousin, Mary E. Lee (33) in 1915 and died in April 1929 at the age of 86. The death certificate notes her parents as Samuel and Caroline but note her as widowed, although her name remained

Francis and there is no record of a husband. Her death certificate notes that she was *black*.

6.2.3. - Caroline 'Carrie' F Sands Francis (1847-1913) daughter of Samuel Frances III married Ellwood Whipper Hollensworth (1840-1900) in 1880. He was a *Mulatto* man from Philadelphia, but his family had moved to Canada when he was young. He was a highly educated and talented musician who had graduated from Lincoln University in Canada. In 1880 he worked as a music teacher in Camden, NJ. He was listed as *Mulatto* and Carrie was listed as *Black*.[157] In 1900 they were living in Atlantic City, NJ. Ellwood was working as a RR porter. They and the children were all listed as *Black*. Elwood and Carrie were classified as *Mulatto* in the 1910 census with their children. At 63 he was still working as a RR Porter.[158] They were living at 126 N. Ohio Avenue in Atlantic City, NJ in 1914. No further records found. They had 5 children and the whole family identified as *Mulatto* or *Black*.

6.2.4. - Sarah E. Sands Francis (1848-?) 4th child of Samuel Francis III and Caroline Sands was noted in the 1855 census at the age of 7 as *Black*. No further records were found.

6.2.5. - Edward Sands Francis (1849–1885) 5th child of Samuel Francis III and Caroline (Sands) was born in New York City about 1849. In 1860 at the age of 12 in New Rochelle, Westchester, NY he was working as a Colored domestic in a boarding house.159 In the 1870 census he was listed as Colored. He apparently died at the age of 37 in 1885 in Flatbush, NY.160 He did marry but his wife's name is not known. They had 1 son:

6.2.5.1.- David Beaumont Francis (1875-?). David B. married Ella Teneyk and he was noted as owning a barber shop in Queens in 1910. In 1925 David was noted as the 49 year old Superintendent of a club, *mulatto*, and 2nd wife Adelyn, also *mulatto*. David B and Ella had one son:

6.2.5.1.1 - Edgar Samuel Teneyk Francis (1895-1933). He worked as a cook, *black*, in the 1915 census. He was a pipefitter in 1917 and entered the military that year. All records show he was *black*. He became a bank cashier after the war and died in Brooklyn. He is buried in Cypress Hill National Cemetery, noted as Sgt. Co. 1, 367th NY Infantry. He and his wife Susan had 3 children. All identified as *black*.

6.2.6.- Jeremiah J Sands Francis (1851-) 6th child of Samuel Fraunces III was born in New York City in 1851. He married Annie Livingston in 1868 and both were noted as *Black* in the marriage documents. By 1870 he was living with his parents again. In 1878 he married Mary Elizabeth Dunleavy in Manhattan. In 1911 he was a *black* elevator operator in NYC.

6.3. - **John Lewis Stevens Francis** (1810-after 1860), 3rd child of Samuel M. Fraunces and Elizabeth (Stevens) was apparently lighter skinned. He married Rebecca B. Henicut (1818 -?) from Rhode Island and the family was listed as *Mulatto* in 1850 and again in 1855 New York Census. The 1860 Census didn't note race. John was a day laborer. They had 5 children, and all were identified as *Mulatto* in the early years or passed as white in later years. John Lewis and Rebecca (Henicut) Francis had the following children:

6.3.1.- Edward L. Henicut Francis (1833-aft 1915) *mulatto*

6.3.2.- Eliza A. Henicut Francis (1836-after 1860) *mulatto*

6.3.3.- Donald Albert Henicut Francis (1842-1885) son of John L. and Rebecca (Henicut) Francis was born in Rhode Island. He was listed as *Mulatto* in the early census records and in his Civil War military enlistment.[161] He joined the 11th US *Colored* Heavy Artillery. He died in Manhattan at the age of 43. Never married and always noted as *Mulatto*.

6.3.4.- George Barret Henicut Francis (1843) son of John L. and Rebecca (Henicut) Francis was a sailor in the Civil War working as a waiter and noted as *Mulatto*.[162] He married Rachel Jones (1845-?) on 14 April 1869 in Manhattan. Both were noted as *Black* in the marriage record. He and Rachel were both noted as *Black* in the 1880 Federal Census when he was working as a waiter and living in New York City.[163]

6.4. - Joseph Stevens Francis (1811-before 1859) was the 4th child of Samuel M. Fraunces and Elizabeth (Stevens). He was born in New York City. He became a butcher in Brooklyn and married a woman named Dinah. In 1850 they were identified as *Black*, and were living close to Sylvia Schenck and her children, also *Black*. In 1855 New York census, Joseph was identified as *Black,* but his wife and children were listed as *Mulatto*. Joseph died before 1859 in New York City as that is when Dinah remarried to a man named Ringgold and had another child. Joseph and Dinah had 6 children who were identified as *Mulatto* or *Black.*

6.4.1 - Lydia Francis (1847-1869) Lydia Francis (1847- 1869) daughter of Joseph Francis was born in 1847 and married John Russell. She died young at the age of 23 in Dec 1869 and was always identified as *Black.*[164]

6.4.2 - Francis died at birth (1848-1848) died at birth.

6.4.3 - Edward B. Francis (1849-?) son of Joseph Francis was born in Brooklyn. He was listed as *Mulatto* in the 1855 census. In 1865 he was working as a chair caner and living with his mother Diana and noted as *Black.* In 1870 he was working as a cigar maker, noted as *Black.* He married Catherine 'Kate' Lucas and in 1880 was running a restaurant in Indianapolis, Indiana. He was listed as *Black*; wife and children were listed as *Mulatto.*

6.4.4.- Abraham S. Francis (1850-?) son of Joseph Francis was born in Brooklyn, He worked as a chair caner in 1865 and was noted as *Black.* He married a woman named Maria about 1870. In the early 1870's Abraham was listed as a clergyman in Manhattan living in Brooklyn. In the 1880 census Abraham was working as a truck man in Brooklyn where the family apparently remained. Abraham and Maria had one child named Tiny. All were identified as *Black.* There are no confirmed records found after 1880.

6.4.5 - Charlotte Francis (1855-1855) died young

6.4.6 - F. William Francis (1855-?) son of Joseph Francis was born in Brooklyn. He was working as a car man in the 1870 census and identified as *Black.* He married a woman named Charlotte, also *Black.* There are no confirmed records found after 1880 when he was working as a waiter in Brooklyn at the age of 24. Charlotte was keeping house, and both were listed as *Mulatto*.

6.5. - **William H. Stevens Francis** (1815-?) the youngest child of Samuel M. Fraunces and Elizabeth (Stevens) married a woman named Marie. In the 1840 census, his mother Betsey Stevens Fraunces, he and his 2 brothers were living in Ward 5 in NY city with a free colored female 24-35. William was working as a waiter in Brooklyn in the 1855 census and noted as *Black*. He moved to Poughkeepsie, NY and worked there as a whitewasher in 1870. His aunt, Hannah Louisa Dally Fraunces (84) was living with William and his wife, Marie in the 1870 census in Poughkeepsie, NY. She was then 84. William and Marie had a son – all were noted as *Black* in 1870 census:

6.5.1. James Francis (1849-?)

7 - Sophia Dally (Fraunces) Gomez (1776-1860)

Sophia, 7th child of Samuel and Elizabeth (Dally) Fraunces, was born about 1776 in New York City. No birth or marriage records have been found. It is believed she was married to John Gomez, a *free Black male* 45+, with a *free Black male* under 14 (son Ernest), a *free Black female* under 14 (unknown daughter) and *free Black female* 26-44 (Sophia) in Ward 5 of New York City in the 1820 census. In the 1830 Census, Sophia Gomes was found in Ward 5 in New York, living on Church St. Her daughter and 3 grandchildren were apparently living with her. The 1840 Ward 5 census notes Sophia as a *free Black female* 56+, living next to Samuel Francis III, *free Colored male* 24-36 and his wife, Caroline (Sands) Francis, *free Colored female* 24-36; his mother 'Betsy' Francis (widow of Samuel M., Sophia's sister in law) *a free Colored female* 36-56; Betsey's daughter Elizabeth Francis, *free Colored female*, 24-36 and 3 *Colored males* 24-36, Betsey's sons John, Joseph, and William.

Sophia and John Gomez had the following children:

7.1. Ernest Gomez (1807-?)

7.2. Daughter Gomez (1808-?)

7.1. Ernest Gomez was the only son of John and Sophia (Fraunces) Gomez. On 18 April 1822 he went missing and his parents placed an ad asking for information about him. The ad read: *"TO THE PUBLIC: Left his father's house early on the morning of the 10th inst. a lad whose names is ERNEST GOMEZ; aged fifteen years; very tall for his age; of* *a dark complexion, rather pale, and of a thin visage with a prominent nose; dark eyes; short chestnut curled hair; he bites his nails very much. His clothes, a fine blue coattee with a small black collar; a black cloth waistcoat; dark mixed pantaloons; laced shoes; he wore a yellow fur cap and took with him a large cape dark big coat, with an old hat. His disconsolate parents have reason to suppose that he has been seduced aboard some vessel navigating the North or East Rivers or aboard of some outward bound vessel – Should any merchant, captain of any vessel, sailor, or citizen have seen or heard of a lad of the above description and name, they will confer a very great favor on his afflicted and aged parents (as he is their only son) by giving information at No. 39 Vesey St. "[165]* The term *dark complexion* usually referred to *negros* or *mulattos*. And 'rather pale' would show he was a light skinned black or mulatto. Ernest was never found. There was a later record of an Ernest Gomez, born in NY, who arrived back in NY from Bordeaux with a wife and 4 children. His passport stated he was born in NY on 19 Dec 1809. That date is 2 years later than the presumed date for Ernest based on the ad so this may not be the correct Ernest, however the description is quite similar, noting a long curved nose, 6' tall, with a dark complexion.

7.2 Daughter Gomez apparently married and had 3 children. Nothing is known of her husband. She and her children were found with their mother and grandmother Sophia in the 1830 census in New York, Ward 5. All identified as *Black*.

8 - Hannah Louisa Dally Fraunces (1784-after 1870)

Hannah was the last child (possibly a grandchild) of Samuel and Elizabeth (Dally) Fraunces. She was baptized in 1784 at Trinity Church in New York with Gifford and Hannah Dally and her sister Elizabeth as godparents. At this time, Elizabeth (Dally) Fraunces would have been 44 years old, somewhat old to have a child. Hannah was possibly a child of Andrew, Margaret Amelia, or Elizabeth, all unmarried at the time.

Hannah's father, Samuel Fraunces, died in Philadelphia on 10 October 1795. She was 11 at the time. Her mother was still alive as were most of her brothers and sisters. Her brother Samuel M Fraunces was named executor of Samuel's estate and guardian of Hannah L. Sophia was 20 and probably married.

Hannah may have married. There was a Hannah Francis noted as the colored wife of John Ricker in the Dutch Reformed Church in 1812, in NYC. Ricker was apparently white. This couple shows up again in 1857 where John was a driver living at 581 3rd Avenue. Wives were not listed at this time. In 1860, Elizabeth "Betsy" Francis lived at 15 Marion St with her son Joseph. From 1863-1868, Hannah Francis lived at 17 Marion St, noted as a colored, nurse. She finally appears in the 1870 census as Hannah Francis (84), living with her nephew, William Francis, a whitewasher, his wife Mary and son James in Poughkeepsie, NY. Henry was youngest son of Betsy and Samuel M, her original guardian at the death of her father. They all identified as *Black*. She presumably died soon after this census.

Several trees have claimed that Hannah Louisa Fraunces was the Hannah Darrah and that married David Kelley. This theory is not supported by any evidence and is contrary to other evidence above was well as extensive investigation of the prominent Darrah family. Hannah Darrah was born to Rebecca Thompson and William B Darrah in 1777-1779. Hannah Fraunces was born in 1784 per baptism records, a 7 year difference in birth dates. Hannah Darrah is noted as being born in Bucks County, PA. Hannah Fraunces was born in NY City. This theory continues that Hannah Fraunces was adopted by William Darrah after the death of her father Samuel, in 1795 and took Darrah's last name. This seems highly unlikely. Hannah Fraunces had a living mother, sisters, and brothers so there would have been no reason for an 11 year old to be adopted by an outside family. At that time, fostering was common but last names did not change in those cases. Hannah Darrah (29) married David Kelley (24) in 11 Oct 1806 in Philadelphia. By 1806, Hannah Fraunces (22), her mother and Samuel M and his wife Betsy had all moved to New York City where Andrew and Sarah Fraunces, Catherine and Cornelius Smock, Sarah and TC Campbell, and Sophia and John Gomez all lived. I do hope that others will correct their trees to reflect the extensive research done on this matter.

The presence of Black children in the extended Fraunces family conclusively proves that Samuel Fraunces was of mixed race.

Bibliography

Albion R G, Labaree, B, Baker, W. New England and the Sea, (1970), Mystic Seaport Museum, Mystic, CT.

Ancestry.com. England & Wales, Non-Conformist and Non-Parochial Registers, 1567-1970, Vital records

Ancestry.com. UK American Loyalist Claims, 1776-1834, Original petitions

Ancestry.com. Will of David Pye (1786): NY Wills and Probate Records

Auchmuty, Robert. Report to Britain Following Capture of Ft. Washington and Ft. Lee, (1776)

Balestier, Joseph N. Historical Sketches of Holland Lodge, delivered as an Address 29 Nov 1861, (1862), Master, Reprinted 1878

Baker, William Spohn. Washington After the Revolution, (1898), Philadelphia, J B Lippincott Co

Barret, Walter. Old Merchants of New York City, (1862), New York, Carleton Publishing

Bayles, W Harrison. Old Taverns of New York, (1915), New York, Frank Allaben Genealogical Company

Brown, Christopher Leslie. Moral Capital: Foundations of British Abolitionism, The University of North Carolina Press (2012) Project MUSE, muse.jhu.edu/book/42651

Burrows, Edwin G. Forgotten patriots: The Untold Story of American Prisoners During the Revolutionary War, New York, (2010) Basic Books

Clinton, Henry. The Henry Clinton papers: 1736-1850: Letter from A Gautier to S DeLancey, 3 Jan 1781

353

Bibliography

Conrad, Dennis M, Parks, Roger N, and King. Martha J ed. The Papers of Nathanial Green: Nathanial Green (1781-1782), Rhode Island Historical Society

Crackel, Theodore J, ed. The Papers of George Washington Digital Edition, George Washington et al, Charlottesville: University of Virginia Press Rotunda (2008-2022)

Crews, Ed. Drinking in Colonial America, (2007), Colonial Williamsburg Foundation

Dept of State. Continental Congress Papers, MS, No. 41, III

Dir, Morgan, ed. History of the Parish of Trinity Church in the City of NY, Part II, 9th rector (1901), New York, Putnam Press

Ellis, Joseph. The Quartet: Orchestrating the Second American Revolution 1783-1789, Vintage Books Edition, May 2015, Penguin Random House LLC

FamilySearch.org. PA Births and Christenings

Flexnor, James Thomas. George Washington and the New Nation: (1783-1793), (1970), New York, Little Brown

Ford, Worthington C et al ed. Journals of the Continental Congress 1774-1789, Washington, DC, Government Printing Office

Franks, David C. The New York Directory (New York, 1787), Journals, XXVIII, 207 208, (1785), March 28, 1785

Freeman, Douglass Southall. George Washington, Volume VI: Patriot and President, 1784-1793, (1954), New York, Charles Scribner's Sons

Genealogybank.com. various newspapers

George Washington Bicentennial Commission. History of George Washington: Bicentennial Celebration, Volume III, (1932), Literature Series, Washington, DC

Green, Richard C. Demon of Discord, (2002), article, www.library.csi.cuny.edu

Grundy, J Owen. The History of Jersey City, 1609-1976, Jersey City, NJ, Progress Printing Co Inc. 1976

Horner, William. Of Men and Things, (1934), Philadelphia Evening Bulletin, 22 Feb 1934

Ketchum, Richard R. The Winter Soldiers, (1973), New York, Doubleday & Co

Livesay, Daniel Alan. Children of Uncertain Fortune: Mixed Race Migration from the West Indies to Britain 1750-1820, (2010), Univ. of Michigan PhD Thesis

Lossing, Benson J. Field Book of the Revolution, Vol 1-3, (1851) Harper

Ludlum, David M. Early American Winters, 1604-1820, (1966), American Meteorological Society

Lyon, J.B. ed. First-Thirtieth Annual Report – 1896-1925 to the Legislature of the State of NY, Original Documents (1920), American Scenic and Historic Preservation Society, Albany

McAnear, Beverly. The Place of the Freeman in Old New York, (1940) New York History, 21(4), 418-430. http://www.jstore/stable/23134736

McCullough, David. 1776, (2005), New York, Simon and Schuster

Bibliography

Magra, C. P. (2007). The New England Cod Fishing Industry and Maritime Dimensions of the American Revolution. *Enterprise & Society*, 8(4), 799–806. http://www.jstor.org/stable/23700768

Mercantile Association of New York. New York City During the American Revolution, New York, Collection of Original Papers (1861)

Montagne, Prosper. Larousse Gastronomique, (1938)

Munves, James. Thomas Jefferson and the Declaration of Independence, "First Reading of the Declaration of Independence in NY", (1978), Harper's Weekly: Sat 9 July 1870

National Archives and Records Administration. US Civil War Draft Registration Records, Original records, 1863-1865

National Archives and Records Administration. US Dept of State: Office of the Historian: Accounts Records, Cash Book, 19 Jan 1785 Original records

National Park Service. African Burial Ground, Wikipedia,

Newspapers: Genealogybank.com and Newspapers.com

NYCAGO.org. St. Paul's Chapel, Trinity Parish

New York Genealogical and Biographical Record. Records of Trinity Church

Papas, Philip. Renegade Revolutionary: The Life of Charles Lee, (2014), New York, NYU Press

Roberts, James Arthur. New York in the Revolution as Colony and State: Vol II, Original records of the State Comptroller's Office (1996) University of Michigan

Smith, Thomas E. V. City of New York in the Year of Washington's Inauguration, New York, (1889), Trows Printing and Bookbinding Co

Smith, Jaqueline. Halloween History: The Legend of Sleepy Hollow, (2013), New York Historical Society Museum and Library

Stokes, I.N. Phelps. Iconography of Manhattan Island Vol 1-6, New York, (1915), Dodd Publishing

Thane, Ellsworth. Washington's Lady, (1960) New York, Dodd Mead

Valdez y Cocom, Mario. The Blurred Racial Lines of Famous Families: The Fairfaxes and George Washington, (1995) PBS episode

Vickers, Daniel. Farmers and Fishermen, (1994), Univ. of NC Press

Washington, George et al. George Washington Papers at the Library of Congress, Series 2, Letter books 3, Aug 1793, (1741-1799)

Wikipedia. David Mathews, 43rd mayor of NY

End Notes

1754 - Arrival

[1] NY Mercury: 19 August 1754, issue 106, page 1, letter for Samuel Francis.

[2] New York Historical Society: Roll of Freemen in City of New York.

[3] National Park Service, African Burial Ground, Manhattan.

[4] Iconography of Manhattan Island, I N Phelps Stokes, 1928, Archive.org, Chronology: English period 1664-1763, pg 679

[5] New York Genealogical and Biographical Record, 1938, page 283: Note: Dutch Reformed Church was also marrying interracial couples long before and after this marriage so there would have been no impediment to this even if he was acknowledged as Mulatto.

[6] Children of Uncertain Fortune: Mixed Race Migration from the West Indies to Britain, 1750-1820, Daniel Alan Livesay

[7] Mario Valdes, "The Fairfaxes and George Washington", *The Blurred Racial Lines of Famous Families, Frontline,* PBS. Note: Valdes interprets historical documents as suggesting that Sarah Walker was of partial African descent from her maternal line. Her husband Fairfax was concerned about the progress of his mixed-race children in the world. Valdes has found that a later descendant tried to cover up this aspect of the family's history by eliminating parts of letters when quoting family documents. "Col. Gale has indeed kindly offered to take the care of safe conducting my eldest son George, upwards of seven years old but I judged it too forward to send him before I had yours or some one of his Uncles' or Aunts' invitation, altho' I have no reason to doubt any of their indulgences to a poor West India boy especially as he has the marks in his visage that will always testify his parentage."

[8] Children of Uncertain Fortune: Mixed Race Migration from the West Indies to Britain, 1750-1820, Daniel Alan Livesay

1756 - Friends

[9] New York Gazette, 14 May 1759 issue 137, page 3

[10] NYCAGO.org: St. Paul's Chapel – Trinity Parish

1762 – Queen's Head

[11] NY Mercury: May 28, 1757

[12] Royal Gazette: 17 March 1781, property for sale

[13] Iconography of Manhattan, Vol 4, Liber Mortgage I:258-59

[14] NY Gazette, Issue 225, page 1, 4 April 1763

[15] Iconography of Manhattan, Vol 4, page 705: Mortgages, I: 268-269

[16] New York Gazette: 19 April 1762, Issue 174, page 3

[17] Iconography of Manhattan, Vol 4, p705: Sanford, Chan. Rep, IV:660

[18] Larouse Gastronimique

[19] Rivington's New York Gazeteer, 7 Oct 1773: Issue 25, page 3

1763 – Restaurants

1764 – Tension

[20] Iconography of Manhattan, Vol 4, p 740: NY Post Boy, 6 Dec 1764

[21] Iconography of Manhattan, Vol 4, p 740: NY Gazette 4 March 1764

[22] Iconography of Manhattan, Vol 4, 745: NY Gazette, 3 Dec 1764

1765 – Riots

[23] FamilySearch.com: PA Births and Christenings, 1709-1950, Batch C72588-9, GS Film # 1490578: She was baptized on 27 Jan 1766 at Christ Church and St. Peters in Philadelphia

[24] (New York City during the American Revolution: Collection of original papers)

1766 – Repeal

[25] Demon of Discord:
http://www.library.csi.cuny.edu/archives/pdfs/14%20Demon%20of%20disco
rd%20205_222.pdf

[26] Iconography of Manhattan, Vol 4, p 705: Liber Mortgages I: 511-512

1767 – Taxes

[27] Iconography of Manhattan, Vol 4, p 705: NY Mercury, 18 Feb 1766.

[28] Iconography of Manhattan, Vol 4, page 705:

[29] Old Merchants of New York City: Walter Barret, 1865

[30] Pennsylvania Chronical: 3 Aug 1767, Vol 1 Issue 28, Page 112

1768 – Vauxhall

[31] PA Births and Christenings on FamilySearch.com, Batch C72588-9, GS Film 1490578: She was baptized at Christ Church and St. Peters in Philadelphia on 6 March 1768

[32] New York Gazette and Weekly Mercury, I 1331, p 3, July 4, 1768

[33] Pennsylvania Gazette: 20 Aug 1752

[34] New York Gazette and Weekly Mercury, July 25, 1768

[35] Weekly Mercury: August 17, 1772

[36] New York Gazette and Weekly Mercury: 2 April 1770, I 962, p 4

[37] The Old Merchants of New York City, Walter Barret, 1865

[38] The New-York Weekly Journal: May 13, 1773

[39] New York Journal, Issue 1445, page 143, Sept 13, 1770

[40] New York Gazette, 26 March 1770, Issue 1421, Page 1

1769 – Choices

1770 – Massacres

1771 - Quiet

1772 – Unity

1773 – Tea

[41] Iconography of Manhattan, Vol 5, Page 1116

[42] New York Gazette and Mercury: 4 Oct 1773, Issue 1145, page 2

1774 – Intolerable

[43] Iconography of Manhattan, Vol 4, p 859: NY Journal 14 July 1774

[44] Iconography of Manhattan, Vol 4, p 869: Voucher, Comptrollers Ofc.

Fig. 2: 1776 Map of Manhattan:
Library of Congress 2002623929

1775 – War
45 Christopher Paul Magra (2006), New England Cod Fishing Industry and Maritime Dimension of the American Revolution, Univ. of Pittsburgh, PhD Thesis Albion, Baker and Labaree, New England and the Sea, 30. Because the Massachusetts fishing industry took such a majority of the share of the catch from the entire region, and maintained such a large proportion of fishermen and fishing vessels, Daniel Vickers has gone so far as to assert that during the colonial period the New England and Massachusetts fishing industries "can be treated as roughly equivalent." Vickers, Farmers and Fishermen, 154, Table 4

[46] The New England Cod Fishing Industry and Maritime Dimension of the American Revolution: Christopher Paul Magra, PhD, Univ. of Pittsburgh, 2006

[47] Iconography of Manhattan, Vol 4, p 889: NY Mercury 29 May 1775

[48]

[49] Chronology of NY in the American Revolution
www.hudsonrivervalley.org/

[50] Iconography of Manhattan, Vol 4, p 884: Rivington's Gazetteer, 11 May 1775

[51] Iconography of Manhattan, Vol 4, p 983: John Hancock letter to Dorothy Quincy, 7 May 1775

[52] Iconography of Manhattan, Vol 4, p 894: Biographical Notes Concerning General Richard Montgomery, Louise Livingston Hunt (1876)

[53] Iconography of Manhattan, Vol 4, p 877: New York Mercury 3 and 10 July 1775

[54] Iconography of Manhattan, Vol 4, p 900: Poems of Philip Freneau; written chiefly during the late War (1786) 321

[55] Iconography of Manhattan, Vol 4, Page 922

1776 – Assassination

[56] Iconography of Manhattan, Vol 4, p 923: MS in Library of Congress, box 43, pp 339-340

[57] Iconography of Manhattan, Vol 5, p 991: letter from a British soldier stationed on Staten Island: *Washington's headquarters later removed to city hall upon discovery of a design to seize and deliver his person to Gov. Tryon; for which a drummer, who had deserted from the Royal Welch Fusiliers, was apprehended, and hanged. A pardon and rewards were repeatedly offered to this young lad (not exceeding 18 years of age) if he would impeach his associates, but he continued inflexibly secret and died resolute.*

[58] New York Historical Manuscripts: Revolutionary Papers, Petition of Philander Forbes, 19 May 1777

[59] Letter of William Eustis, a surgeon (and possibly the Dr. who confirmed the poison) to Dr. David Townsend dated 18 June 1776.

[60] Connecticut Journal, November 27, 1776, as found in The Invincible Frenzy, Colonel Joel Stone: Founder of Gananoque, Ontario. Retrieved November 17, 2013

[61] Forgotten Patriots: The Untold Story of American Prisoners During the Revolutionary War, Burrows, Edwin G., Basic Books 2008

[62] Harper's Weekly: Sat 9 July 1870: The Declaration of Independence quotes Lossing's Field Book of the Revolution as noting the reading was on the Common, done by one of Washington's aides.

[63] 1776, David McCullough, quoting Joseph Plumb Martin

[64] 1776, David McCullough, page 212

[65] Iconography of Manhattan Island, Vol 1

[66] The Winter Soldiers, Ketchum, Richard R., New York: Doubleday & Co. Inc. 1973. p156

1777 – Spies

1778 – Prisoners

[67] Report to Britain following the capture of Ft. Washington and Ft. Lee, 1776, Robert Auchmuty

[68] Renegade Revolutionary: The Life of Charles Lee, Philip Pappas, NY University Press 2014.

[69] Washington letter to Charles Scott, 25 September 1778 in the George Washington Papers at the Library of Congress, Washington, D.C.

[70] MS. Department of State, Continental Congress Papers, No. 41, III, 292-295, memorial of Fraunces to Congress dated at New York, March 5, 1785.

[71] Iconography of Manhattan, Vol 5, P 1074, Royal Gazette, Aug 29, 1778.

[72] Ibid: Vol 5 page 1074, November 14

[73] American Prisoners of the Revolution, Danske Dandridge, 1911

[74] New York State: Battleground of the Revolutionary War, Hamilton Fish (1976) page 145

[75] New York Mirror: September 10, 1831

1779 – Occupation

[76] Iconography of Manhattan, Stokes, Vol 5, page 1092

[77] Iconography of Manhattan, Stokes, Vol 5, page 1094

[78] George Washington, Circular Letter to the States Regarding Supplies, 16 December 1779, George Washington Papers at the Library of Congress, 1741-1799: Series 4. General Correspondence 1697-1799

[79] The Papers of General Nathanael Greene, Vol. 2, eds. Richard K. Showman and Robert E. McCarthy, Chapel Hill: University of North Carolina Press, 2005, 230

1780 – Treason

[80] Early American Winters, 1604-1820, David Ludlam

[81] Iconography of Manhattan, Stokes, Vol 5, page 1082

[82] American Incomes 1774-1860, Peter H Lindert and Jeffrey G Williamson, *eml.berkeley.edu/~webfac/cromer/e211_f12/LindertWilliamson.pdf*

[83] Iconography of Manhattan, Vol 5, P 1110

[84] Iconography of Manhattan, Vol 5, P 1116

[85] History of Jersey City 1609-1976, Grundy, J Owen, p 24

[86] Culpepper: A Virginia's History through 1920, Eugene Scheel, 1982, Culpepper Historical Society.

[87] Memoir of Col. Benjamin Tallmadge, Benjamin Tallmadge

[88] Ibid

[89] Iconography of Manhattan, Vol 5, P 1117, diary of William Smith.

[90] Loudonhistory.org/history/revolutionary-war-john-champe

[91] Southern Literary Messenger, Vol. 4, Thomas W White, 1838, page 523

1781 – Discontent

[92] Clinton Papers: A Gautier to DeLancey, 3 Jan 1781

[93] Memoirs III, 438-441, Sept 13, 1781

[94] Iconography of Manhattan, Vol 5, P 1781, NY Mercury, 19 March 1781.

Fig. 3: Portrait of Samuel Fraunces:
Art by Rosemary Palermo from etching

1782 – Peace

[95] NY in the Revolution, Vol II, page 40

[96] Memoirs of Boston King:
http://collections.ic.gc.ca/blackloyalists/documents/diaries/kingmemoirs.htm

[97] A Sketch of Fraunces Tavern and Those Connected with Its History, Henry R Drowne (1919)

1783 – Powderkeg

[98] Thirtieth Annual Report - 1896-1925, Legislature of the State of NY

[99] Moral Capital: Foundations of British Abolitionism, Christopher Leslie Brown, North Carolina Press, 2005, page 299

[100] Book of Negroes, www.blackpast.org

[101] Iconography of Manhattan, Vol 5, P 1165: Jrnl of Congress IV: 231

[102] Pension Acts: An Overview of Revolutionary War Pension and Bounty Land Legislation, Will Graves, http://revwarapps.org/revwar-pension-acts.htm

[103] The Quartet: Orchestrating the 2nd American Revolution 1783-1789, Joseph J. Ellis, 2015

[104] Writings of George Washington, 27 June 1783, Nov 1784, John C Ftizpatrick, ed. (1931-44) p 22

[105] History of the Parish of Trinity Church in the City of NY, Part II, p 256]

[106] The George Washington Papers, Library of Congress, 1741-1799, Nov-Dec 1783, Expenses

[107] New York in the Revolution, Vol II, page 167

[108] George Washington Papers, Library of Congress, 1741-1799, Series 5, Financial Papers

[109] Field Book of the Revolution, Lossing

[110] The George Washington Papers, Library of Congress, 1741-1799, Nov-Dec 1783 Expense Account

1784 – Civilians

[111] Independent Gazette, New York: 22 Jan 1784, Issue XII, page 1

[112] George Washington Papers, Library of Congress, 1741-1799, Series 4, General Correspondence, March 1, 1784

[113] Iconography of Manhattan, Vol 5, p 1194: NY Gazetteer and Country Journal, Sept 3, 1784

1785 – Depression

[114] Trinity Church record, 27 Aug 1784

[115] US Dept of State, Office of the Historian, Accounts Records, Cash Book, 19 Jan 1785: a cartman was paid cash to haul 2 cases belonging to the office from City Hall where they had been delivered by mistake.

[116] Memorials addressed to Congress, 1775-88, Record Group 360, M247, Reel 49, National Archives, Washington, DC

[117] Library of Congress: Journals of the Continental Congress, Vol. 28, page 208

[118] Iconography of Manhattan, Vol 5, p 1200: Liber Deeds XLII: 414

[119] George Washington Papers, Library of Congress, 1741-1799: Series 4, General Correspondence, 26 June 1785

[120] Will of David Pye, Rockland, NY 7 Jan 1796: NY Wills and Probate Records, 1659-1999, Ancestry.com

1786 – Troubles

1787 – Constitution

[121] Iconography of Manhattan, Vol 5, p 1227: Daily Advertiser, 8 May 1788

[122] NY Genealogical and Biographical Society, Records of Trinity Church, 1944, page 35.

[123] Iconography of Manhattan, Vol 5, p 1234: NY Daily Gazette: Dec 30, 1788

1788 – Ratification

1789 – Steward

[124] NY Genealogical and Biographical Society, New York City Marriages, 1944, page 36

[125] NY Genealogical and Biographical Society, Trinity Church Records, 1960, page 171

[126] New York Gazette, Issue 111, page 443

[127] New York Packet, Issue 905, page 3

[128] George Washington, Volume VI: Patriot and President, 1784-1793 Douglas Southall Freeman, Charles Scribner's Sons: New York, 1954, p. 199-200

[129] Washington After the Revolution, William Spohn Baker, J.B. Lippincott Company: Philadelphia, 1898, p. 138

[130] Washington's Lady, Elworth Thane, Dodd, Mead: New York, 1960 p. 281-282

[131] History of George Washington: Bicentennial Celebration, Volume III Literature Series, George Washington Bicentennial Commission: Washington, DC, 1932, p. 280

[132] New York Gazette, 9 Nov 1787

[133] Historical Sketches of Holland Lodge, Delivered as an Address 29 Nov 1861 by Joseph Balestier, Master, Reprinted 1878: Appendix

[134] Old Taverns of NY, W. Harrison Bayles, 1915, page 339: archive.org

[135] NY Genealogical and Biographical Society, Records of Reformed Dutch Church in NY, Aug 1789

[136] Iconography of Manhattan, Vol 5, p 1255: NY Packet Oct 3, 1789

[137] Old Taverns of NY, W. Harrison Bayles, 1915, page 345

1790 – Philadelphia

[138] Iconography of Manhattan, Vol 5, P 1262: Gazette of the US, 10 Feb 1790

1791 – Slaves

[139] per George Parke Custis

1793 – Fevers

[140] George Washington Papers at the Library of Congress, 1741-1799: Series 2, Letterbooks 3 Aug 1793

[141] George Washington Papers at the Library of Congress, 1741-1799: Series 5, General Correspondence 23 Oct 1793

1794 – Retirement

[142] Philadelphia County Deed Book D, 39-122, Andrew G. Fraunces to Jacob Hull

1795 – Death

[143] Gazette of the US, Philadelphia, PA: 17 June 1795, Vol.VII, Is 143, p1

[144] Contrary to some stories, this was not the Tun Tavern, which was also on Water Street, and is famous as the location of the founding of the US Marine Corps. The original Tun Tavern was built in 1685 by Samuel Carpenter and was located at Water Street and Tun Alley. The Tun Tavern burned down in 1781.

[145] Iconography of Manhattan, Vol 4, page 923: MS in Library of Congress, box 43, pp 339-340

[146] Iconography of Manhattan, Vol 5, Page 1110

[147] NYGBR, 1872, selected abstracts. 1702 marriage

[148] New York Gazette, 21 May 1798, issue 2965, page 3
[149] Philadelphia Public Ledger: 25 May 1852, Vol. XXXII, Iss 53, Page 1

[150] New York Daily Advertiser, 27 Aug 1794, Volume X, issue 2974, page 4

[151] Gazette of the United States, Philadelphia, PA, 22 Sept 1796, Volume X, Issue 1260, page 4

[152] Year: *1850*; Census Place: New York Ward 8 District 1, New York, New York; Roll: *M432-541*; Page: *26A*; Image: *56*

[153] Ibid

[154] Year: *1870*; Census Place: <u>Elizabeth Ward 3, Union, New Jersey</u>; Roll: *M593_890*; Page: *439A*; Image: *277*; Family History Library Film: *552389*

[155] Year: 1850; Census Place: <u>New York Ward 7 District 2, New York</u>, New York; Roll: M432_540; Page: 360B; Image: 355

[156] <u>New York State Census, 1855</u>, Ancestry.com

[157] Year: 1880; Census Place: <u>Camden, Camden, New Jersey</u>; Roll: 774; Family History Film: 1254774; Page: 366B; Enumeration District: 054; Image: 0377

[158] Year: 1910; Census Place: <u>Atlantic City Ward 3, Atlantic, New Jersey</u>; Roll: T624_867; Page: 5B; Enumeration District: 0018; FHL microfilm: 1374880

[159] Year: 1860; Census Place: <u>New Rochelle, Westchester, New York</u>; Roll: M653_882; Page: 424; Image: 425; Family History Library Film: 803882

[160] <u>New York Death Index, 1862-1948</u>, Ancestry.com

[161] Year: *1880*; Census Place: <u>Indianapolis, Marion, Indiana</u>; Roll: *294*; Family History Film: *1254294*; Page: *130C*; Enumeration District: *110*; Image: *0733*

[162] Year: *1880*; Census Place: <u>Brooklyn, Kings, New York</u>; Roll: *841*; Family History Film: *1254841*; Page: *512A*; Enumeration District: *021*; Image: *0503*

[163] Year: *1870*; Census Place: <u>Brooklyn Ward 11, Kings, New York</u>; Roll: *M593_952*; Page: *23B*; Image: *50*; Family History Library Film: *552451*

[165] <u>National Advocate, NY</u>: 19 April 1822, Vol X, Issue 2659, Page 1

Go to your local VA ELIGIBILITY office to enroll and ask for primary care

73128422R00233